COME HOME
TO YOUR CHILDREN

How Families Can Survive and Thrive on One Income

FRANK AND AYESHA JONES

Published in 1997 by Stoddart Publishing Co. Limited
34 Lesmill Road, Toronto, Canada M3B 2T6
85 River Rock Drive, Suite 202, Buffalo, New York 14207

Stoddart Books are distributed in Canada by General Distribution Services
Inc., 34 Lesmill Road, Toronto, Canada M3B 2T6. Tel. (416) 445-3333;
fax (416) 445-5967; e-mail Customer Service@ccmailgw.genpub.com

For information about U.S. publication and distribution of Stoddart Books,
contact 85 River Rock Drive, Suite 202, Buffalo, New York 14207.
Toll-free Tel.1-800-805-1083; toll-free fax 1-800-481-6207;
e-mail gdsinc@genpub.com

01 00 99 98 97   1 2 3 4 5

Cataloguing in Publication Data available from
the National Library of Canada.

ISBN 0-7737-58569

Cover design: Pekoe Jones
Author photo: Dick Loek
Design and typesetting: Kinetics Design & Illustration
Printed and bound in Canada

We acknowledge the Canada Council for the Arts and the Ontario Arts Council
for their support of our publishing program.

*For our children
and grandchildren*

Contents

Acknowledgments

Many voices went into the making of this book.

We are grateful for the help we received from Dr. William Sears in San Diego, Penelope Leach in London, Dr. Burton L. White in Boston, and Dr. T. Elliott Barker of Midland, Ontario — champions all in the cause of giving children a better life.

We were overwhelmed by the graciousness of families who, often on short notice and with only a sketchy idea of what we were about, welcomed us into their homes and allowed us to ask them all sorts of personal questions. Even beyond that, we got special help from members of Mothers at Home in and around Washington, D.C., and, in particular, that group's able and untiring public relations director, Marion Gormley. We'd like to thank, too, our editors at Stoddart, Lynne Missen and Elizabeth d'Anjou, for their patience, encouragement, and skill. For Lynne the arguments presented here were more than academic: just after the book was published she went on maternity leave.

Introduction
"Hi, Mom!"

*I*s this you?

- Dashing into the toy store at the airport to grab a souvenir from your business trip for your daughter, trying somehow to make up for missing the concert at her preschool.
- Asking yourself, "How can I leave my baby when I go back to work at the end of my maternity leave tomorrow? It's all gone so fast. Couldn't we find some way I didn't have to go?"
- Confronting your three-year-old's tears as you leave in the morning, promising: "I'll bring you a Superman if you'll be good."

Guilt — it seems to have become part of your makeup. You love your job; you love your family. Yet somehow there never seems to be enough time for both. You feel trapped with nowhere to turn. It's bills, bills, bills waiting to be paid. You keep telling yourself, "We both have to work to survive." But at what price?

Your days are a rushed blur. Up before light, hurry the still-sleepy children through breakfast, then off to the day-care center or the child minder. At work: worry. "What will I do if she falls ill?"

Or, if the children are school age, the three-o'clock anxiety: "Did they go straight home? What are they doing?" But once you're home, no time to worry — get the supper on the table, do the laundry, sit 'em in front of the television or, if they're lucky, tell 'em a quick bedtime story. Because soon the alarm will go and it will be time to start the routine all over again.

And the worst is, you know you're losing something you can never have again. These precious years can never be repeated — and you're not there with them to enjoy them. It's the price we're paying for our rush-rush, dual-income lifestyle. Someone else may well see your child take his first step, utter her first word.

You're smart, you're educated, you could give them so much if there were more time. You know they'll turn out fine anyway, but in your heart there's a tiny fear. You read the newspapers, watch the TV news: the items about drugs and teenage violence and crime, about latchkey kids and drinking and more. Children have never had greater need for support. Yet the amount of time we spend with them today is down 40 percent from the previous generation.

All the experts agree that the first three years are the most crucial in a child's life in terms of creating a loving and empathetic individual. Yet many children spend those years being shunted from one low-paid child-care worker to another, learning an indelible lesson: never trust anyone, because they'll be gone tomorrow. It's reached the point where, according to George Washington University sociologist Amitai Etzioni, "single parents may do better than two-career absentee parents" because at least the single parent is more likely to be at home with the child.

In Etzioni's widely circulated report, tellingly titled *The Parenting Deficit*, he talks about parents who "flew the coop." The fact is, he writes, "parenting cannot be carried out over the phone, however well meaning and loving the calls may be. It requires physical presence. The notion of 'quality time' (not to mention 'quality phone calls') is a lame excuse for parental absence." Echoing a theme many child-rearing experts are now coming around to, he emphasizes, "Quality time occurs within quantity time." As you spend time with your children — fishing, gardening, camping, or just eating a meal — there are unpredictable moments when an opening occurs and education takes hold."

But for too many children, says Etzioni, the reality is "substandard care and all-too-frequent warehousing of children with overworked parents trying frantically to make up the deficit in their spare time." As Figure 1 illustrates, most full-time working parents spend less than four hours a day with their kids.

Figure 1   Time Parents Spend with Their Children

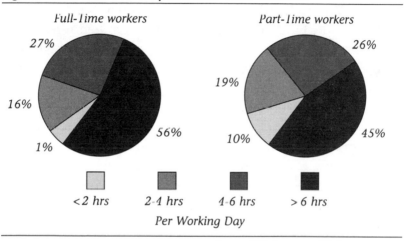

Source: U.K. Parents at Work survey, 1995.

It would be difficult not to believe there is a relationship between increasingly absent parents and increasingly troubled youth. Dr. Paul Steinhauer, a psychiatrist at the world-famous Hospital for Sick Children in Toronto, predicted in 1980 that teenage delinquency, suicide, vandalism, and violence would rise dramatically in the years ahead in the face of increasing divorce, two-income families, and father absenteeism, all of which cause children to miss out on vital parental contact in the earliest years.

Dr. Steinhauer has seen his predictions come depressingly true. Today, he says, almost one child in five has a psychiatric disorder. What we used to call the innocence of childhood is being tainted by exposure to TV violence, playground bullying, drugs, booze, and, ultimately, despair. Today's new parents can read the numbers. Many feel a profound disquiet when they learn, for instance, that violent crimes by youth aged twelve to seventeen doubled between 1986 and 1992, and that teen suicide has climbed to the point where it is the second leading cause of death for teens. Street kids are to be seen in every large city.

In its 1994 landmark report on children, *Starting Points*, the Carnegie Corporation says America's children under three and their families "are in trouble, and their plight worsens every day." More than half of all mothers, it reports, return to work within a year of their baby's birth (our research turned up cases of many mothers returning within six weeks and sometimes even two weeks after the birth of a child), and "many of their infants and toddlers spend thirty-five or more hours per week in substandard child care." No wonder one in three U.S. children starts kindergarten unprepared to learn.

"Home alone" is not just the title of a cute movie; it's a description of the tragic situation of millions of school-age children. One U.S. study found that thirteen-year-olds who take care of themselves for eleven or more hours a week are twice as likely to use marijuana, tobacco, and alcohol. More than a million American children go home daily to an empty house where there are guns. A Toronto newspaper actually ran a "service" feature at the start of the summer holidays advising working parents on how to keep in touch with children who were home on their own.

It would not be fair to suggest that all these problems would magically disappear if parents stayed home. Neither is it right to say your child will turn out badly if you both work; many children of two working parents grow up happy and healthy. There are no guarantees, and bringing up children is certainly not a one-size-fits-all proposition. But more and more dual-income couples are starting to wonder if their children are not paying too high a price for today's work-work economy. A few facts and figures:

- In 1993, 53 percent of women told *Yankelovich Monitor* that they would quit work to be with their families if they could afford to; five years earlier the figure was only 38 percent.

- The Canadian Council on Social Development in 1996 reported that 50 percent of working mothers and 36 percent of working fathers have difficulty managing family time. Similar numbers of working parents reported feeling stress and depression.
- In a 1994 U.S. National Commission on Children survey, 59 percent of respondents said they needed more time with their families.
- In Canada, one in five working parents with a child under twelve told Angus Reid pollsters in 1994 that they "feel very guilty" about the time they spend at work away from their children. A 1991 Decima poll reported that 70 percent of women would make child-rearing their top priority if they could afford it.

Says Heidi Brennan, public policy director for the Virginia-based organization Mothers at Home: "The working mothers of this country are dying for someone to say it's okay to stay home."

Instead, they hear from the media a million reasons why they can't: that they won't survive financially; that they'll have to give up on all their career goals; that they'll vegetate. Everyone seems to be telling you, "You need two incomes to survive today."

We're here to say that you don't. You *can* come home to your children.

We know a good deal about being home with children. We reared six on one income. We didn't plan on six — we just got started, rather liked having them, and kept going.

But having set off along this well-populated path, we were faced with a dilemma: how to feed and house our growing brood? Child care of any sort was out of the question — too expensive. After the birth of our second child, Ayesha quit her job as an operating room nurse and stayed home with Frank Jr. and Farida. Then, through the sixties and seventies, babies arrived at more or less regular intervals: Bryn, Ivor, Yasmin, and Fazia.

Frank's salary as a newspaper reporter was sorely stretched. How did we manage? We were oddballs even for our time, practicing voluntary simplicity before anyone had invented the term.

We furnished our home from the Sally Ann and the Crippled Civilians (yes, it was really called that!), and grew our own fruit and vegetables. Ayesha sewed clothes for herself and the children, baked bread, made jams and preserves. *Consumer Reports* became our bible.

Yet we lived well. We took the children on regular vacations, usually camping, but once to Britain and once to Aruba, to see where Ayesha had grown up. We purchased an old, three-story house in the city (where we still live) and eventually bought an abandoned farm for a recreation retreat.

There were other, less tangible, benefits too. We lived in several cities and in two countries during that time, but one thing remained constant: the first words any kid uttered coming through the door were almost invariably "Hi, mom!" And almost as invariably they got an answer. In their early years they had their mom's full — if occasionally distraught — attention. All through their school years they had the comfort (and maybe the occasional discomfort) of knowing there'd be a parent there when they got home.

"That was then, this is now," you may be saying. "Can't be done today!" But you'd be wrong. We're not basing this book simply on our own experiences. We're drawing on the experiences of nearly one hundred Canadian and American families contacted in the course of our research.

Many have a parent at home full-time. But today there are other options, and, as thousands of parents are discovering, conditions are better now than at any period in the last twenty years for spending more time with your kids. Since the high-pressure eighties, a revolution has occurred in the world of work, a lot of it due to the computer. For many the workplace is becoming more family-friendly — even if the basic driving force behind this trend is economic.

Statistics Canada, for instance, reports that the number of employees doing all or part of their work at home increased by 50 percent between 1991 and 1995, to one million. Nearly a third of working women with preschool children by 1995 were working flextime schedules — meaning they could adjust their work times to make minimum use of child care and share home duties with their husbands — and another third were working part-time. Self-employment is the other big trend of the nineties, with 2.1 million Canadians now operating their own businesses. Fifty-seven percent of women with their own businesses are operating them from home.

There are other big changes afoot. Lower interest rates are making it possible for people to refinance their mortgages at substantial savings, reducing the need for second incomes. And, in reaction to the unbridled consumerism of the 1980s, more and more people are embracing voluntary simplicity as a viable lifestyle. It means a family needs less money to get by — perhaps one income, or one main income plus a smaller one from a part-time job or a small home business.

Social changes are happening too. A kid coming home after school now is not unlikely to shout "Hi, dad" as she comes through the door. More fathers — although still not nearly enough — are recognizing the importance of their roles at home. And where isolation has been the main drawback for women staying home in recent decades, more community groups, and even groups from the professions, are giving mothers at home a greater sense of self-worth.

But many of us still don't quite believe it. We are stuck in a mind-set where nearly all parents work all the time and only a tiny minority stay home. Evelyn Dresher, of Mothers Are Women, a group of mostly university-educated Ottawa mothers, has done research that shows in most Western countries — including Canada and the United States — about a third of parents are home with their children, a third are working full-time, and a third form a floating population, doing part-time jobs or working off and on. The notion of "Mommy Wars," where the interests of working mothers are thought to be diametrically opposed to those of moms at home, is a myth. Today, with so many options open, many mothers at home are working in one way or another, while many mothers working full-time are looking for more flexible answers to their needs.

Women in senior jobs and the professions are most often

constrained by the mythology of the 1980s. While their mothers, in the 1950s and 1960s, were expected to stay home with their kids, today's most educated women are expected to return to work — generally, very quickly after having a baby. Many of these mothers expected to fit children into their career plans almost without breaking stride. It would be hectic for a while, they figured, but they'd survive.

But today many highly senior, professional women, often to their own bemusement, are finding themselves home with their children. In the weeks after their babies were born they found themselves with feelings they could never have anticipated. Suddenly their worlds — before so broad and free — shrank to focus exclusively on a unique, tiny being. And, far from resenting this new tie, they reveled in it. Why didn't someone tell them they'd feel this way? Wasn't there some way they could be there to enjoy it to the full?

Most, often with tears and regrets, returned to work, at least after their first child. But many, maybe not until their second child was born, have stopped to say, "Look here, what's really important in our lives as parents and in the lives of our children?" With creativity and support, they have found ways to be there for their children.

In the interval, many have realized that although some employers are more flexible now in helping parents, the work world in general, and particularly that of the highly paid professional, has become immeasurably more hostile to families than ever. Many parents in important jobs are working longer and longer hours and seeing less and less of their children. They're part of what in Britain has come to be called "the long-hours culture." Ambition and materialism are part of the explanation. But in an age when the bottom line is everything, people are also just plain scared that if they don't work as hard as the boss they'll find themselves on the rubbish heap.

Figure 2, from a British survey, shows the high degree of dissatisfaction this culture breeds in its workers as it relates to family life. Over 60 percent of respondents objected to the way their jobs kept them from seeing their children.

Figure 2   Negative Effects of Work on Family Life

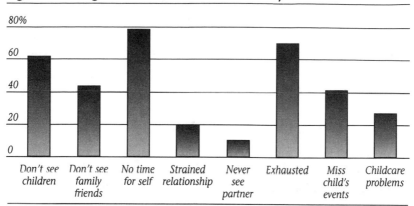

Source: U.K. Parents at Work survey, 1995.

We became aware of the long-hours culture in our own neighborhood when, out walking the dog at seven or eight in the morning, we'd see dads pushing infants in strollers. We thought they were just taking baby for a walk. It was only when we noticed them bringing home their children at six or seven o'clock that we realized the babies had spent ten or twelve hours with the child minder or at the day-care center. We frequently see more nannies with toddlers than parents at the local playground — on weekends! Even babies put in workaholic hours now.

It's reached a point where a London group called Parents at Work, declaring, "Britain's long-hours culture is seriously undermining the quality of family life," announced that June 21, 1996, would mark the first annual observance of Go Home on Time Day. It could hardly be called a holiday, but it was a start. "So many people are just terrified to leave on time," explained Lucy Daniels, of Parents at Work. "It's getting worse and worse. We felt we had to remind people they have a home to go to."

As Bruce O'Hara, Canadian author of *Working Harder Isn't Working*, a study of the long-hours culture, puts it, dual-income families in the squeezed nineties "have a high standard of living — and a low quality of life." But is the standard of living really that high? Many couples discover when they take a close look at their budgets that child care and other expenses can wipe out part or even all of that second income. *The Toronto Star*, in March

1997, had an accountant examine the books of a couple with one child who were earning together in excess of $100,000. This wife's income was $33,000, but they found that after taxes, child care, and other costs associated with her job, she was only clearing $7,000.

We may have reached a turning point. In the 1970s and '80s, women entered the workforce in unprecedented numbers, peaking in the early '90s at about 60 percent in the United States and Britain, for instance, and above 70 percent in Canada and Sweden. By that time about half the women with preschool children were working. But since then, the proportion of women working has leveled out in most countries, including the United States, and has even taken a dip in Canada. (For a look at how some other Western countries compare, see Table 1.)

Table 1   Mothers Working

	With Children under 18	*With Children under 3*
United States	*65%*	*53%*
Canada	*67%*	*58%*
United Kingdom	*59%*	*37%*
Denmark	*86%*	*84%*
Germany (West)	*48%*	*40%*
France	*66%*	*60%*
Italy	*44%*	*45%*
Sweden	*89%*	*86%*

Source: Population Bulletin, 1992.

The recession of the early 1990s could be part of the explanation. But there also seems to be a dawning realization that real wealth — the sort that makes life worth living — is not measured in gross salary figures, but in areas such as family life.

Demographic shifts may lead to far more parents staying home in the future. Dr. Sherry Cooper, chief economist at the Canadian financial house Nesbitt Burns, predicts that the proportion of traditional families — dad at work, mom at home — will increase from a low of 28 percent in the mid-1980s to, by the year 2005, close to the 1960s level of 44 percent. As the baby boomers enter their forties and fifties, she says, the available "marriage pool" of younger women will shrink while the number of eligible men, including older divorced men "dipping back" for a younger partner, grows. She believes this amounts to a classic scenario for a resurgence of traditional family life.

"In my generation," says Dr. Cooper, "there was a feeling you were selling out if you stayed home." Now, she says, she can point to countless cases in her own high-pressure business of women who have stepped aside to be home with their children. The trend, she says, is already having an impact on the economy, with one-income families buying smaller, cheaper homes and favoring discount warehouses.

New Yorker Richard Hokenson, chief economist at Donaldson, Lufkin & Jenretta, a demographer by training, in 1994 identified what he calls the beginning of "a demographic sea change." He too predicts the decline of the two-income family and the re-emergence of the one-paycheck family, pointing to falling interest rates as a significant factor driving the trend. With lower mortgage rates, he says, many families have rushed to refinance their mortgages, the lower monthly payments allowing one partner to stay home with the children. Indeed, many of the families we interviewed for this book reported that one of the first things they did on deciding to have a parent stay home was to refinance their mortgages.

So, how on earth *can* parents today afford to be home? This is not 1955, or even 1965. In the last decade, family incomes in most countries were actually dropping while the cost of living — not to mention the tax burden — was increasing. That was one reason many mothers entered the workforce — it was a question of family survival. So how can they quit now?

For some parents, there really is no choice in the matter: their incomes have been eroded to the point where they really need two jobs to make ends meet. Other parents have little choice but to be home for different reasons. If we were starting our large family today, for example, one of us would still have to be there unless we won the lottery and could employ a team of caregivers. Then there are parents whose options are severely limited because their children have special needs. A family where there is a child with disabilities, for example, will incur many additional expenses and confront unique emotional and practical difficulties relating to child care. We couldn't possibly deal with all the questions this situation raises, many of which are covered, however, in *Yes You Can: A Guide for Parents of Children with Disabilities* (Stoddart, 1997).

This book is aimed at parents who, whether they know it or not, really do have choices about whether to stay home with their children; who feel they are getting only the abridged versions of their children's lives, with the good bits left out; yet who feel so boxed in financially that they think they simply couldn't survive on one or maybe one and a half incomes.

It's for moms and dads — though especially moms, who face the dilemma more often — who find themselves torn between their attachment to their children and the enjoyment and challenge they derive from their careers; who fear that if they don't grab the chance now to enjoy their children, it will be too late later on; yet who worry that if they do stay home they're selling out a great education and abandoning all chances of career advancement.

What's the trick to being happily at home? In preparing this book, we drew on what we know from our own experience — which is a lot. But we also spoke to today's experts: families at various income levels who are finding ways to do it. Many wrote to us about their experiences after reading Frank's columns on the subject in *The Toronto Star*. We also conducted lengthy interviews with some thirty families in southern Ontario, upstate New York, and in and around Washington, D.C. The issues, we discovered, are precisely the same on both sides of the Canada–U.S. border, just as they are in every other country where dual-income families are trying to sort out the conflict between work and family life.

We looked for answers to questions like:

- How can we afford it?
- Which of us should stay home?
- How do I avoid being lonely and isolated?

- How long should I stay home?
- What is my spouse's role?
- What if we split up?
- How can I help my children benefit the most from my being home?
- How can I keep my career options alive while I'm home?
- How can I resume my career later?

What we came back with was no sure-fire ten-step program for being home with your kids. There are almost as many answers to these questions as there are families. Instead, we offer a menu of solutions from which you may want to pick the answers that best suit your situation.

The task of preparing to stay home starts with getting your financial house in order, but there's a whole lot more to it than that. Whether you make a success of being at home can depend on such things as the kind of neighborhood where you choose to live, and on your attitude toward material possessions — and perhaps your children's attitudes. We met parents who, thanks usually to the computer, have launched whole new careers from home. And others who, when the time seemed right, resumed their careers.

More than anything we confirmed what we already really knew: that the success or failure of a parent's foray into stay-at-home life depends as much as anything on the attitude of his or her spouse. Many told us they had found a new domestic tranquility and that their marriages had actually been strengthened by the decision to give more time to their children.

We were intrigued to discover that many parents are building bonus benefits into the experience of being at home. For instance, with breast-feeding shown now to be far and away the best way to start your child off, many women take advantage of being home to breast-feed their children for the first year or two. A surprising number of dads and moms are home-schooling their children — not because they disapprove of schools so much as because, being home, they fall into an easy pattern of instructing their children in a natural and casual fashion. Still others use the opportunity of being home to start their children on a vegetarian or near-vegetarian diet, or, with their kids, to grow much of their food organically. Deciding to stay home with your children, in fact, often seems to be the first step toward adopting a close-to-the-earth, home-based, spare-the-planet way of life.

And there's a big bonus too for the whole community when parents stay home. It's usually the stay-at-home moms and dads who run the local toy libraries or play groups, volunteer at preschool or kindergarten, help on school trips or sports programs, and, quite often, are there to help a working neighbor when a sick child needs to be picked up from school or even looked after for the day.

Few of the women (or men!) we interviewed remotely resemble the June Cleaver image often ascribed to mothers at home by the out-of-touch media.

"When I first stayed home," Deborah Fallows, a former university teacher, told us, "I was a little bit afraid because I envisioned it being a bit like the life my mom had — you know, the moms of the 1950s who thought they had to keep the perfect house and wear aprons and make perfect meals and have perfect kids. I don't like to do housework, and I don't even like to cook much, although I very much enjoyed the time I spent with the kids. It took me a long time to understand that I could reinvent the way I wanted to be home with the kids, and I could set my own standards." Fallows, whose husband, Jim, had once been a speechwriter for President Jimmy Carter, managed to research and write a book, *A Mother's Work* (Houghton-Mifflin, 1985) while caring for her boys, Tommy and Tad.

"We look at [being home] as a broadening of the choices for women," says Evelyn Dresher. Her group, Mothers Are Women, has its own magazine, *Homebase*, and is active on the Internet. "We are feminists; it's not a question of regressing to the fifties — we're on the cutting edge." Dresher's group and others like it, such as Mothers at Home and Canada's Kids First, are serving notice that a mom at home these days is just as likely to have a law degree and her own legislative agenda as an apron and an apple pie recipe.

They speak for parents who are taking the long view. A woman who has reached the middle years now can reasonably expect to live into her nineties or even make it beyond a hundred. These parents see the childhood years as brief. "It's not very long," says Paula Brook, a Vancouver magazine editor who came home to be with her daughters, Abby, aged fourteen, and Shira, twelve. "I probably have another forty-five years of life."

Choose to stay home with your children and in the first five years of their lives they'll have ten thousand hours of your time they would otherwise have spent with others. And time you might otherwise have spent punching a keyboard or attending meetings. "If something comes up [with the children] and you're at the office, just too bad," says Brook. "The kids are not young for that long and I couldn't stand the fact that I was missing dozens, hundreds of opportunities just so that we could pay the mortgage."

The title of this book may seem like an arrow aimed at the heart of the working mother. That is not our intention, however. If anything, our message is aimed more at fathers than at mothers, because it is most often they who are most out of touch and absent from their children's lives. We'll say it again and again in this book: where women (or men) choose to stay home, what they need more than anything is the active support and understanding of their spouses. *Come Home to Your Children* is also aimed at society itself, and is an appeal for policies that support families instead of isolating and impoverishing them.

More than anything, though, we hope this book causes parents and parents-to-be to consider how we, as parents and as a society, are treating our children. Are our children being made to bear the cost of our affluent lifestyle? We hope the stories relating how other parents are managing to spend time with their children will help them to see through the myths surrounding the home-versus-work conflict and realize that, yes indeed, you can come home to your children.

Deciding to Stay Home

1

The Mothers in Withrow Park

*I*t's a summer morning in Withrow Park. Children shout in the playground, a group of nannies gathers under a silver maple with their small charges, and a dozen new mothers, their babies parked in those trendy new strollers with the big yellow or green wheels, stretch and bend, taking part in an exercise program called "Baby and Me." It's what life is supposed to be about: sun-dappled shade, children's voices, and young mothers enjoying their babies.

Yet, as the Withrow Park mothers finish their sit-ups and gather around a picnic table to talk, it's obvious some of them are unhappy. Their babies are mostly four and five months old, and the mothers, in their late twenties and their thirties, most with successful careers, are approaching decision day. Some of them have already decided to return to work and now are only apprehensive about that first morning when they leave their babies with someone else. "I wonder about when he's upset and I'm not there," says one mother, "and I dread coming home that first day, wondering if I'm going to get the big smile."

At least she's decided what she's going to do. Some of the other young mothers, who had their return-to-work plans all figured out before baby arrived, are surprised at how they feel now, and are reconsidering their decisions.

"I had no idea my feelings would be so intense," says Lisa Howarth, cradling baby Ahren, five months. "I always defined myself by my job." Lisa, who is events manager at the Heart and Stroke Foundation, explains, "I had no intention of staying home, but once he came along the idea of going back became extremely painful. I probably spent the first three or four months trying to think of some alternative not to go back to work."

Sarah McGarr, finance manager for a large restaurant chain, whose baby, Jack, is only three months old, tells how she received a call yesterday from her employer asking if she could start back working part-time from home. She said no. "I thought, gee, I'll never get this six months back again — it's now or never." But she is torn about what to do when her leave is up. Night after night, she says, she and her husband thrash over when and whether she'll go back to work. "I'm not sure what I'm going to do," she says. "If I stay home we could manage financially, but I feel I have so much invested in my career. Yet right now Jack is my priority." She adds: "It's funny. When I'm talking about going back and leaving him, my milk is flowing and I'm getting myself in a hell of a mess."

Withrow Park is in a middle-class neighborhood of older homes in Toronto, but you could find women like Sarah and Lisa in Chicago, in Dallas, in London, in Vancouver, in Sydney. In nearly every country where women have made giant steps toward equality in the workplace, new mothers are facing an agonizing conflict: my job or my baby.

It wasn't supposed to happen this way. Day-care, home-care providers, nannies — a whole army of willing child workers has been mobilized so that mothers can return to their jobs and careers as soon as possible. For many parents that's a satisfactory answer, and the only real problem is ensuring there's enough surrogate care of an acceptable standard.

But for millions of mothers it's an answer that doesn't allow for their hormones. It's a topic you'll find women talking about endlessly at mom-and-tot play groups in church basements, around office coffee wagons, in pediatricians' waiting rooms, and in plush executive offices: how to reconcile the world of work with the powerful, often overwhelming emotions a mother feels. "It's all women at work talk about," says a consumer product expert who has made her own compromise by working at home with a nanny to handle the minute-to-minute baby problems.

Growing up, many of these women got the best of educations and believed they could go as far in their chosen careers as their abilities would take them. The only thing no one told them about was the impact having a child might have on them.

Penelope Leach, a leading British child psychologist whose syndicated television show is seen throughout North America, has an explanation for this remarkable parental unpreparedness. "It's very hard to break past the feelings concerning pregnancy and birth," she told us when we went to see her in London. "It's very hard to make pregnant couples think about afterwards at all, which is why there is so little preparation for parenthood.

"In the past everyone treated birth like the climax, as if that was the be-all and end-all instead of the beginning. Now I think people really try, but it's very hard to make young couples focus until that day is over." The conflict mothers feel, she says, is much more common than we realize — and is too easily accepted as inevitable: "It's taken for granted that women returning to the workplace in three months or six months will be going through hell. It's almost accepted, as if you have to go through this initiation — 'We know you're miserable, dear, but . . .'"

Leach, whose book *Your Baby and Child* is a bestseller, faced her own crisis when her son Matthew nearly died of viral meningitis at age two. She was working, with a nanny at home, "but the conflict became absolutely impossible," she recalls. "There wasn't the family-friendly attitude and the flexibility at work that I desperately needed to do right by him, so I quit. I was working for the Medical Research Council, in the child development unit — and the joke is, I was working on attachment issues!" Her laugh still has an edge of bitterness.

We're moving, however slowly, toward sexual equality in most countries, and we'll meet some men in this book who have assumed the primary caregiver role in their children's lives. But it is still over-whelmingly mothers who feel the most intense need to bond with their infants, especially in the first weeks and months of a baby's life. In prehistory it was that powerful, instinctive attraction that ensured the child's survival, and millions of years of conditioning, it turns out, are not easily put aside or forgotten to accommodate career ambitions and modern corporate requirements.

But this message of biology is one a lot of institutions — employers, governments, universities — want to ignore. It's not fashionable to tell young women how strongly attached they may feel to their babies. Instead, society tells them they can have it all — they can deliver their babies and be back at work in no time with child-care problems neatly taken care of. And no one wants to tell mothers what it will be like that first day when they leave their babies to return to work. For many it will be a heartbreaking moment, a realization that, even though they are still a parent and the most important person in their child's life, they are giving up a significant part of their shared future together. The day-care center may be bright as a pin, the nanny they have hired may be loving and competent, yet they know they are sacrificing hours and days and weeks in their children's lives that won't come again.

The Withrow Park women are luckier than many mothers in other countries. Under the fairly generous Canadian laws, these moms receive maternity benefits amounting to about half of their pay for the first six months after their babies are born. In the United States, even if women are lucky enough to be among the 40 percent covered by a new federal law, they have only twelve weeks' maternity leave — with no guaranteed pay. In Britain there is no legal requirement for employers even to grant maternity leave. In some European countries, on the other hand, standard leave can be as long as three years. Table 2 shows the range of maternity (and paternity) benefits available in a number of countries.

But whenever it is, the day a mother must return to work often arrives far sooner than she wants it to. The mother's instincts may be telling her she should be concentrating her life around this tiny new being and letting the rest of the world go by — yet colleagues, friends, family members, and sometimes her husband are telling her she must go back to work. It's expected of her.

Table 2   Parental Leaves

Canada:	*10 weeks for mother plus 15 transferable (mother or father). Pay: 55 percent of insurable earnings from employment insurance*
U.S.:	*12 weeks, transferable, employer under no obligation to pay employee for period away*
Australia:	*12 months, transferable, no pay requirement*
Denmark:	*10 weeks shared plus 6 months nontransferable for each parent, plus 6 months for each parent with employer's permission. Pay: 67 percent*
Finland:	*11 months, supplemented by child-care leave up to age 3, partially transferable. Pay: 75 percent*
France:	*3 years, transferable, pay requirement only for second and subsequent children*
Germany:	*3 years, transferable, means-tested benefit for first two years*
Greece:	*6 months, 3 months for each parent, no payment*
Italy:	*6 months, transferable. Pay: 30 percent*
Netherlands:	*12 months, 6 months nontransferable for each parent, no pay requirement*
New Zealand:	*12 months, transferable, no pay requirement*
Norway:	*42 to 52 weeks, father 4 weeks nontransferable. Pay: 100 percent if parent opts for 42 weeks, 80 percent for whole period if parent chooses 52 weeks*
Spain:	*3 years, transferable, no payment*
Sweden:	*15 months, 30 days nontransferable for each parent, remainder transferable. Pay: variable, commencing at 85 percent*
United Kingdom:	*no legal requirements*

"Before my daughter was born," says Kareen Climenhaga, "I said if I could get a job I would go back to work teaching. I was just working in a store then and it wouldn't be worth the cost of the day care, but if I could get into my field . . . I haven't got a teaching job, though — I haven't applied. I don't think you can ever know what it's going to be like being home — how hard it can be, and how wonderful. Right now I can't imagine going away and leaving her with someone else. I feel I can't survive without her. So I'll stay home at least for another year. Every year I'll probably go through the same thing. It's tight — we can pay the mortgage, but our car is on its last legs. My husband is okay with that, but he wants to stay home too." She muses, "Maybe we'll end up taking turns," then laughs, "but I'm nursing her, so I have the inside track."

For several of these women, the arrival of their babies, and the conflicting emotions they feel, are threatening to disrupt long-laid plans they and their husbands have made to buy larger homes, usually in the suburbs. "If I stay home," says a confused Sarah McGarr, whose boss has asked her to resume work part-time, "it will mean we're in the house we're in now longer than we would like. When number two comes along it will be a bit tight." So far, she says, she's resisting the temptation to work part-time. She fears her boss would soon be putting pressure on her to do extra work, and in her present state of mind, baby Jack would win out and her work would suffer.

"I definitely want to be part of the business world," she explains, "but I'm not sure how I'm going to keep up the pace. My work is fairly demanding. I work fifty or sixty hours a week and one weekend every month, and I spend ninety minutes commuting every day. My husband's job is fairly demanding too. He's a marketing manager and he works a ten- or twelve-hour day and brings some work home at night. Some weeks he's pretty ragged."

She has put Jack down on the waiting list for a day-care center, but now she's not so sure. "I'm a bit uncomfortable with the idea of putting a six-month-old baby in a day-care center. My father's comment is that babies are very resilient. He understands that I'm torn, but I think he would like to see me stay in the workforce. He says, 'Look at all the kids now, they're looked after by caregivers, and they all seem to be fine.' I say, 'Yeah, but they're not grown up yet!'"

Louise Christie is talking about how the arrival of Hunter four months ago altered her plans. For the past six years she worked in her husband's firm. "That wasn't what I wanted to be doing for the rest of my life. But having Hunter was a revelation. I loved to be involved in the whole childbirth process. I'm going to take a night course and become a childbirth educator."

That's not unusual, the exercise instructor, Skylar Hill-Jackson, tells them. She has seen many new mothers change careers after having a baby, often giving up a business career for something less competitive like childbirth education. Children, she says, change your ideas. In her case, she says, she and her husband sold their home so they could expose their three children to the experience of living in France for a year. "It gave us a whole new perspective on living here," she says. "We learned how to cut costs — and it's amazing how simple you can make your life."

One of the happiest mothers here today is Fiona McKnight. She's just heard that the firm she works for is willing to arrange for her to work two days a week. "I think two days will be just the right amount," she says, playing with five-month-old Max. "It will keep my brain ticking over, but I won't be away from him too much. The money from working the two days is not essential, but it makes things a little easier." Their three-bedroom semi-detached home, she says, is a little cramped, and they'd planned to buy a bigger house in the suburbs, but that will have to wait. "If we have another baby in a couple of years, at that point we'll have to make a decision."

Stella Margaritis tells the others how, before her daughter arrived, she worked for eighteen months caring for another woman's child. "I saw his growth in that time, the changes. It's not something I would want to miss with her," she says, nuzzling five-month-old Zoe. "The mother of the little boy I looked after was really struggling. She was forty and she really missed her baby. She would call and say, 'How are you guys doing today?' and she would want to know every little detail, what he said, what he had eaten. She was telling me, 'Stay home with your baby — don't go to work.'"

But it's not that easy. Stella says her husband, who is in software development, works from home on contract, and feels he has to work all the harder because she's not working. He puts in ten-hour days normally, but works eighteen-hour days if she's away visiting her parents. They had been making extra payments on their mortgage to pay it off faster, but now they are back to paying the minimum, and their furnace is on its last legs. They might, she says, have to consider selling their house, or she might care for someone else's child at home.

"I went to college, but I have never had a real job," says Stella. "If I stay home, by the time my next child comes, I will be in my thirties and I will be unemployable. That's what worries me."

Across the park we hear the voices of children in a summer program singing "If You're Happy and You Know It." Lisa Howarth, Ahren's mother, is anything but happy. She and her husband, Tim McCutcheon, have only recently moved to the city, and Tim has just started his first job as a research analyst. They signed for a $189,000 house on a Saturday and Lisa found she was pregnant on Sunday. They got the mortgage on the basis of having two incomes, and now Lisa feels she's locked in, with no choice but to return to her job at the Heart and Stroke Foundation.

"I guess it was when we filled out our income tax return we realized, this is real. I tried everything to stay home. I contacted a lot of people about setting up an at-home business, and I looked into working part-time. But we just can't take the risk. There's too much uncertainty in the job market, and our mortgage payment is $850 every two weeks."

Making it harder, Lisa now realizes they made a mistake buying a house in an area where there are few children and so few moms at home they're having a hard time even finding a child-care provider. "I want Ahren to make the connections as he grows up. I remember how great it was for me growing up and being able to play in the lane or out on the street, having friends to go to next door. But I wouldn't feel comfortable with him out on the street where we are now. I'd like to live in this area. I really enjoy walking up here when the school gets out, and seeing all the children."

"I was hard on stay-at-home moms in the past," says Lisa, who is twenty-eight. "I was someone quite committed to my career, and I don't think I had any kind of appreciation of what it takes to stay home. It's a tough spot to be in. I have a number of friends at work who have had babies recently, and they're all struggling with it too."

As she swings Ahren like a little airplane, her mind keeps coming back to her difficult choice. "I found it was destroying my ability to enjoy being with him now. I was counting the weeks until I had to go back and obsessing on how I could avoid that. Now I'm trying to forget that by counting the time I have had with him. This is my twenty-third week, and I have nine more."

The mothers are stowing their diaper bags under their strollers before heading home for lunch. "See you next week," they tell each other. Of course, one or two will not be here next week. For them this was an all-too-brief golden interlude when they could be with their babies before work called them back. For others, changed by the experience of motherhood, the "interlude" will stretch into months and years, maybe a lifetime. The next few weeks will determine into which category each one falls. We'll return at the end of the book to check again which paths these women are taking.

2

What Babies Need

*I*t's the most natural thing in the world for new parents, especially new mothers, to feel overwhelmed. Suddenly they're responsible for the life of this tiny, apparently fragile human being — no wonder they feel anxious and inadequate. It's always been that way, and the fortunate mothers have always been able to turn to their mothers or more experienced friends for advice on everything from whether to pick up a crying baby to breast-feeding difficulties.

But parents now have a fresh set of problems to deal with. In the past, everyone knew approximately what they were supposed to do: dads went to work and earned money, moms stayed home and looked after the children, and financially everybody managed the best they could. But look at the questions that come up now in our more fluid turn-of-the-millennium society. What does dad do now when the sexes are supposedly equal? Who will do what for this new baby? What happens to mom's career if she stays home too long? How will the bills get paid? And if mom and dad are not there, who will look after the baby? No one has any hard and fast answers.

Attachment and the "Irrational Passion"

However, there is one very basic question for all parents, and if you can answer that the rest tend to fall into place. That question is: What do babies need?

"Every baby," writes Penelope Leach in her book *Children First* (Knopf, 1994), "needs at least one special person to attach herself to. It is through that first love relationship that she will learn about herself, other people and the world, experience emotions and learn to cope with them, move through egocentric baby love into trust and eventually towards empathy and then the altruism that will one day enable her to give another person what she needs for herself now."

Who qualifies as that one special person? "Mothers start out with an irreplaceable biological advantage in relating to their infants," writes Leach, "and fathers start out with a lesser one, which still puts them ahead of any outsider."

Dr. Burton L. White, the dean of American child researchers and author of the perennial bestseller *The First Three Years of Life* (Prentice-Hall, 1986), expands the field somewhat. Drawing on decades of experience with thousands of families, he says that for every baby there are potentially six people who are likely to feel what he calls "the irrational passion" — i.e., unstinting love. They are the baby's two parents and four grandparents.

We can identify with his words. Just when we thought the challenges of parenthood were behind us, we found ourselves unexpectedly bowled over once again by "the irrational passion" when, as a result of a family tragedy, we took over the care of a grandson just a few weeks old. He stayed with us for nine months, making an impact on our lives — as we did on his — that will never be erased. For three months of that time he was with us at our second home in Wales where Frank was writing a book.

Now we never see the bluebells flower there in spring without remembering how he tried to form the letter F for flower, or drive down the lane we've named after him without recalling how he'd laugh when Frank would honk the car horn at every bend. Like many grandparents these days who, thanks to divorce and other family turmoil, find themselves plunged back into caring for little ones, we found it was the most intense, exhausting, and wonderfully satisfying experience of our lives.

What is that special emotion that parents (and grandparents) feel? It's called attachment, and it was beautifully described by Deborah Fallows, a Washington academic who chose to stay home with her children. "The bond between parents and children is incredibly strong," she wrote in *A Woman's Work*, one of the first feminist-era books to describe the importance of a parent at home. "The love between them is special; it grows for so many years without judgment, without limit. Parents simply love their children beyond all bounds, often as much for their weaknesses and their faults as for their strengths and gifts."

What we're talking about is really a mutual reward system. You can produce all sorts of rational reasons for staying home with your children: breast-feeding, giving them emotional support, and so on. But right down at the very root of things, you do it to please yourself, to experience that surrender of the self and the joy that comes from a baby's responses. If you're *not* doing it to please yourself, the perfectly proper thing to do is to carry on with your life and, if it's possible at all, put baby in the hands of one of the other people capable of giving that special love.

The last thing you want, says Dr. Bill Sears, a San Diego pediatrician who, with his wife, Martha, a nurse, has written a number of books on bringing up children, is a parent who is incompetent or resentful. Other than that, he says, "I don't think there's any deep psychology here, it's just common sense. You just can't pay anyone to do what a parent will do. Definitely children are better at home with the parent for the first three years . . . We have eight children, and children do have these moods when they are not so likeable, but the parent still has unconditional love for that child."

In *The Baby Book* (Little, Brown, 1993), the Searses have produced a blueprint for attachment parenting. It begins even before baby is born, they suggest, when the parents educate themselves and do everything they can to ensure a tranquil — and, if possible, nonsurgical — birth. They advise getting to know your baby early through examination and touch, and keeping the baby in your hospital room so you can respond instantly to its cries. They urge mothers to breast-feed, and fathers to support this choice. They believe that rather than distancing your baby in a stroller you should "wear" your baby, binding it to your body in a sling-like carrier — just the way indigenous people all over the world have carried their babies for thousands of years.

Fathers are not excluded from attachment parenting. They are, say the Searses, indispensable, supporting mom and pinch-hitting while she's away. "Nothing," they write, "matures a man more than becoming an involved father."

Far from creating a "clingy" child later, babies who develop a secure attachment with their mothers and fathers in the first year are able to tolerate separation better later, since they have learned to feel secure and are more contented.

Does all this mean that only the most traditional way of bringing up baby, with mother providing nearly all the care, is likely to work? Not at all! Our eyes were opened by the range of alternatives new parents are coming up with.

One of the many happy (and, in this case, exceedingly pretty) babies we met on our travels was Morgan, a chubby, eleven-month-old girl with laughing, sky-blue eyes. And why wouldn't she be happy? She has the best of all possible worlds. Her mother, Beth Baskin, is an outreach worker in a downtown church (essentially doing the work of a minister), while her father, Keith Nunn, is a graphic artist and band singer. It's Keith who is at home caring for Morgan, but Beth isn't exactly left out; when we met the family in their little two-bedroom terrace house in Toronto, Beth was breast-feeding her daughter.

They manage it all by making Morgan a part of their everyday lives. Beth works just a ten-minute ride away on the streetcar, and quite often Keith will put Morgan in the stroller and they'll walk to meet Beth for lunch. If Keith has a meeting with a client, he'll drop Morgan at Beth's office. And one day a week, Keith's dad, a college teacher, looks after Morgan so Keith can get some work done.

So who's the "real mom" here? Sometimes it can get confusing. "Last night at baseball," said Beth, "suddenly Morgan looked around and she couldn't see her dad, and as soon as he came in sight it was arms out to him. She sat with him for quite a while until she realized she hadn't had her milk, and then it was, hmmm, I'm missing something." Missing her mom, of course.

How does the interaction between baby and special person (or persons) really work? According to Dr. Sears, "Babies develop from a cue response: they give the cue, they get the response. That's how they gain self-esteem. If they give the cue and the parent responds, they learn they have value. 'I'm special, I'm worth something because someone responds to me.' They learn social skills, they learn language, and no one's going to respond like a parent."

Day Care

If a child's "special people" aren't available, chances are he or she is looked after in day care of some kind. Day cares vary wildly in quality; some are, frankly, dangerous, while others are clean and stimulating.

But even a good day care, in Dr. Sears' view, doesn't cut it. "Other kids at day care don't respond to kids the way a parent would, and the day-care provider can't respond to several children the way she could to one." There is also, on average, a 41 percent staff turnover annually in American day-care centers.

Penelope Leach too has expressed reservations about day care. The day we went to see her in London — with moms and babies arriving at her Victorian home for a photo session for a new illustrated version of *Your Baby and Child* — the newspapers were headlining a new U.S. National Institute of Health study on day care and attachment. Many had interpreted it as saying day care does no harm.

"That's not what the report said at all," insists Leach. "It said, if the relationship between the mother and child was extremely close and empathetic, then being in day care up to forty hours a week would not have any discernible effect on it. In other words, a really good relationship is very resilient. But we also know the longer the hours the more the risk, and the bigger the group in day care the more the risk." The 1994 Carnegie survey of day-care quality found that only one in seven centers met top standards, and was, she says, "the most appalling indictment of infant day care."

Deborah Fallows, in *A Woman's Work*, was one of the first to question day-care standards. "But I think the argument has changed," she says now. "In the mid-1980s day care was seen as the great answer, and I was very rough in my book on day-care centers. I visited a lot of them and wrote about what I saw, and that was the lightning rod that attracted a lot of criticism. Now I think there's been a lot more written about standards in day-care centers so the argument is more that we have to have day-care centers, but they really have to be good — which is what I was saying.

"I think one of the most enlightening things you can do as a parent is to spend time with your kids wherever it is they are going to spend eight or ten or twelve hours a day. When I visited those centers I had people say, you're the first parent we've ever had drop by during the day. I would say, make regular visits to the day care at unannounced times, and stay long enough so that the pretensions drop away and you can see how it really operates. And think about the experiences and perceptions your child is having every single day and then think about what it would be like for him to be at home instead. And don't be complacent — always make that decision over and over again: Are we doing the right thing?"

Will a home-reared child automatically turn out better? There are no guarantees. Dr. Burton White says because child research is so subjective and comparisons are so difficult, we've yet to see the ultimate study proving that the child at home fares best. "But I think there's a great deal of indirect evidence," he told us, "that says the ingredients for the best possible beginning in life are best provided by somebody who has an extraordinary attachment to this new human being. Over a long period of years," he said, "I've done more research than anyone who's lived on the circumstances that exist when a child develops wonderfully well — and they always feature a huge amount of time from one or more of these six people — the parents or grandparents."

Without conclusive proof, he said, "what we do is tell people they are dealing with something pretty precious to them — their child's future — and the wisest course of action is to be conservative. And the conservative position, indubitably, is that parents and grandparents are the best people to raise children."

Dr. White tries to get at what's best for children by looking at the best-adjusted children. His friend, Canadian psychiatrist Dr. T. Elliott Barker, whom we met at his office in the small town of Midland, in Ontario, takes the opposite tack: his patients have included some of society's most dangerous men, and he's pretty sure what made them that way. Dr. Barker worked with psychopaths at an institution for the criminally insane. It was a patient, a convicted murderer, who told him, "Don't waste your time here. You're dealing with losers. They're losers at the beginning, and they're losers at the end. You can spend your life here, and you won't do anything." It was out of his own sense of frustration at not being able to achieve change in his patients' lives that Dr. Barker decided to go back to where the trouble begins: in childhood. He quit and founded a small, maverick organization called the Canadian Society for the Prevention of Cruelty to Children, which publishes a monthly journal, *Empathetic Parenting*. Dr. Barker's mission: to get children a better start in life so they won't end up like the untreatable patient-prisoners he once dealt with.

"I'm known as 'the cement doctor,'" he told us. "Because I believe that in the first three years of life the cement hardens in the mold. If you want to change things after that, you need a hammer and chisel. If you want to do things right in a child's life, never mind when they are six or twelve or any other age, it's the first three years that are damned important. If you're going to make time in your life for a child, that's the time to do it."

Dr. Barker has the perfect metaphor to describe the importance of the first three years: "A child who does not receive enough love in the first three years is like a leaky pail," he says. "You can keep filling it and filling it afterwards, but the pail can never be filled. Such a person may spend a lifetime looking for what he or she can never achieve: enough affection. However, a child who *is* nurtured properly in the first three years has the gift of being able to give to others."

The shaggy-haired doctor whose outspoken views now have a following across the continent believes proper preparation begins even before conception. "What has to be decided beforehand is what priority you are going to give that baby. Are you going to be a two-income family with all the perks and toys, or is the baby going to alter your lifestyle and what you do? Is the mother going to breast-feed the baby until the child no longer needs it — whether that's for six months or three years? And is the dad going to be there as backup, to give support, whether that's looking after baby while his wife goes to bingo or changing diapers in the night? But most of all, will he value what his wife is doing?"

Dr. Paul Steinhauer, the Toronto psychiatrist who is one of North America's leading child advocates, adds his own warning. Without that all-important early contact and attachment, he says, "what you are going to see is a child that will never reach his intellectual potential." Like many leading child experts and advocates, Dr. Steinhauer has been circumspect in the past about offending working parents and day-care advocates. But in a television interview with the Canadian Broadcasting Corporation's *Medicine Show* in December 1996, Dr. Steinhauer did not mince words:

"What we have to do in families is somehow to find ways where parents can have more time and energy to devote to parenting. Families need to look at how much of their time they're investing in working and how much is invested in parenting. There will be some families that will have no choice but to take on two full-time jobs. There are other families who have a choice and who are choosing to have both parents work full-time. I think they need to be aware that this may have implications for the development of their children."

The Nanny "Solution"

Many young professionals, reluctant to entrust their children to day care, have hit on what they think is the perfect answer to their problem: the nanny. A whole generation of adults has grown up on the saccharine wisdom of Mary Poppins. But even if such perfect nannies existed outside of fiction, is leaving your children with a hired helper all day long really an ideal arrangement?

For hard-pressed working couples who can afford it, the nanny may seem the best of several less-than-ideal alternatives. At least the children will be seeing the same person every day and all day, will be in their own home, and, if the nanny is carefully chosen, will have the benefit of competent and loving care. Right?

Well, maybe. Many children receive wonderful, attentive care from nannies. But in many cases, couples, unable to afford a properly trained nanny, hire what are effectively low-wage, Third-World domestic workers to look after their children. Make no mistake, we are full of admiration for women who frequently work hard and long, living lonely lives gaining a foothold in their new country, often sending nearly all their money home to their families. But an employee who has no formal training or qualifications, who finds Western culture completely foreign, and who is only just learning English, however loving and hardworking, suffers from many disadvantages as a child minder.

It's a particularly serious concern that many of these overseas workers speak only rudimentary English, and hence can rarely offer the child the interplay, the constant talk, rhymes, and games that are the foundation of language. It would be nice to say that children with overseas nannies have the benefit of being reared in two languages, but in truth, overwhelmed by culture barriers and lacking any child-care training, immigrant "nannies" from poor countries often hardly speak to their charges at all. The fact is your child may be better off in a good day-care center than with this sort of "nanny" care.

But what if the nanny is loving, knowledgeable, and culturally in tune? Then the match may be perfect. Too perfect, in fact; the nanny may become "Mommy."

A while back, Frank received a letter from a couple who said they had the perfect nanny looking after their infant daughter. He spent half a day with the nanny and child, and could only agree — she was wonderful. The child loved this terrific young woman who did so much with her and who obviously returned her affection. At the end, though, he came away rather saddened that the parents were missing out on all this love and these exciting years. And what would happen, he wondered, if this wonderful alternative "mother" left? "Nanny jealousy," in fact, is not unknown. In our own circle we have seen parents become unnecessarily picky and critical of a competent nanny, apparently out of guilt and a hidden resentment that the nanny is so well loved by the child.

With the best will in the world, a nanny can't help building a wall between parent and child. This phenomenon was described to us from painful experience by Diane Fisher, a Washington-area psychologist who returned to practice when her first son, Colin, was eleven months old, but who is now at home with her three children.

She relates: "By the time we had two boys and one was six and one four, we had a live-in nanny who did everything for us. I would come home and the boys would have had their dinner and would be bathed. The laundry was folded, the house was immaculate.

"She was fabulous and everyone thought we should be thrilled and that there was absolutely nothing wrong with our lives now. My husband is a cardiologist, I had this big practice, everything was handled. And, you know, I just didn't like it. I felt I was spending an enormous amount of money for someone else to live my life. When I'd tell my friends I wasn't happy, that I was still stressed out, they'd say, you need someone to do the cooking, or you need a nanny who drives so you will feel better. So I would just write more checks. And I'd still wonder why it wasn't working. It wasn't that I wasn't writing enough checks! But it's amazing how seductive that reasoning is. And meanwhile you're getting farther and farther away from your children.

"You know, I would walk in, the nanny would be there with our four-year-old and I would say, 'Well, I'm going to the grocery store, everything okay?' and she would say, 'Yeah, everything's okay.' So why am I going to take my child away to go to the grocery store? And off I'd go, on my own. So the most basic interaction was preempted by the presence of the nanny. I wasn't as close to my children in that period because I wasn't schlepping them along with me every day.

"I think kids get a lot out of going to the post office, riding on mom's hip, or carrying the packages or picking apples. They get so much more out of that than sitting home with the nanny playing intellectually stimulating games. But when all your colleagues have nannies and your neighbors have nannies it's so hard to know what's wrong until you do it for a while. You get so accustomed to handing them over. There's a removal from the child. We can all get to that point. And the more removed you get, the more numb you are to the fact you're missing anything.

"There was another irony too. When I was doing therapy with patients and wasn't with my children, I felt I was trying to repair people whose parents had been preoccupied, who somehow hadn't given them what they needed. And I was trying to repair it as a therapist while my own children sat at home with a nanny. I've known other therapists who felt the same way — that when their own children were about thirteen they would be telling someone how their parents didn't have time for them."

Breast-Feeding: The At-Home Bonus

There's no longer any argument; all the experts are agreed that breast milk simply gives a baby the best start in life. Every few months it seems there's a new study showing yet another hitherto unsuspected benefit from breast-feeding, including:

- Breast milk is free, which means the poorest mother, given reasonable health, can offer her baby just as good a diet as the richest. And nearly all mothers, if given proper help at the start, can breast-feed.
- Breast-feeding provides baby with protection against allergies, respiratory illnesses, ear infections, and gastrointestinal illnesses.
- For the mother, breast-feeding provides protection against premenopausal breast cancer; the longer she breast-feeds, the greater the degree of protection.

• In later life, the mother who has breast-fed is four times less likely to suffer osteoporosis, the crippling loss of bone mass.

But these are only spinoff benefits. The two instant and over-whelming advantages of breast milk are that it is Nature's perfect growth food, and that it provides the baby with the other com-modities it needs most: its mother's time and touch.

Breast-feeding was, of course, the only way babies got fed in an earlier age, and it still is today in many poorer countries (although the baby formula companies are making inroads nearly every-where). But in richer countries there is an interesting trend: the higher a woman's education, the longer she is likely to breast-feed (see Table 3). It's not hard to understand why this is so; educated women have access to the latest information on the advantages of breast-feeding, and also have access to better medical care, which includes pediatricians who are likely to urge them to breast-feed. It's sad but true that the advantages enjoyed by the children of educated, better-off parents start right at birth, even when the benefit comes free.

Table 3   Breast-Feeding and Education

Percentage of mothers breast-feeding by educational standing, U.S.

In Hospital	1986	1988	1990	1992	1994
All mothers	56.9	54.3	51.5	54.2	57.4
Grade school education	33.6	31.4	31.6	35.9	38.8
High school education	48.1	44.9	41.3	43.9	47.7
College education	74.7	72.2	69.8	70.9	72.9
At 5–6 Months	1986	1988	1990	1992	1994
All mothers	23.1	21.1	19.0	20.4	21.3
Grade school education	13.3	10.9	11.3	14.3	15.5
High school education	16.6	14.7	12.8	13.8	14.9
College education	35.4	33.0	30.0	30.7	31.2

Source: La Leche League.

Not surprisingly, nearly all the mothers at home with infants we interviewed for this book were breast-feeding. Our sessions were not interrupted by any consulting of the clock to check on feeding time. The babies didn't cry; they didn't need to. Only a hint of restlessness, and they were put on the breast. There was no formula bottle to prepare or finish or wash. No worry about whether baby was getting enough — the baby took as much as it needed, then stopped.

We were witnessing a rite familiar to us from the time our own children were growing up: the slowing down of life to a baby's pace. One of our most treasured family photographs is of a tranquil moment when our youngest, Fazia, was on the breast. Yet, in today's two-income tear-around, not only are parents' lives speeded up as if someone is pressing the fast-forward button, but babies' lives too become rushed. They learn quickly that they must fit the schedule, that the bottle comes at feeding time, not a moment sooner, and that, too often, instead of being snuggled against a mother's human warmth, they must content themselves with a plastic formula bottle propped against a pillow.

But talk to doctors who believe profoundly in the benefits of breast-feeding and you would think from the problems they encounter that they were promoting bootleg gin or some dangerous drug. They are up against two implacable enemies: the ruthless formula industry, dedicated to making breast-feeding as unpopular as possible in the name of profit, and today's rush-rush lifestyle that insists on making babies fit adults' needs instead of the other way around.

Part of the problem is that a whole generation of women in North America, the United Kingdom, and many other Western countries — the mothers of today's mothers — forgot about breast-feeding, deluded by the sly arguments of the formula industry that the bottle was so much simpler, so much more scientific. The nadir was reached in North America in the early 1970s, when only 25 percent of babies got even a first taste of breast milk. The result today: a generation of new mothers whose moms, rather than advising and supporting them, are inclined to say, "Why bother, dear? I didn't, and look how you turned out!" Even today, it's frowned upon to breast-feed in public, and any woman who breast-feeds until her child is two or three is in for rude stares and snide remarks.

But breast-feeding is gradually climbing back into favor, and now about 60 percent of mothers start breast-feeding in the United States and 74 percent in Canada. (These figures conceal the fact that far smaller percentages of poor women breast-feed, especially in the United States, where a massive federal program provides poor mothers with free formula.) The bad news is that, of those who start, a quarter quit by the end of the first month, and by six months only 20 percent are still breast-feeding. That compares with a 70 percent three-month breast-feeding rate among women in Norway and Sweden, where, incidentally, maternity leave can be as long as 15 months or a year. The world leader in breast-feeding, ironically, is strife-torn Rwanda, where 90 percent of mothers are still breast-feeding after six months.

Mothers, as we have seen, can work and breast-feed. Dr. Jack Newman, head of the breast-feeding clinic at Doctors' Hospital in Toronto, says that by six months — the time at which maternity leave runs out for most Canadian women — babies are usually eating solid foods and it's practical to breast-feed them before and after work without the need for putting them on a bottle.

Mothers often phone him at the point they are returning to work, saying, "My baby won't take a bottle."

Figure 3   Breast-Feeding: How Long

Canadian Children under 2 years, 1994

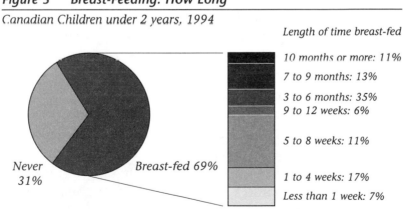

Length of time breast-fed

10 months or more: 11%

7 to 9 months: 13%

3 to 6 months: 35%
9 to 12 weeks: 6%

5 to 8 weeks: 11%

1 to 4 weeks: 17%

Less than 1 week: 7%

Never
31%

Breast-fed 69%

Source: Canadian Council on Social Development.

He tells them, "'Why give it?' At between six and seven months a baby can usually learn to drink from a cup. A baby doesn't ever have to have a bottle."

How long should a baby breast-feed? As you can see from Figure 3, nearly 90 percent of children are no longer breast-feeding by a year old. Yet if we compare ourselves to primates in the wild, Dr. Newman says, the equivalent for humans would be two to four years. A one- to two-year-old child who breast-feeds is getting about 30 percent of its nutrients from the breast. One of his own children was almost four when weaned. The issue at that point is not nutrients, but time and contact.

"I find it laughable," he said, "that someone can make an argument that a baby at the breast is the same as a baby stuck on to a piece of plastic or rubber. It can't be. Children need time and they need to be with their mother. As they grow older, of course, the father becomes more important. But we can accept that fathers and mothers have different roles. Being a mother is one of the most important careers there is; a good mother is doing as much good as the president of IBM." Some people would say more.

It distresses Dr. Newman that some feminists see breast-feeding as a symbol of the chains still holding women back. "It's a big issue in women's health," he says. "Women are empowered when they breast-feed. Even if they don't have a cent in their pockets, they can feed their babies for four to six months."

You need more than a cent or two to feed a baby any other way these days. The La Leche League, which promotes breast-feeding internationally, calculated for us that in North America formula for a year costs more than $850 U.S. ($1,200 CDN). Then there's the cost of bottles, nipples, bottle refills, and other supplies. And for what? After a century of trying, the formula firms have not come up with anything close to mother's milk.

Dr. Newman: "They are only superficially similar. If you look at the individual amino acids that occur in formula, they are really much different from the ones that occur in breast milk. People say, 'Where's the proof breast milk is better?' I say, why do I have to provide proof it's better when breast milk is the normal physiological food for infants while you're saying it's okay to give them this other stuff that doesn't even come close to breast milk!"

The fact is, though, that many working women, especially in the United States, where maternity leave can be six weeks or even less, would rather not start breast-feeding at all because they have to go back to work so soon, while others speak of the pressure they feel to wean as the time for returning approaches. The chance to breast-feed for as long as the mother and baby want to is one of the great bonuses that comes with being at home.

Says Dr. Bill Sears: "Most moms who decide to stay home for a year or two — and that's the new trend — will say, well, I'm going to stay home so I'll make the most of it. And with the new studies showing the superiority of mother's milk for immunities, for brain-building, and all the good health benefits, I'll give my child my milk for a year or two. No care provider can do that. It's just the basic nurturing, the love and attention, even when the child is not being so lovable."

You Can't Imagine What It's Like

Sandra and Jim Kenzie live in a large contemporary house among tall trees on the Niagara Escarpment in Ontario. Jim is a well-known automobile writer, and for years, since Beth quit her job teaching nursing at university, they have managed on one uncertain income. Adding to the challenge, Jim's job involves frequent trips overseas. When she needed help, Sandra turned to the La Leche League, and found it in spades.

I had been teaching pediatric and obstetric nursing for ten years when I stayed home to have Megan. Initially I looked on parenting as a kind of temporary interlude. I thought originally that I was going to stay home perhaps for the first year. Then I would go back to work part-time. It was the perfect job to combine with parenting. If I'd had an easy baby it might have happened.

But I knew Megan didn't do well being left with other people. Only my mom or Jim could have looked after her, and I kept putting off going back to work. Jim was very supportive of my staying home. And after I read *The First Three Years of Life* by

Burton White, I felt I should stay home for at least that long. And then I became pregnant with my second one, Meredith.

The way I adjusted to Jim's travel was having my own support system, having friends I could talk to on the phone or go and visit. So I created my own life instead of sitting here every day alone with the kids. It's hard to find because so many people are working, but I found it through the La Leche League.

It was amazing to me, attending La Leche meetings, that a lot of what I had been taught about breast-feeding as a student nurse and would then teach mothers often wasn't very helpful — things like, get your baby on a schedule right away, don't feed them more than once every three hours, and give them bottles of water after feeding because they're not getting enough fluid from the breast. A lot of those things were routine in hospital at that time. It was only after seeing mothers at La Leche who were completely successful at breast-feeding that I realized a lot of what I had learned as a nurse was not helpful.

At La Leche the message was, if it feels right to you, it's probably what you should be doing. They didn't give me a lot of advice, they just supported me in what was good for me. And they didn't tell me, 'You need to get away from your baby.' I found it was more than a breast-feeding organization. I found what a lot of mothers need in those early months and years is to feel confident about their parenting. When I brought Megan home the hospital gave me a free pack with the formula and everything, and when they do that it's enough to sow doubt in the mother's mind: 'Maybe I won't be able to breast-feed, but at least I've got this here if I need it.'

If you send the mother home saying, 'You can do it,' without having the bottle of formula there, it's often the difference between success and failure. So much of the time mothers are being told what to do, and if they're not doing it they must be doing everything wrong. But I found La Leche was a very accepting group and allowed people to parent the way they felt was instinctively right. I guess after a year or so I felt I wanted to be part of the organization to help mothers.

At my first La Leche meeting I said I was just going to nurse for six months, but Megan was a child who seemed to need the closeness of nursing and I couldn't even imagine weaning her at that point. So we just grew together and I became comfortable nursing an older baby and then a toddler. I remember at an early La Leche meeting seeing a woman breast-feeding a two-year-old, and I couldn't imagine doing that. It's just not common in our culture to nurse two- and three-year-olds, yet look at the rest of the world and the average for weaning is three or four. You can't imagine what it's like until you've experienced it. The nursing, when it's past the infant stage, is very much a relationship thing, a closeness, an intimacy. Just lately they've found that the antibodies in breast milk are actually higher when the child is one or two than when it's an infant. It's almost as if it's Nature's way of protecting the child as it moves away from its mother.

Sandra Kenzie was a professional who thought she knew all there was to know about breast-feeding, until her own personal experiences demonstrated how little she knew. Doctors, nurses, and community workers are more aware all the time of the benefits of breast-feeding, and you're likely to get better advice today than Sandra did a few years back. At the same time, many women feel under pressure to wean their babies at the earliest possible moment in order to get back to work. By that point, the battle may already be lost. A better idea: just as you and your husband attended pre-natal classes together to prepare for the birth, read all you can ahead of time about breast-feeding. Your public library and the La Leche League in your town are good sources of material.

It still won't be easy. An older generation of women figures they got by with bottle-feeding, so what's the fuss? Society is still not especially understanding of the need to breast-feed, especially in public or semipublic locations. And the woman who intends breast-feeding for six months, a year, or longer is likely to encounter raised eyebrows, even from her friends.

Sandra's advice is to first make sure your partner is on side and sympathetic, and then to become involved in a support group, either at your church, parent–child center, or the La Leche League.

If we've talked rather a lot about breast-feeding, it's because it is at the very heart of this chapter on what babies need. The truth is, if we as a society want happy, well-adjusted children, we need to put their needs first, rather than force them to conform to our needs.

As we've seen, babies need at least one special person on whom they can rely. It doesn't mean that one person must be there night and day answering exclusively to their needs, but certainly baby should be in no doubt as to who that special person is. The mother who breast-feeds (and nearly all mothers can, with proper instruction) can hardly help filling that special role.

The rewards are mutual. No one's saying that a new baby doesn't mean a lot of work and fatigue. But if baby is contented most of the time, its mom and dad are going to reap the enjoyment and thrills that, after all, most of us anticipate when a new human being enters the world.

3

What About My Career?

*T*he classic conundrum of the modern woman is baby versus career. But it is — or should be — an issue for men, too. How many of *their* career plans are they willing to sacrifice or put on hold in order to give their children more of their time and their love? Men can be quick to fall back on traditional modes where it is primarily a woman's role to care for the baby. Frank would be the first to admit that he sometimes took full advantage of the dads' loophole, using his career as an out to avoid parental responsibilities.

It's better today. We encountered many fathers who are making much more of a contribution in the home than their dads did. But in most families responsibility for the children still ultimately falls on the woman, which means she has the hard choices to make.

Do you see yourself in this picture? Maybe you were the first in your family to go to university. Or maybe your parents were professionals and there were high expectations of you, as a woman and as a daughter.

You did well at school. It was a proud day when your mom and dad presented you with a briefcase bearing your initials and you headed off to your first job. Or you put "M.D." up beside your name on the office door. You were bucking centuries of male dominance. You needed to be better than most men to succeed — and you were. The rewards were just beginning: respect, a bit more money and what it could buy; prospects of advancement.

Your marriage until this point had been a fifty-fifty partnership; you'd never settle for less. The two of you were talking about buying the house you've always dreamed of — maybe next year. And in a year or two, vacations in Europe, or wherever. Why not!

That's the way it was looking. Then a baby arrives, and suddenly it's all thrown into question. Everything that happened before was easy by comparison. Every step was logical: school, job, marriage. Now it's as if your instincts are telling you to tear it all down. It's the hardest thing you've ever had to face as you are tormented by the interaction of four issues: your career, your marriage, your economic survival, and the new baby.

Are there any ways out of this maze? Happily, there are, but they all involve some radical shifts in outlook. The first solution that occurs to many new mothers is that they'll switch to part-time work. But as some of our Withrow Park mothers discovered, that's not always so easy. Your employer or business partners may not be willing to cooperate; and if they are, "part-time" may be a guise just to get you back to work, where you'll quickly find yourself once again working all the hours God sends.

A switch in careers to one where you work at home or operate your own business from home are alternatives we'll look at later. In each case there's one snag: new parents often don't realize how totally time-consuming and exhausting it is caring for a baby. There are also any number of variations you can work out with your spouse to share the burden: staggered shift work, part-time work, weekend work, and so on. The drawback here is you may not get to see much of one another! Perhaps the answer that comes closest to allowing a woman to hold on to her career and her baby is sequencing.

Sequencing

The idea of sequencing was first spelled out by Arlene Rossen Cardozo in a book of that name published in 1986 (Collier), although a generation of career women had been practicing it for years before. Sequencing is one way of having it all — but not at the same time.

Cardozo says women should get the best possible education, pursue their careers, then, when the time seems appropriate, break away to raise their children, returning to their careers again when they feel the time is right. It combines, she believes, "the best of modern feminism with the best of traditional mothering."

Instead of juggling career and family as many young career women try to do, says Cardozo, sequencing offers them a chance to balance their lives. Ideally, she suggests, a couple should anticipate this career interruption, saving for it, so there will be as smooth a transition as possible at the time the first child is born and they switch to living on one income.

Cardozo starts out by rejecting the idea, promoted then as now to young women, that they can have children and pursue their careers in exactly the same fashion that men have always pursued theirs. This myth, she writes, implies a clear separation between *having* a child and *raising* a child, because surrogate care must fill the gap when the mother works.

Even when Cardozo was writing, many women were rejecting the superwoman model. These were women, she wrote, who knew they were as capable as any man professionally, yet didn't want that fact to impede them as women.

The first objection many women would make to Cardozo's plan is that picking up their careers after being away for a few years might not be easy. But the consequences of taking time off may not be as bad as you think.

When Edith U. Fierst, a Washington lawyer, interviewed some fifty successful career women in their fifties and sixties, she found that "many of today's most successful women had a sequencing pattern in their lives. I think many young women today don't know this. As far as I know, they're not considering it because they don't realize how many women have succeeded who have taken a few years off."

Some Successful Sequencers

A case in point: Sandra Day O'Connor, an Associate Justice in the U.S. Supreme Court and mother of three. O'Connor dropped out of practice for five years when she couldn't find anyone to look after her second child. "I worried that it would be hard to get back into the practice of law if I left it for a time," she later wrote to a young lawyer expecting her first child who had asked her advice. "But I engaged in various volunteer projects during those years at home. I also helped write and grade bar exams, served as a juvenile court referee, and took some bankruptcy trustee assignments just to keep some contact with the legal profession. It turned out just fine in the long run, and I am glad I stayed home for those years."

O'Connor hits on the single most important factor for women at home who don't want to lose sight of their careers: remaining *au courant* in their fields.

But there are, as Judge O'Connor makes clear, many ways you can accomplish the "keeping up" that is so essential if you want to step back into the job later. These include:

- Keeping in touch with colleagues through regular social contact, so you'll be aware of opportunities as they arise later. Beware, though — it may take superhuman effort to resist boring them with details of your wonderchild's latest achievement!
- Improving your qualifications with classes and seminars.
- Starting a small home business related to your career.
- Focusing on volunteer activity that will look good on your curriculum vitae and give you the skills you need when the time comes to return.

For a textbook example of how sequencing works, we called on Sandra Evans, an engineer living in Mississauga, Ontario. As we arrived, she was playing a card game with her six-year-old daughter, Christine, who was home from school with an upset tummy.

Giving her a glass of Seven-Up and a consoling cuddle, Sandra then led us downstairs to her "dungeon" to show us the other side of her life.

With no small pride she sat down at the keyboard of one of her two computers to show us her project: designing a circuit board for a hotel chain's automatic guest checkout system.

Sandra met her husband, Frank, in engineering school at McMaster University. For nine years after they married, Sandra worked for Bell Telephone, latterly as a supervising engineer. But all along, Sandra, who came from a family of six, intended being home — just like her mother had been — when children arrived. "We planned for me being home," she said. "That's why I didn't have Christine until I was thirty. Basically what we did was save, save, save. We bought the house in 1983 and we aimed to pay it off fast, so we socked everything into it while we were both working. We paid off the last of it in 1989, and then we took a holiday in Europe to celebrate. That was just before I got pregnant." She then quit her job to be home with Christine and, later, Valerie, who is three and a half.

It was lonely at first being home, she admitted, and she missed her workmates. "On our street there was only one other at-home parent, and she started going to work part-time. But we're lucky enough to have the park behind us, and when Christine was born I took down the name and number of everyone I met there. I think maybe they thought I was a little crazy, but afterward everybody loved it. Mostly they were parents at home or working shifts, and soon we had like a little group and we used to go on outings with the children. Frank and I would host a barbecue for the group on our deck, everyone would bring something, and it ended up being a lot of fun."

Her part-time freelance computer programing work was bringing in about $7,500 CDN ($5,500 U.S.) a year, a far cry from the salary six or seven times as large that she had collected at Bell six years earlier. But she found the work, which she lined up through her previous contacts in the business, very satisfying. Besides, business was slow with the firm where Frank worked nearby, and she felt she had to do what she could in case he lost his job.

Three months later, when we checked in with Sandra again, she had gone back to work at Bell. She'd been offered exactly the job she wanted, with lots of challenge. "It's hectic. I still find it hard leaving the girls, and not having a hand in the school" (Sandra had been a volunteer at Christine's school while she was at home). Frank was taking the two girls to school in the morning on his way to work, and they would be looked after either by a neighbor or a babysitter — nursing student — when they got home. One reason she went back, says Sandra, was to make sure there was enough money to pay for the girls' post-secondary education later, "but I feel very satisfied that I was home for those years," she added. "I wanted to ingrain our values into our children rather than have someone else bring them up. I mean respect and good manners. If they see you care and are willing to take the time and explain things, and you're there to listen to them, then they're more apt to listen to you when they get older."

Sandra and Frank, who earned about $70,000 ($50,400 U.S.) when Sandra was home, have been able to follow the Cardozo plan so well, they believe, because neither of them is a big spender. "I hate shopping," says Sandra, and Frank, she says, doesn't rush out and buy "toys." "We talk about what we're going to get before we get it," she emphasizes.

She didn't deny that there were costs to sequencing: "We have a drug plan with Frank's work, but when I left Bell I lost my pension plan and dental plan." But in their case these were only temporary losses — now Sandra is back at work they are fully covered again.

Sequencing worked so well for the Evans couple partly because they planned for it. They may be the exceptions, however. Among the couples we interviewed, at least half were taken by surprise by their feelings when their baby arrived. Because they hadn't planned for a drop in income, typically these mothers went back to work, but felt increasingly frustrated at missing out on their babies' important early development. From her studies, Cardozo found that a mother with these conflicts commonly makes the break with work when the baby is between ten and fourteen months old, or when a second one comes along and she decides she's not going to miss out a second time.

This is exactly what happened to Julie Roper. She was a news reporter on a major Toronto television station when she and her husband, John, a real estate executive, had their first baby. "I was lucky," she said. "At the station we got ten months' maternity leave, part of it unpaid." Her only concern as the months went by was their attempts to sell their expensive condominium, which was not really suitable for a baby. The value of the condo was going down steadily as the real estate market dropped.

"So as it came time for me to make a decision, and we'd lost our shirts on the condo — all our savings, about $100,000 [CDN; $72,000 U.S.] — and it still hadn't sold, I knew I should go back as a safety net. I had been cooped up in the condo for ten months and I missed my friends and the job. I wanted to see what it was like to be a working mother, so I jumped right back in."

Roper hired a nanny to look after her son, David, and went back to work. "And for the first few months," she explains, "to the great relief of my husband, I loved it. It was exciting. I felt I had the world by the tail. I didn't feel I was missing anything. The baby slept morning and afternoon. All I was missing was when he was awake at lunchtime.

"I could go straight to my assignment of the day, usually leaving at ten or so when the baby was already asleep. My husband would come home at five or six, and I would come later — about seven — because of being on air. I didn't have a job as far as I was concerned — it was just a way of life that I got paid for. I remember interviewing General Norman Schwarzkopf, and that was a lot of fun, and feeling, I've still got my wheels and my cell phone, *and* I've got this great baby at home. I had that feeling of having it all, that package we were sold as women twenty years ago.

"But suddenly, as time went by, the baby wasn't napping as much and would be awake when I left. And it reached the point where I was walking out every morning crying and I would redo my face and start the day again. I thought, the baby's safe, the house is spotless, it's all easy. So what's the big complaint here? It was me. It was heartstrings.

"All of a sudden everything affected me. The thing about being a mother is very true. I'd go to the Hospital for Sick Children to do something on liver transplants and I'd end up in tears at the press conference, and that would never have happened to me before. I would have been thinking about the story, about what's a good TV clip, thinking about it totally journalistically. And then I'd rush to phone home to see if he was okay.

"After a few months of that I said to my husband, do what we have to, give the condo away, we'll move in with my parents if necessary, but I'm not leaving this child. I can't. We ended up with two offers for the condo and sold it for what was a good price at the time."

Julie and John eventually bought a house in Aurora, an hour north of Toronto. By then Julie was six months pregnant with their second child, Sarah; she quit her job and is still home. When the children are in school, she says, will be the time to look at her career again.

Julie and John's story is fairly typical in many ways, including the fact that it was Julie, the mom, who felt the urge to stay home; John leaving his job was not seriously considered. So why *doesn't* dad stay home? Well, in some cases, he does; we'll have more to say on that in Chapter 7. But Cardozo believes nature programs women to nurture, particularly in the baby's early years. The difference often emerges when the moment arrives to leave the baby with a caregiver. It's not fair to generalize, but a number of mothers told us how surprised they were that their modern, enlightened husbands could kiss the baby and go to work without a second thought, while they were torn apart at leaving.

Some Expert Opinions

Sequencing has been greeted by many thoughtful people as the best way to reconcile the conflicting demands of careers and children. "It has to be a very large part of the answer," Penelope Leach told us in London. "I get so irritated when people ask 'Can women have it all?' The answer is yes, but not all at once."

We asked Betty Freidan, the feminist who originally drew attention to the plight of mothers with no choice but to be home, for her view. Most women staying home now, she said, "don't intend to bow out altogether from their professions and careers. But careers are still structured for men who have wives at home to take care of the details." Women, she said, need more realistic choices, including a shorter work week, longer paid parental leaves, part-time work that comes with job security and benefits, and generous tax deductions that apply both to those caring for their own children at home and those using day care. And where women take time away from the workforce to rear their children, "we need provisions so that people can get back in more easily."

This last point is a concern echoed by Ellen Gallinsky, co-founder of the New York–based Family and Work Institute, a nonprofit research outfit. "There need to be real supports for people wanting to get back into the workplace," she told us. "It's hard starting out again when you're forty or forty-five. But a lot of my friends stayed home, and they've all made it back in."

Spreading the Word

Despite the fact that many experts find sequencing to be a sound answer, young women rarely learn about this alternative as they launch their careers. The impact of having a baby still comes as a shock to many of them. One group that's trying to change that is Lawyers at Home, a rapidly growing Washington mothers' group that Carlie Sorensen Dixon helped found in 1990. Dixon was a partner in a firm of tax lawyers when she chose to stay home with her first son, Peter. She says the group, which is part of her local Women's Bar Association, brings together everyone from mothers planning to return to full-time law practice when their children are older, to women who just want to keep their hand in by taking the occasional pro bono legal case, to lawyers who simply want to be at-home moms.

Says Dixon: "We hold a yearly evening forum at local universities so that women in law school get a chance to talk about issues like 'How am I going to be a lawyer and a mother too?'" If she'd heard about these issues when she was in law school, she says, she would have been in a better position to choose between tax law, a highly demanding specialty involving deadlines and huge workloads, and a specialty like trusts and estates, a more leisurely type of practice that allows for part-time work and more time at home.

Only now, says Dixon, who was forty-three when we spoke to her at her home in Georgetown, are young women in college and in the professions starting to ask these questions. "In my generation we never thought about these things. Marriage and children were simply not in the picture. It was going as far as you could in a man's work and on men's terms, which clearly involved a full-time week. So it was really trying to become like a man and trying to negate the female side of yourself."

Staying Home

As she interviewed more and more career women who had chosen to stay home, Cardozo found many had become so turned off by their former high-pressure lives that they vowed never to return. Instead they negotiated deals to work part-time, often at home, for their former employers, or they started their own home businesses or consultancies. Others, usually with husbands earning decent salaries, opted for rewarding volunteer work, often fulfilling earlier ambitions that had been put aside for practical considerations.

It's not hard to understand why this would happen. The early months and years with small children are hectic and tiring, but parents at home also learn to value their freedom and the chance to set their own pace and priorities, so it's often hard for them to return to a nine-to-five life. Being with their children also gives many parents a new perspective on life, a different notion of what's important. And when the time comes to get back on the career track, you'll hear them say, "My children seem to need me more than ever."

Many of the women we interviewed — who, a few years ago, would have been surprised indeed if you'd told them they would be contented to stay home with their children — found themselves in this situation.

I Am So Glad to Be Out of the Rat Race

Betty Walter, for instance, is a former high-powered Washington bureaucrat who is home with her two boys, John, aged four and a half, and Mark, three. She's now thirty-four, and doesn't plan on returning to work any time soon.

I remember in college filling out a survey form about expectations, and one of the questions was "How many children do you expect to have?" I put down "five." It asked, "Do you expect to work full-time, part-time, or be at home?" I put down "full-time." You can see just how unrealistic I was! Although I felt I would have children, I just felt that work was going to be an essential part of who I was and that I would never find personal fulfillment by spending a lot of time with kids. I couldn't imagine what women at home did.

I guess I really defined myself by my career, and I did very well. I worked for the Environmental Protection Agency, essentially as a project manager. I had been promoted every year and I had reached a salary level of about $60,000 [U.S.; $83,000 CDN] — pretty darn good for my age. My mom didn't go to college, and I think she always regretted it, so I think there was a strong expectation that my sisters and I would follow that path. I went to a women's college where the emphasis is very much on women succeeding, and the women we celebrated either didn't have children or their kids were older.

I remember getting together with a couple, he had worked with my husband and his wife was at home. I was pregnant at the time with John, and I remember saying, "Oh, I couldn't ever imagine quitting my job — I just don't think kids are that interesting." She said she found them absolutely fascinating and took it upon herself to explain how interesting they are. I remember thinking, I just didn't know what to ask her. That's how it is; at-home mothers read the papers too and have opinions, but people don't think to ask them.

I had built up enough leave to be home with John for three or four months. I was totally convinced it was going to work; I was going to make it work. My husband, Mike, was the one who seemed to be feeling regretful that I was going back to work. He is seventeen years older than I am, so his perspective is somewhat different from mine. His daughter was three when his first marriage broke up, and I think he had sad feelings that he had not been able to spend time with her. He feels it's important for kids to have their parents close to them.

But we had refinanced our house, switching from a thirty-year mortgage to a fifteen-year one needing a bigger payment, and that made it very hard to live on one income. We were counting on my salary. Also, my husband's daughter was going to college soon and we wanted to continue to put money aside for her.

But I enjoyed being home with John immensely. It was exhausting, but I loved being with him. I was astounded how much he changed from day to day. I felt I could see the hair growing on his head; I could see it! I remember just spending hours and hours being with him, having him on the carpet, holding him, nursing him. I guess I realized how dependent he was on me. It was a profound thing. I just wasn't prepared for how helpless he was. It was a sudden realization, how much he needed me.

But those feelings didn't prevent me from wanting to go back to work. I didn't wean him, I pumped at work and brought the milk home so that my friend, Joyce, who was looking after him, could give it to him the next day. I look back on it now in a comical way: I was so determined he would have my breast milk, yet I was also determined not to give him me! It's not just the milk — it's being there.

I think it was part of my superwoman complex: you know, "I'm going to do everything everybody says I should, and I'm going to succeed and I'm going to be wonderful." I think that's one thing parenthood has changed for me, giving me a different sense of what really is important. It doesn't matter whether other people think I'm wonderful. What matters is my kids and whether they are happy and well-adjusted.

At the start I was working three days a week. I was working on perhaps the most satisfying project of my life, running a study of radon gas in American homes. It was important, and I had about eight people working for me. It pushed me to the very limit of my skills. But I was badly conflicted. It was hard driving John in the morning to Joyce's and having him put his arms out to her. I would leave him there at six-thirty in the morning and pick him up at five-thirty at night. I was happy that he was adjusting so well — the last thing I would have wanted was for him to have been screaming when I was dropping him off. On the other hand, she was with my kid, and I wasn't. She was the one who called me and told me his first tooth was coming out. That just sort of hit me. She wasn't being rancorous about it — she was excited.

Then Joyce couldn't look after him any more and we switched John to a day-care center at my husband's work at the Department of Transportation. Only now we had to pay for him on a five-days-a-week basis, and it was more expensive, so I switched to working four days a week. I can't tell you how exhausting it was getting up in the morning. I felt like I was packing to go to the airport every morning and then unpacking again when I got home. Mike would bathe him while I was getting dinner and doing the laundry. I was glad I was still breast-feeding because that meant at least I had to be with him. But it was rushed, I felt like a cow, to me it was not rewarding at all. It was the quintessential example of the tradeoffs you make: I am not with my child during the day because I'm working, and when I am with him, I am overwhelmed. He wakes up in the morning and he's cranky, and I have to say "you must eat now because we have to leave in twenty minutes."

The thing is, John has asthma, and this became evident when I stopped breast-feeding him at twelve months. At the day care John would often be on the borderline of just getting sick. I would think, if he can just get through today, I'll take him to the doctor tomorrow. My attitude was, let's get him through this. It's not something of which I'm proud, but I think it's something that happens a lot. I know there were children in the day-care center who were sicker than John, and their parents were never telling the day care to call them if the child got sicker and needed to be taken home. And that's something I was doing too.

It was a good day care in the sense that his needs were being met, but I didn't feel he was getting the love and attention he had been getting with Joyce. And then there was an opening at the day care where I worked and we moved him there. I really liked the women, I had never had a problem, but he did not make the transition as easily as I expected. I guess it was another indication to me that you can't just take your kid and say, okay, you're a round widget, I'll fit you into a round hole. He would totally fall apart when it was time for me to leave. I would leave with him screaming bloody murder and reaching for me while the day-care worker held him. It was horrible. I would come down at ten o'clock and look in just to reassure myself he was okay.

I was in total conflict. I'd be thinking, "I can't go through another day of this," and the next minute, "This is wonderful, I love this job!" I can't tell you how complicated it felt. I continued to be astounded at how much he was changing, and I felt I was missing out. Plus I got pregnant, and it's really much harder to go through the whole routine with two as opposed to one. There was the financial thing too — the feeling that we needed my money for the mortgage. And then my husband got a raise, which helped. And he put pressure on me.

When I left to have Mark I told them at work I would be back, and if I had been a pain in the butt about it with my husband, I probably could have gone back to work. But he told me — these were his words: "When you decided to have a second child, you made a choice about what's important to you. You can't continue balancing these things and have everything come out right."

I would say it took me about six months after separating from my job to decide that I had fully embraced being at home. When I'd been home with John, one of the things I did was get hooked up with a neighborhood play group. We were about eight mothers at home, and we rotated to different people's homes each week. They were incredibly generous to me and I stayed hooked up to them, meeting with them every Friday even when I returned to work. And that was something that really helped me with the transition. It was not as if I came home and there was nobody.

I guess it was a feeling of relief. I was happy to have made the decision and have the wondering over with. There was a certain sense of calm. Now I needed to do the things to make my life happy instead of having it come to me. I needed to have my husband help me when I needed help, I needed to have him praise me if he wasn't doing it enough. I needed to set up some time to meet my girlfriends in the park to talk. Once I was home I felt I really needed to have things for myself because children can totally encompass you. I started creative writing, which I had put on hold since I had gone to graduate school.

I found there were some problems I couldn't solve, like how to keep John busy while I was nursing Mark. He was so incredibly jealous. Even to this day I haven't solved the problem. Or when I'd get a call during the day from my husband, John would start screaming. That's probably been the biggest challenge I've had with him. You're not around people all day and then when you get on the phone your kid is still demanding you focus on him. Those things are extremely hard to adjust to. I've had to modify my expectations and learn to relax, and we're starting to see improvements. I'm a lot more relaxed about potty training this time too.

These days too I'm much more careful with money than I used to be. I don't buy suits any more; I go to Kmart. And we ended up refinancing again at a lower rate about the time Mark was born. I don't want to make it appear we're living from paycheck to paycheck; it would be untruthful to say our standard of living has suffered significantly. But we're saving less and I guess I feel a little bit of guilt spending money because I'm not making it.

In many ways my life reflects my mother's life. Our roles are very gender-typical: you know, my husband pays the bills and I take care of the house. But I think there are subtle differences. My husband helps around the house in ways my father never did. My husband folds laundry every night, and he will do a lot of the grocery shopping.

I don't have the fears my mother had, such as, "If my husband died whatever would I do?" My life would change definitely, and it wouldn't be as nice as it is now, but I wouldn't ever have to worry about going on welfare or depending on the social safety net. My husband is extremely involved with the boys. My dad — and

I don't want to be critical of him because he was a good dad — just did not devote a lot of time to us kids. He was very much focused on his career. He would come home at the end of the day and turn on the television because he was pooped out. My husband is as tired as my father was, but he knows these boys need him, and they're excited when he comes home.

My mom — well, she's wonderful at going with the flow, at being relaxed. She really knows how to pace herself, and I don't do that as well. But being home has helped. I have more opportunity to concentrate on meals that are pleasing for everyone, to focus on creating a pleasant atmosphere. I think we all benefit from that. As to going back to work, if something happened to my husband I would have to consider it, but at this point in my life I am so glad to be out of the rat race.

> *One writing effort was to have important results: she submitted a story to* Welcome Home, *the magazine produced by Mothers at Home, the non-partisan mothers' group, ended up volunteering for them, and is now chairman of the board.*

————————

Staying home was, of course, a huge decision for the career women we met. Especially if you've invested a lot of your identity in your job, you may well worry that once you're home, you'll feel trapped, like the pliant suburban housewife zombies in the movie *The Stepford Wives*. Cardozo says there's no reason why you should, providing five conditions are met:

- You have a clear idea of who you are and why you're at home raising your children.
- The community reinforces your values.
- You makes a clear distinction between, ugh! housework, and the much more important work of caring for your children.
- You have time to develop interests outside the family.
- You have a supportive husband who backs you up in what you're doing.

We would expand on this last condition. Beyond being simply supportive, husbands should be home more, not less, and play a larger, not a smaller, role in caring for their children. They should never feel they've been "let off the hook" because their wives are home. And even if they need to travel — especially if they need to travel! — husbands need to find ways to boost the morale of their wives at home.

"Jim is very good about this," said Sandra Kenzie, the woman whose car correspondent husband travels the world. "When I would have doubts when they were little, he would talk to me about what a good job I was doing. He always told me I was doing the most important job."

Should we be surprised after all that so many women in careers are willing to make a complete U-turn in their lives? Women have always seen their lives as a series of chapters, each with its beginning and end, far more than men have. In adopting an uninterrupted linear career path they were adapting to an essentially male pattern of progress. Now we're seeing that for both genders there are many more life and career choices than we had ever thought.

4

Can We Afford It?

*I*f you're used to living on two incomes, the notion of staying home might seem like taking a flying leap into bankruptcy. Maybe you've used both incomes to qualify for the maximum mortgage; probably you have two sets of car payments; perhaps you're also running outstanding credit card balances. Even if you're not shouldering a big debt burden, the money from those two incomes has a habit of disappearing. A car-repair bill here, a meal out there, and suddenly there's not much left. No wonder cutting your income by up to 50 percent seems a little, well, rash.

But, as we'll explain in this and future chapters, the prospect isn't really as crazy as it appears. Cutting back is easier than you might think, once you have a clear idea where your money's going. And you'll be surprised at the economies that arise simply from the decision to stay home.

The most important thing is to plan. Plan all you can. When Larry Burkett, author of *Women Leaving the Workplace* (Moody Press, 1995), surveyed 600 working mothers who had decided to return home, almost 60 percent said they had made the decision impulsively. More than 90 percent said that if they had to do it again, they'd plan better. Of those forced to return to work against their instincts, almost 100 percent said the reason they had had to return unwillingly was lack of planning before they quit.

It's so easy when a new baby arrives to be swayed by your emotions. Emotions are what babies are about. That's why the human race survives: because the newborn child demands our love and attention. It's easy to say, "I'll stay home and we'll muddle through somehow," and indeed some couples do muddle through. But some don't, and end up with both parents back at work and a lingering feeling of failure.

To avoid this and other unpleasant situations, begin by asking hard questions about your finances. The earlier you confront the facts the better. If you are already on top of your finances, you're a step ahead of the game, ready to pick and choose among the advice that follows.

Where the Money Goes

Whether you're looking ahead and want to stay home when your baby arrives, or are currently on maternity leave and wondering how you can avoid returning to work, or have decided you want to quit to stay home with your already existing family, the first thing you need to know is what happens to your money.

Try recording every penny you get and every penny you spend for a month. (Total it week by week and start afresh each Monday morning or you'll tend to lose interest.) Keeping track is harder than you might think; the banks and credit card companies have devised so many ways to separate you from your cash that you almost need to be a mastermind — or have a computer — to keep track. It's easy to make a cash withdrawal with your ATM card, but much harder to track where the money goes afterwards! It's so simple to pay for the groceries with your debit card, so you don't worry about spending more than the cash in your wallet allows. Above all, it's so hard to resist buying whatever takes your fancy when all you need do is sign the credit card slip. The end result is often you never see your money: it can leak away through so many holes in your wallet that many people never at any single moment have a true picture of what's happening with their finances.

That's why it's so important to keep records of your spending. It's easiest if you have a computer and personal finance software, but there's nothing the matter with an old-fashioned notebook and pencil, either. At the end of the month, the figures may shock you. But they'll also help you to see what is essential spending and what is discretionary. How much of your money is going on what really matters to you, and how much is being wasted on interest charges, meals out and small indulgences that add up?

Credit Cards

Because interest rates on credit card balances are the most onerous — commonly running 20 or 30 percent or more — any credit card debt should be cleaned up first. It's very easy to get on the credit card merry-go-round — pay a little off this month, add a little more next month — and darned hard to get off.

There is only one certain way, in fact, and that's to buy nothing on credit. That's right: nothing. The trouble with plastic is that if you use it for buying a pair of shoes for the baby, why not use it for a restaurant meal you don't have the cash for? And if for that, why not for that $300 suit you don't really need, but which is on at this fantastic sale price right now? During our more stringent years we always kept one credit card, but it was only for emergencies.

These days the banks are countering criticism of their high credit card interest rates by offering low-interest cards (a typical rate is 9 percent). Don't let them fool you. Your goal is not to have an unpaid balance at all, so the interest rate doesn't really matter.

The first cards to toss out should be the most expensive ones: the high-fee cards that will supposedly make it cheaper for you to buy a car or take a holiday in Hawaii. For every dollar you spend, you get points towards air miles or high-price items like cars. In fact, unless you're a real big spender, the benefit often doesn't even cover the card's annual fee. And, after all, the whole point of this exercise is not to be a real big spender.

So get a no-fee, no-frills credit card — they can still be found — and keep it for emergencies. If you can bear to, get rid of ATM cards and debit cards too. We manage without them, and we find the trip to the credit union for cash wonderfully bracing, as well as a useful discipline on our spending habits.

Unless you must have one for tax bookkeeping purposes, ditch any oil company cards; they make it easier for you to drive more without noticing the financial sting, and force you to buy at that one station when there may be cheaper gasoline across the street.

Your Mortgage

In general, pay off your debts is our main advice, but the mortgage may be a different matter. For most of us the mortgage is simply too large to pay off any time soon. If mortgage payments are a major impediment to your staying home, you have two choices: either sell the house and move to a more modest one, or refinance to reduce the payments.

Lower mortgage rates in Canada, the United States, and Europe in recent years have been a major factor in allowing more parents to stay home with their children. If you're lucky, your mortgage term will expire around the time you decide to stay home, and you can take advantage of lower rates when renewing the mortgage. If your mortgage still has several years to run, there will be a penalty, usually amounting to six months' interest, for switching it to the lower rate; it may not be worth it. A rule of thumb is that it's worth refinacing only if the current rate is two full percentage points lower than what you're paying. The monthly payment on a $100,000 mortgage amortized for fifteen years, for instance, drops from $1,015 at 9 percent to $899 at 7 percent.

Another alternative is extending the term of your amortization. Normally we wouldn't suggest adding to your debt burden, which is what this amounts to. But you need to look at your life as a series of "need periods." The time when your children are small is a high-need period when postponing mortgage repayment can be justified. Later, if finances become easier through pay raises or both partners returning to full-time or full- and part-time work, you can pump more money into the mortgage again. To take the example of the mortgage above, at 7 percent, the monthly payment falls from $899 to $666 if you extend the amortization period from fifteen years to thirty years.

For those who are highly disciplined in money matters, John Clode, a Burlington, Ontario, financial adviser, told us of another useful device: the line of credit. You replace your mortgage with a line of credit at your credit union or bank, using your house as equity. The advantage is that you are free to pay off the loan as fast as you like without penalties, but if you hit a rough spot, as long as you keep up your interest payments no one comes calling for the principal. The line of credit is also available as a source of emergency funds if you run into a problem.

Car Loans

We'll have a lot more to say about cars and how much we really need them — or don't need them — in Chapter 12. For now, we say: check your car loan(s). If you financed through the dealer you may be paying far too high an interest rate. Have your financial planner, bank, or credit union check it over to figure out the rate you're really paying. If the figures are not good, we suggest, if possible, paying off the loan and borrowing instead from your bank or credit union. Remember, too, if you have any savings bonds or securities, use them to back the loan; you'll save a point or two on interest if your loan is secured.

Life Insurance

When our young family started arriving, we made a mistake many young couples do: we bought whole-life, or cash-value, insurance. It offered the minimum amount of life coverage for the maximum cost. Why were we foolish enough to buy it? The lure dangled in front of us was that this was a way of saving money as well as insuring, and that there would be a big cash payout years down the road. When we finally came to our senses and cashed in the useless policy, we received only a paltry sum in "savings."

In the years when your family is young you need maximum coverage on the income earner, and that means term insurance. Term insurance is life coverage, pure and simple, for a specified period; if, pray God, you don't die, you don't get anything back. You don't buy into a "savings plan" when you buy a chicken at the grocery, and neither should you expect a savings plan when you buy life insurance. Get life insurance from the insurance company, but do your saving elsewhere.

How much life insurance do you need? Be realistic. You shouldn't expect to totally replace the breadwinner if he or she should die because that will probably mean you're giving over too many of your living assets to insurance premiums. Think about what your options would be in the event of a catastrophe: Would the other spouse return to work? Sell the house for something smaller? Couples commonly carry mortgage insurance that would pay off the mortgage at the time of death, plus term insurance at work amounting to two years or more of salary.

Financial adviser John Clode gives the example of a client who has $150,000 of insurance at work, plus mortgage insurance to take care of his at-home wife and several school-age children in the case of his demise. It sounds a lot, but is that enough? Calculating a return of twelve percent, this amount would provide a mortgage-free home and an income of only $18,000 a year. His suggestion: buy another $150,000 or $200,000 of term insurance to bring the potential income to around $35,000.

There may also be some justification for insuring the parent at home; if he or she died there would need to be alternative child-care arrangements. But there's no justification at all for the insurance industry scam of putting life insurance on children. It's a tragedy if a child dies, but it's not a major economic loss.

House and Car Insurance

When our annual home insurance bill arrived, we noticed one part of the coverage involved a $250 CDN ($180 U.S.) deductible. We asked our agent what it would cost if the deductible were $1,000 ($720 U.S.), like the other deductibles on our bill. Answer: $113 ($81 U.S.) less. In other words, we were paying more than $100 ($72 U.S.) for only $750 ($540 U.S.) of coverage. Of course, we opted for the $1,000 deductible.

There are a couple of lessons here. First, never pay your car or home insurance bills without going over them in detail. You'd be surprised how many times additional coverage is sneaked in without your knowledge. Second, only insure against the really big risks. Make sure, for instance, to have hefty public liability insurance on your car for damage you might cause other people's property and persons, but if your car is four or five years old consider canceling your collision coverage — if your car is even modestly damaged in an accident, the company will want to write it off and pay you only the depreciated value. Finally, generally speaking, it's best to go for maximum deductibles; there's no point in making small claims against insurance companies because they'll get it back from you in future premiums.

Taxes

In our research we discovered the issues affecting parents who want to stay home are identical in almost every regard on both sides of the U.S.–Canadian border. But taxes are an exception.

In Canada, the government gives working couples favored treatment. For instance, a two-income couple with two children and a combined income of $60,000 CDN will pay $6,780 less in income taxes than a one-income family with the same income, once you factor in a $2,113 child-care benefit that is not open to the single-earner family to claim. Although the House of Commons, responding to a campaign by the at-home parents group Kids First, voted 129 to 63 in November 1996 in favor of a special additional tax credit for caregivers at home, the federal government had not acted at the time of writing.

In the United States, because deductions can only be claimed against the first income in a two-income family, the second income earner will actually end up paying a greater proportion of earnings in tax than the higher-earning partner.

But Ray Loewe, a financial planner in Marlton, New Jersey, has one tip that we know from experience applies in just about every country: being self-employed is one sure way to pay less taxes. "I've been in business for myself for a long time," he told us. "You don't have to make as much money, and your dollars go further. When you buy a car, it's deductible, and vacations can be tagged on to a business trip, making a lot of the cost deductible." But be aware of one thing: if you start your own business, make sure to pay your taxes on time. That's one debt trap you don't want to fall into!

The Mom and Dad Factor

Many of the at-home parents we spoke to told us about a source of funds they had found close to home: their parents. With their own financial crises behind them, some parents are able to help their grown children buy their houses, extend them loans, or even give them money. In these times when, especially in Canada, older people are being hit by higher taxes and seeing their pensions clawed back by ever-more avaricious governments, it makes sense to make low-interest or no-interest loans to one's children at a time in their lives when they most need the money. Some older couples get around the tax problem by giving their kids interest-free loans. If the kids then want to buy them a couple of airplane tickets to Florida now and then, no one's going to call that taxable income. . . . Some older parents, of course, are not in a position to contribute financially. But for many who are, the idea of helping to give their grandchildren a better start in life by having a mom or dad at home is an attractive one.

Second Family Blues

Child support payments and alimony often loom large in the budgets of "second families." A second (or third) wife will often have the feeling she's only working to support the children (or even wife) from her husband's earlier marriage. Does she really have the option to stay home with her own child? The answer is that it comes down simply to an income problem. The payments can't be postponed or avoided, so it's a question of figuring whether there's enough income to go around. In one case we encountered, the couple had actually saved the college expenses for the husband's two children from an earlier marriage (high income earners, these!) before the wife decided to stay home.

Even in situations where incomes are reasonably high, difficult financial issues will arise in blended families that move to one income. Dad may not be able to take his son from his previous marriage skiing, or buy his daughter that expensive birthday present. There needs to be some frank talk and clear explanation of why the budget will be tighter in future, so the kids don't get the feeling dad just doesn't love them as much any more. It helps if the first wife is informed and sympathetic about your choice.

Savings

Every sensible budget starts with the admonition "Pay yourself first." Instead of saving what's left over, financial planners always suggest you put away money at the start. That advice is as good in this situation as anywhere. As we suggested earlier, switch over to *living* on one income as soon as you possibly can, then save the second income while you still have it. A savings pillow will be invaluable when the baby arrives to allow for those unexpected expenses.

Even if you are already surrounded by the patter of little feet, we highly recommend a savings program, no matter how modest. In Canada, Britain, and other countries, the monthly baby bonus paid to all parents was traditionally a painless way to put aside money for the future. Now, in Canada anyway, only those with modest incomes receive the child benefit. It's still a good savings opportunity for those who qualify for it. Maybe there's another payment you receive on a regular basis that you can put away without feeling its loss too much — and any tax rebate or other windfall that comes your way we suggest you apply either to debt reduction or to savings.

Why save? The biggest reason is psychological: it gives a sense of progress, of being in charge of your fate. You'll also feel better if you're saving toward your children's education, and there will always be surprise bills that come along. Being able to pay them out of savings instead of borrowing may mean the difference between success and failure as you walk the budgetary tightrope.

Budgets

Once you have a clear idea where your money is going now, you'll be in better shape to decide where it should go in the future. Appendix I shows a sample budget outline as well as some "typical" family expenditure tables. But a budget is only a theory. For it to be translated into a workable plan, you need to continue keeping tabs on your detailed expenditures month by month. For the story of one family that learned that lesson the hard way, read on.

The Turning Point Was Seeing a Financial Planner

Linda leads us into the dining area to show us her prize possession: the family computer. It has, she says, transformed her life. Two years ago Steve and Linda Ryan owed all sorts of money on their credit cards, were up to their ears in car problems, and thought they might even have to sell their home.

But they were certain about one thing: they wanted Linda to remain at home with their four children. So they went for advice to financial planner John Clode.

The meeting with him was a turning point. Gradually the Ryans pulled out of their steep financial dive and began saving money. But it was the computer, bought with a small inheritance they received from Steve's grandmother, that really put them in charge of their finances.

The Ryans live in Mississauga, Ontario. She's thirty-nine, he's thirty-eight. With Steve's salary as a research engineer and the money Linda makes caring for children in her home, they have a total income of about $70,000 CDN ($50,400 U.S.). Their children are Emily, aged ten, Alex, nine, Carley, five, and Claire, three.

Steve: We took a premarriage course before we were even engaged and it was clear from that we were really connecting. Everyone taking the course had to put down their future plans: house, children, and so on. Then it was compared with their partner's. We hadn't realized how compatible we were until we saw how far apart other people were. We had talked out a lot of these things, but it was clear a lot of people didn't share goals. We wondered afterward what became of them. . . .

Linda: We were pretty clear we both wanted four children, and one thing I knew for sure was I wanted to stay home with them. I had actually worked in day-care centers while I was in high school and going to college. I enjoyed it, to be honest, but there was the turnover of teachers and the fact that not all kids connect — there are always kids that nobody can handle and no one likes. My mom was home with me, and I can remember coming home and smelling supper cooking. I want my kids to have that.

Steve: Nineteen eighty-five was a big year for us. We became officially engaged in January, got married two months later, then Linda was pregnant in April, and we had Emily at the end of the year. I also got my layoff at Atomic Energy of Canada, although I knew it was coming. I'd already found my present job, and we used money from my separation package (along with money Linda had received from an earlier AEC layoff) to buy a townhouse. So the transition worked perfectly.

Linda: Having my first was a lot more work than I expected. When you have one child, that child takes 100 percent of your time. Once you have two, the pressure is off because they play with each other. Another mother and I organized a moms' group in the townhouse development. There were sixteen moms at home and we used to meet in the park on Wednesday mornings. We were just organizing a babysitting exchange when we bought this house and moved away. It was hard moving here in a way because I was afraid to give that up.

We had this wonderful townhouse, but the kitchen was small, with no eating area, and there was no ground-floor family room. I couldn't live with that. And we wanted a backyard. You couldn't see where the kids were. It made sense for us to move here in a lot of ways — except economically. We paid $95,000 [CDN; $68,500 U.S.] for the townhouse, but moving here we paid $170,000 [$122,500 U.S.]. And it was farther for Steve: from there it was a thirty-minute drive to work; from here it's forty-five minutes or an hour. He leaves at six-thirty in the morning and gets home about five-thirty, unless there's been an accident or heavy traffic; then it can take two hours. What we spend on gas is crazy. It used to be about $35 [$25 U.S.] a week before, but now Steve has a more economical car and it's about $25 [$18 U.S.].

Steve: I could look for another job. But my job now — I help to develop new devices for handicapped children — is with families and I really love my work. But it costs so much to live here. And it's the wear and tear on me, too — two hours on the road, and then it's not fair for me to be coming home exhausted when Linda's tired too from having the kids all day.

Linda: As far as money was concerned, we didn't plan. We figured we would find a way. But our vehicles, both of them ten years old, were costing us a fortune. We had to replace the engine in our old van. Then Steve's mom gave us a car that her husband was trading in. But we had a terrible spring. Steve and Alex were in a car accident. The lovely car that she had given us was totaled, and the van was on its last legs. So we took a $20,000 [$14,400 U.S.] loan from Steve's mom and bought the little car for Steve to go back and forth to work, and a '94 van with two airbags. With four children, we need a van.

I was always thrifty. We buy in bulk — that way you can save 30 percent on your money. That's a good investment — a lot more than the bank will give you. Also, we're mostly vegetarian, and I buy nearly all our produce at a local little supermarket where the prices are great. For vacations we used to spend a week at a cottage, but that was $700 [$500 U.S.]. So the last couple of years we've been adding to our camping equipment and going camping. We hardly eat out at all, and if we go to a movie we go to the cut rate one that charges $1.50. And then we take our own snacks. We get most of our clothes from hand-me-downs and garage sales and rummage sales.

But still, every time we had a child we seemed to go into debt, and this last time, with Claire, it seemed a lot harder to recover.

Steve: We were also paying quite a bit of interest on credit cards. We had a negative balance, and we just couldn't seem to get it back to zero. We were four or five thousand dollars in the hole on the credit cards.

Linda: There were times we had to borrow on our credit card to pay our mortgage because Steve's paycheck was coming a few days later. We had to do whatever we had to do to survive. There's no question, though, of me going to work full-time. We could never afford to put our children into day care.

I think the turning point in our lives was going to see a financial planner. We heard about him through neighbors of ours across the road who were on the point of losing their home, and who had gone to see him. We considered whether it would pay us to sell the house, invest the money, and rent a place closer to Steve's work. We could live with one vehicle, save on maintenance and insurance, and so on. Our house is at the point where it's going to need new windows and other expenses. On balance it was very close. But it wasn't the right move for us to make because we are at the point where we are starting to pay down our mortgage. It will be paid off in twelve or fourteen years.

We had been saving our child-tax credit and we had $5,000 [$3,600 U.S.] saved. The planner recommended we have a Registered Retirement Savings Plan [an RRSP, equivalent to a U.S. IRA] and now we have $100 a month [$72 U.S.] going into that. Plus we had some left over after buying the cars, and Steve's mom told us to put that into the RRSP too, so now we have about $12,000 [$8,650 U.S.] in mutual funds. That money is for the kids. It's good knowing it will be there for their education if they so choose. Really, we've come a long way in the last six months.

Steve: Getting the computer was a godsend. Linda took a course in money management and she does the bookkeeping.

Linda: I do a monthly report on how much we spend in each category. Our spending money is the hardest to keep track of.

The pace of our lives is still crazy. In the morning I have eight children here because I also look after children before and after school. At lunchtime I have five or six. And I still have extra children here while I'm trying to cook supper because some don't leave until six or so.

The only thing that makes it bearable is knowing that I am doing the right thing by being home with them. When the school calls and a kid is sick, I'm there in two minutes. They can come home if they're not feeling well. I do volunteer work at the school; I feel connected. I know their teachers well, I can talk to them, and I know what goes on at the school. I don't see adults during the day too much. I talk to my mom on the phone every day and when I go to get the kids from school I talk to the moms there.

Steve: You always want to see yourself twelve or fifteen years down the road. We never really had the opportunity to do that before. We were always fighting brush fires. It's nice to know we're putting something away.

The Ryan Budget

No two families are going to have the same budget, of course. You have to tailor yours to your needs. But just to give you an idea of where one family's money comes from and goes, here's Linda and Steve Ryan's budget for the month of May 1996. (All figures are in Canadian dollars.)

Income

Steve's take-home pay	2,839.43
Day-care income	1,668.00
Child-tax credit (invested in mutual funds for the children)	257.88
Income tax refund	450.00
Licence rebate on totaled car	47.50
Other income	253.88
Total income	**$5,516.69**

Expenses

Car		OTC drugs	18.15
Gasoline, car (for commuting)	154.13	**Education**	
		Books	18.66
Gasoline, van	103.04	Cubs	
Automobile insurance	205.54	(including trip for	
Parking	6.40	Steve, Emily, and Alex)	124.64
Cellphone		Explorers	5.00
(mainly for Steve's work)	36.97	School expenses,	
Home		crafts, trips	30.14
Maintenance		**Entertainment/Vacation**	
(mostly garden supplies)	163.84	Eating out	27.29
Mortgage		Baseball tickets	28.40
(including property taxes)	985.17	Bowling	8.00
Home insurance	33.75	Cable television	44.38
Garage sales	85.00	Lottery	6.00
Housewares	16.08	Toys and games	4.56
Stationery	12.04	Video purchase	19.06
Electricity	85.00	Video rental	7.33
Heating		Vacation camping fee	230.00
(including furnace repair)	121.94	Camping gear	349.83
Telephone	31.62	**Debt Payments & Savings**	
Water/sewage/garbage	81.29	Bank loan, principal	
Basic Household Goods		and interest	307.81
Clothing	157.41	Credit card	169.94
Computer software	6.89	Mutual funds	240.00
Groceries		Registered Retirement	
(including food		Savings Plans (IRA)	450.00
for child care)	954.31	**Miscellaneous**	
Newspaper	22.47	Charitable donations	66.00
Health & Hygiene		Gifts (birthdays, etc.)	193.49
Eyecare	25.00	Life insurance	42.32
Personal care		Allowances	28.00
(including diapers)	114.87	Photographs	49.41

Total expenses	**$5,871.17**
Deficit	**$354.48**

Of course, the Ryans' budget, like any family's, goes up and down, depending on major expenses that month. May was an expensive month because, among other things, they paid their camping fee in advance for their vacation in the summer, as well as buying camping equipment. The spring is also the boom season for garage sales, when Linda stocks up on clothes and other items for the rest of the year. In addition, Linda's income from child care fluctuates, going down toward the summer. So, although they were in the red in May, the Ryans' six-month budget shows a total credit of $4,600 CDN ($3,300 U.S.).

Recording all their expenditures has given Linda a new insight into where their money goes. "It's shocking when you write it all down," she says. Shocking, but essential. Few of us really know where our money goes; most of us don't really care as long as our books are roughly in balance at month's end.

Once you get the hang of recording and budgeting, you're in a much better position than you were before to judge whether it's possible to forgo one income. Especially once you've finished this book, and understand more fully the true costs of working and possible savings in home life, you may be surprised at your new idea of an "affordable" lifestyle.

On the other hand, if you are well and truly caught in the two-income trap, and it's going to take you some time to extricate yourself, you may have to accept that you can't move to one income yet, and consider some alternatives. Before your baby is born, or even after, you could discuss with your spouse whether staggered work-hours could be arranged. It would mean one of you was home with the baby while the other worked, with child care covering any gap when you're both working. It's not an ideal solution by any means: for nothing, you end up only really seeing each other on weekends. And for the mother who is breast-feeding, it poses numerous problems.

Maybe there's another new parent at work or a person close to retirement who would be interested in job-sharing with you, provided your employer is receptive. (You could tell your boss that, according to 1995 Statistics Canada figures, 8 percent of part-time workers share their jobs with another worker.)

Flextime, part-time work, and weekend work all provide other alternatives, each, it must be admitted, bringing its own set of problems.

But if you're ready to start living on one salary or maybe a salary and a half when you've been used to living on two, start right away remembering that every penny counts. It will help if you've put savings aside, because those first months at home are among the toughest. Later, as you get into your stride, all sorts of economies will occur to you and living on less, rather than being a major challenge, will become a source of pride and pleasure.

If you feel apprehensive at first, keep this in mind: by choosing to stay home you're doing what your instincts tell you is best, and you're making a choice that could have a profound effect on your own and your children's future well-being.

As Tonett Wojtasik, at home with Gabrielle, six, and Joshua, three, put it in a letter to us: "Can I afford it? My children can't afford for me *not* to be home."

5

What About My Marriage?

*W*hen you're thinking of staying home with your child, there's an emotional calculation that's almost as essential as the financial ones we've been looking at: a marital stock-taking.

We know now that any kind of major event in our lives is likely to cause stress. Most of us have encountered cases where some dramatic event — perhaps the death of a child or the loss of a job — has had the tragic result of driving a couple apart.

Of course, the arrival of a new baby is almost universally regarded as a joyful event and an important milestone in any relationship. But baby's arrival also imposes stresses and strains, and in the modern context of the dual-income couple these can be severe, and include a number that didn't exist in the days of more traditional families. Whether or not a parent stays home with him, that tiny demanding person in the crib will impose a subtle — or not-so-subtle — rebalancing on your marriage.

Questions such as "Should one of us stay home? If so, which of us? How will we manage?" will cause you to examine, perhaps for the first time, the power balance in your relationship and the priorities you give to your career and your marriage. For women especially the choices are difficult, given the traditional assumption that the mother is usually the primary caregiver.

A New Kind of Relationship

Having started behind the eight ball when it came to finding an interesting job, a woman who has worked hard and moved into an interesting and stimulating career is likely to consider her professional status to be a component of her personal relationships — including her marriage. The arrival of a baby can upset the applecart.

But couples can ride out this tremor if they plan carefully and decide ahead of time how they are going to cope with this new element in their lives. In a sense, it's like starting life together over again, with a new commitment to be mutually supportive. There needs to be frank talk about both partners' careers in terms of both prospects and economic returns. We're not talking here about a rivalry, but about finding the best ways to accommodate what both parents want for themselves and their child. Whatever arrangement is worked out, everyone needs to understand that there will be extra pressures, times when replies will be short and tempers tested.

Tell us about it! We wish now we could have planned better. People often comment on how well Ayesha managed with such a large family. And — this is Frank's opinion now — she did indeed do marvelously. But few people know about the tough days when Frank was traveling to distant parts as a foreign correspondent. Later he made career compromises, but by then the worst was over.

For many couples, once they adjust, having one person at home turns out to be a great boon to their relationship; Lori Demmings, a registered nurse from Stroud, Ontario, wrote to us about the tensions she and her husband felt when she was working twelve-hour shifts at the hospital. "My husband and I had always worked long hours, so, after eight years of marriage, communication between us was suffering. We didn't spend much time focusing on how to make our marriage better. Sometimes he never even bothered to ask why I was crying."

When she was laid off due to government cutbacks, she regarded it as a tragedy. Now Lori, whose son was twelve at the time of the layoff, works part-time. She reports: "Our lives have changed immeasurably, and we don't even miss the money. I have developed a love for healthy cooking and baking, so we eat fewer meals out. Our mortgage is lower and our cars are paid for, which helps. More than that, we seem to have developed a general sense of nonmaterialism. We just don't need as much *stuff* any more. We are more content. I always made time for my son, but now I have time to do some of the things *I* have always wanted to do, like studying yoga and archery.

"I find great satisfaction in all this," continues Lori, who has also begun volunteer work with environmental and literacy groups. "My husband and I have time to communicate our needs to each other, and we are generally a happier couple. My husband enjoys that he doesn't have to come home after a day's work and cook his own supper. My son knows there'll be someone home when he comes home after school. But most of all, life seems to have slowed down, I have lost the 'hurried gruffness' that was so much of my personality before. To any woman who even thinks staying home might be a possibility, I'd say go for it! Or to any man, for that matter!"

Tranquility! That's what parents tell us they discover when they stay home. That's not to say things are exactly peaceful for a mother trying to answer the phone while her two-year-old is having a tantrum and supper is boiling over on the stove. But almost without exception, couples report having more time for each other, to cook meals and to sit down and enjoy them together. Weekends, once a frantic rush of catching up on neglected chores, become a time to go for walks, to really talk about the things that matter, and most of all, to enjoy your children.

Husbands, as psychologist Diane Fisher points out, are often the last to realize the advantages of their wives staying home — especially if the wife is pulling down a large salary. "If a woman is having her first baby and she's a professor or a banker, her husband says, 'Oh, my god, I hope she doesn't tell me she wants to stay home.' And they're not apologetic about this. They're saying 'She's got to keep working; we depend on her income.' And that pressure is evident from the moment the baby is born. That husband is watching: 'Okay, you're on the four-week mark right now, shouldn't you be weaning the baby? And when's the nanny coming in to get used to the baby?' It's a rare husband who says, 'We don't need the big house, we don't need to drive a Jeep Cherokee or a BMW, I'd rather have you home with the kids if that's what you want.'

"But what social status is he going to get out of that? In his kind of circles, it's, 'Yeah, my wife is hauling down $100,000 a year, we're going to Europe with the kids and we're going to bring the nanny because, lemme tell you, we're not going to try and handle the kids by ourselves.'"

Carlie Sorensen Dixon says that when she quit to stay home, her husband resented her somewhat. He was just starting up a business, and "he had been used to having a working wife who brought in a lot of money," she explains. "Now he has this wife who isn't working and he has a child to support. But then he made a 180-degree turn, and he began to feel a strong sense of purpose — that he was needed, that his presence was necessary for our survival. If he didn't go out to work, we wouldn't have a place to live or food on the table. And he loved it. It finally dawned on him that he was playing a marvelous role, that he was appreciated and loved, and this made all the difference in the world to him as a provider. He's come to see what it means to the children, what it means to the family. Obviously I could provide if I had to. But I'm committed to being here, and he loves it. And I think it has been a wonderful thing for our marriage."

More and more qualified women like Sorensen Dixon are recognizing an important truth: that they are *not* in the same position as most of their mothers were, dependent on a man's paycheck for survival. Even if they choose to stay home, they still have their qualifications and can return to the workforce if they have to or want to. Their security and their careers are not sacrificed if they choose to stay home, especially if they keep up to date in their fields.

Divorce: What if Worse Comes to Worst?

Divorce is not a subject we want to think about when the topic is bringing home baby and launching a new chapter in your married life. But it's a subject that can't be avoided. For one thing, concern about possible divorce is an important reason why some women might be reluctant to stay home with their children.

Women know that, in spite of divorce law reforms and tough new initiatives to track "deadbeat dads," they are the ones likely to emerge the financial losers following a divorce: they usually have lower incomes to begin with, and they most often end up with the kids.

For a woman on her own with kids, poverty is often a consequence. In Canada, for instance, the number of single-parent families headed by women nearly tripled between 1961 and 1991, from 272,000 to 786,400. Sixty percent of those families fall below the poverty line. It isn't simply a question of struggling to make do; other figures show that 41 percent of the children of single mothers — poor or not — have at least one emotional, social, or academic problem. That's one-and-a-half to two times greater than the rate for kids coming from two-parent families.

We all think divorce is not something that's going to happen to us. Yet one in three marriages ends in divorce in Canada, and one in two comes unstuck in the United States, so it's sure happening to somebody. Prudent young women today are saying, "If my marriage breaks down, I don't plan on being left penniless." A career is not only a source of satisfaction, it also represents security — no matter what happens.

The question must bear on the mind of any woman — or man, for that matter — considering staying home: "Am I exposing myself to an unreasonable economic risk?" Should a woman, for instance, insist on a contract — a postnuptial agreement in this case — with her husband to make allowance, in the case of a split-up, for the fact that she's at home and has taken a break in her career experience?

If you are seriously considering this option, keep in mind that if a marriage has a shaky foundation, deciding whether to stay home is probably the least of your problems. By its very existence, a contract may exacerbate the problems rather than allay them.

Says Carlie Sorensen Dixon, a lawyer as well as a mom at home: "You need to go into a marriage with an unconditional commitment to be there and to remain mutually supportive of each other." Contracts, she believes, "undermine mutual trust. I think the best thing a woman can do if she wants to stay at home is get herself educated, and keep her big toe in her career through volunteer or professional activity or classes. Even if you have the happiest marriage in the world, your husband can get in a car accident. It's really not something peculiar to divorce. When two people are mutually dependent on each other, something can happen to one of them. You need to set yourself up so that if you have to go back to work for any of a whole host of reasons, you can do that."

Will the woman who chooses to be home be at a financial disadvantage if she has to sue for support and custody in court? Probably not. The general trend in domestic law in recent decades has been toward imposing and enforcing adequate support orders, and ensuring that women have the legal resources to seek their rights. Where custody is concerned, in the absence of any other evidence, judges are inclined to look kindly on the parent who is actually caring for the children.

Consider too that having a parent home is often a valuable defence *against* the eventuality of divorce. It is often the relentless pace of the two-career life that undermines a relationship and puts intolerable pressure on the marriage.

Divorce is a reality of the 1990s for couples of every kind of work status. However, as we'll see in the unusual story of Susan Russell that follows, even divorce doesn't have to mean going back to work.

The Last Person in the World

Susan Russell, a former TV news reporter, is making pita bread, tofu, and beansprouts for lunch for her daughters, Joan, who is seven, and Carol, two years younger. They are vegetarians, grow much of their own food, and live in Boston, New York, an idyllic small town upstate. Susan, who is thirty-seven, is coping with the recent breakup of her marriage to a lawyer ten years her senior.

When we made the decision to have children I had already thought long and hard about the commitment. I knew the only way I could do it was all the way. I think in part I was influenced by my mother because she stayed home and I really benefited from it.

I was definitely one of the lucky ones. My husband was not wealthy, but his income was sufficient. That's not to say we didn't have to make lifestyle choices to afford it. If anything I would say it was harder for my husband because he was used to living fairly extravagantly when he was single. I had a beat-up old Toyota, and the house we had in Buffalo when Joan was born was modest enough. I stopped working a few months before she was born to fix it up. Later we sold it when we moved to a twelve-acre place in the country.

I would say that verbally my husband agreed it was good for me to be home, but when the idea turned into reality I didn't feel the agreement. I felt resentment at one level and, more profoundly, a lack of respect, a lack of acknowledgment that I was working too and working damn hard. And it was a real job.

I wasn't surprised by the amount of work. I think a lot of people have some notion at the beginning that staying home is going to be like a scene out of Norman Rockwell, all fuzzy and warm and cozy. The reality is it has its terrible moments as well as its warm, fuzzy moments. I thought I'd worked hard in the television industry, with long hours, but in TV you do get a break. I was working seven days a week, on call twenty-four hours a day.

The surprise was that I had anticipated getting more help from my spouse, and that didn't come. I think the whole thing freaked him out. He'd been living the single life for so long, free to come and go as he pleased, and that didn't mix well with family needs. I begged and pleaded, could he leave the office by five-thirty just two evenings a week to be home for dinner?

I think sacrifice is seen as a dirty word these days. But you can't expect to put your own needs first when you bring children into the world. I know there are circumstances where both parents are working just to keep a roof over their heads. But I also know there's a whole lot of people who just simply can't give of themselves, and when the kids come along, they run. They don't want to give up their CDs and their boats and their Porsches.

It's hard being home, especially in this society. When we moved to the country, people said, "Are you crazy? You'll be so isolated there." But I was just as isolated in the city. There I was with my little stroller and my baby backpack, walking up and down the street and no one was home. All the parents were working, it was like a ghost town. I used to say to people — half joking and half serious — "Damn this washing machine and this dryer sitting in my house, I would much rather be down at the river with ten other women doing my wash than us all having our own little self-sufficient homes with our own little washer, our own little dryer, our own little everything-we-need." It was a lack of community I felt. I've been home seven or eight years now, and I've found my community. But it means I spend a lot of time driving because my friends are so scattered. All my mother had to do was step out of her side door and there were people around.

Joan was about a year old when we moved to the country. It was a lifestyle choice — my husband was an outdoors kind of person from a farming background, and I love the country. It's been beautiful and a delightful environment to raise our daughters. Being in the country kept us very busy, gardening, enjoying the changing seasons, so it was easy to keep the children involved in things and they didn't need television as a crutch. Now we only take the television set out of the closet when there's something special.

Of course, it's easy to go to the other extreme: "I'm a stay-at-home parent, so to make my job legitimate in everyone else's eyes, I'll become Supermom." You fall into the trap of being your children's entertainment director. I fell into that trap a little bit myself at the start, and that's a big mistake. We're afraid of our children being bored, having nothing to do, not getting the proper stimulation. But boredom is good. The question I hate when the girls wake up in the morning is "What are we going to do today?" I turn it right back on them and say, "Yes, what are you going to do?" It's not my job to provide you with amusement.

The best thing I can do is let them see me as a busy person. They can see me growing food for the family, cooking wholesome, healthy meals, showing pride in our home, repairing clothes. I'm here for them when they need me, but one of my biggest jobs as a parent is teaching them to amuse themselves.

I was with the children just about the whole time; babysitters weren't really in the budget. That's where I think a supportive spouse has to come in. Obviously, my marriage didn't work. It wasn't just the children, there were other issues. But parenting presents enough of a challenge in a strong marriage, and if the marriage has problems, then I think the stay-at-home issue can collapse it.

Now that I'm single people say it must be ten times harder — at least before I had financial security. But this is more honest. There's being lonely alone and there's being lonely when there are two people, and I prefer the honest version. I'm doing everything I did before, only I'm not doing it under the illusion of having a helpmate. I'm not denying my husband's financial contribution, which enabled me to stay home. I don't diminish that at all, but I don't think today that's enough, just to bring home the paycheck.

I am still struggling to stay home. I do some freelance writing from the house and some part-time teaching, but I try to be home when the girls are home. I don't ever want them getting off a school bus with a key in their hand and sitting in an empty house.

I live on a pretty meager budget. The child-support payments go for food, clothing, and shelter. We spend maybe $40 [U.S.; $55 CDN] a week at the grocery store during the off-garden season. We tend to eat seasonally, and in summer, when the garden's going, it may be just five or ten dollars a week, mostly for sundries.

Growing things has always been a love of mine. I don't have a large vegetable patch — it would fit into the average urban lot.

I do grow a lot of root crops like potatoes and carrots, which store very well. We try to eat fresh produce and I even grow things downstairs like indoor greens and alfalfa sprouts. I don't buy prepackaged, prepared anything. I buy raw ingredients, and you wouldn't believe the money that's saved. I also belong to a natural foods co-op in Vermont with six other local families and a truck delivers every month to the house — that's where we get our staples like flour and grains. All that drastically lowers prices.

I think of the work that I do as vital — I don't treat it like drudgery. I treat the smallest task like it's sacred. There's something sacred about making bread, for instance, and the girls can participate in that. We make our own maple syrup from trees in the yard, and yesterday we spent all day picking strawberries and freezing them. We'll make great blender drinks from them in the winter. I freeze blueberries too, and stock up on peaches and apples, which dry real well. The girls love all the vegetables, so a typical dinner will be pasta broccoli, or whatever vegetable is in season. We usually have oatmeal in the morning. We buy it in bulk, just add water, add some frozen blueberries, and there you go!

You can see we live very simply. The extra money I earn goes to pay for them attending a local private school, the Waldorf School. I hope I can afford to keep them there, especially during this period of transition.

I am the last person in the world I ever expected to see divorced. I have been very judgmental in the past about parents who divorce. Now I don't judge until I've walked in someone else's shoes because here I am, walking in those shoes now.

I think my being home has helped the girls through this. In my gut I feel they are very secure. I am their rock, and I'm still here. If we had divorced and then two weeks later I had had to put them in day care and get a job, they would have lost two parents.

But it's still a struggle to stay home. Even the mediator, when we were trying to work out a separation agreement, looked at me and said, "Well, Sue, you're talking about your garden and everything as you're writing up your food costs here, but you're not going to be able to have that garden any more; you're going to have to get out and work." And that was from a woman!

I said, "Excuse me, I *am* working. And I happen to believe I'm doing a very important job. It's that garden that's keeping our food costs down. I'm paying my way; I'm earning my money."

I think children get such a phenomenal sense of their importance from a parent who wants to be with them. It doesn't matter how many toys they have or what a beautiful house they live in or whether they have a Laura Ashley nursery — if mom and dad don't find time to be with them, all that doesn't matter.

Susan Russell has discovered that even after a divorce, there are ways of getting by and still being home for the kids. Many women would consider the sacrifices she's making to stay home to be simply too much. Realistically, without a spouse to share the burden, many women might want to return to work, if only part-time.

The new social reality, in fact, suggests that women have less and less to worry about should death or divorce leave them on their own. In 1995, the British think tank Demos published a report called *Genderquake*, which pointed out that it is young men who are losing out to women in educational attainment, in jobs, in salaries, and in self-esteem. In Canada in late 1996, defying traditional patterns, male unemployment for the fifth year was running ahead of female unemployment. Meanwhile the U.S. Bureau of Labor predicts the fastest-growing employment areas will be in residential care, computer and data processing, health services, child care, and business services — nearly all areas dominated by women.

We are not for a moment suggesting that, if divorce puts paid to your plans to stay home, a full-time job is the perfect answer. It would, after all, take you away from home again. What we are saying, particularly to the woman who is considering staying home, is that income security may not be the worry you thought it was. And when you count in part-time work, working from home, and other choices, the list of options open to a mother on her own is by no means as restricted as people might have you believe.

6

Working Harder — for Less?

*P*eople say it all the time: "It's not what you earn, it's what you get to keep." But how many of us ever take a careful look at what we're really spending our money on, and how much is left over for the things we really want?

Double-income families have prospered mightily in the last couple of decades, according to the statistics. By 1992 the double-income family in Canada with at least one child was earning, on average, $75,700 CDN [$54,500 U.S.], while a similar single-earner family got only $49,600 [$35,700 U.S.]. That means the double-earners were grossing fully 50 percent more than single-income families. But how much better off were they, *really*?

In Canada, as we've seen, with generous child-care tax allowances and an income-tax system tilted in favor of two-income families, the politicians seem to be doing everything they can to get parents out of the house. The tax situation isn't nearly as favorable for double-income families in the United States. And even with tax breaks, that second income, whether earned in North America, Europe, or elsewhere, usually amounts to a lot less than you think. Some people, it turns out, are actually paying for the privilege of working.

Take Julia and Tony Ingram, a young working couple from Lawrence, Kansas, who were featured in a segment of NBC's *Dateline* in May 1996, saying they were both working for their slice of the American dream. "We want our children to have the best," Tony tells the camera. "Unfortunately every time we get close to the dream it changes. And it takes a little bit more money, a little bit harder work, a little bit more shuffle to get that thing."

Tony, who is twenty-nine, earns $28,000 U.S. ($38,900 CDN) as a lineman working for the Sprint telephone company, while Julia, who is twenty-six, earns just under $15,000 U.S. ($20,800 CDN) working the night shift at a garage-door factory. Their combined income comes to $43,000 ($59,700 CDN) — but you should see what they have to do to earn that!

We see Tony getting up at five-thirty a.m. and working out before setting out on his twenty-five-mile commute to work. At nine a.m., Julia gets up with their two boys, four and two. She does errands, gives them lunch, then drives them across town in her late-model sports utility to leave them with her mother while she goes to work at three-thirty p.m. Tony comes home from work in time to pick the boys up and give them supper, bathe them, and put them to bed. Julia finally gets home at two a.m. and goes to bed.

"We're never together any more," complains Julia. "We are separated, individual people who see each other at the weekend and who have two kids."

How long can they keep this up? "As long as it takes," replies Tony. "We've accepted it. It stinks, but we all make sacrifices." Sacrifices for what? The Ingrams are saving to buy a home and for their children to go to college, and that's why Julia works. Are her earnings bringing them nearer their goal?

NBC had Linda Kelley, a home economist and author of *Two Incomes and Still Broke* (Times Books, 1996), analyze the couple's budget. More than a quarter of Julia's earnings goes to income taxes. "That's Uncle Sam's secret," says Kelley. "He's very fond of second-wage earners." Work clothes, two sets of steel-capped boots, and safety glasses Julia needs for her job cost $750 ($1,050

CDN), while she spends $1,550 ($2,150 CDN) on coffee and sandwiches at work.

The couple get an easy ride on child-care expenses — they pay Julia's mother $20 ($28 CDN) a week, and a conservative estimate puts the cost of driving the kids back and forth and Julia driving to work at $1,250 ($1,740 CDN). Because Julia would rather spend her weekend time with the kids than cook, they figure they spend an extra $1,000 ($1,400 CDN) on convenience foods and eating out. Services like haircuts, which they might do themselves if they had more time, cost $500 ($700 CDN), home maintenance that Tony has no time to do, $1,000 ($1,400 CDN). Tony also has to turn down overtime worth roughly $750 ($1,050 CDN) so that he can get home to pick up the boys. Because they don't have time to calculate their finances, they're buying a $2,500 ($3,500 CDN) computer (begging the question of when they will have time to learn to operate it!).

Adding it all up, Kelley breaks the bad news to the Ingrams: It's actually costing them $3,600 ($5,000 CDN) a year for Julia to go out to work. That's how much they're going in the hole.

Julia breaks into tears at the news: "It's such an emotional thing, all this running around and then to find out it's not benefiting you." Kelley tells Julia she'd be better off staying home and caring for someone else's child, doing part-time work, or going to college to qualify for a better job than working at the door factory in the future.

The item doesn't begin to explore how much money the Ingrams could save with Julia at home, how much could be slashed from the grocery bill if she had time for coupon-clipping and bargain-hunting, or the savings they'd have if they could manage without that shiny sports utility vehicle. At the end of the item, though, we learn that Julia, who is expecting their third child, is still working at the factory — for the sake of the family health benefits that go with the job. A closer analysis might show that if she were home they could buy the benefits elsewhere and still be ahead. Certainly if she lived in Canada, where public health benefits are far more generous, it seems likely she would be better off at home.

Newspapers in several U.S. cities have conducted similar exercises to figure out the actual return on a family's second income, and always with results similar to NBC's. In Canada, in 1992, *Chatelaine* magazine calculated that a woman with two preschool children would have to earn more than $25,000 CDN ($18,000 U.S.) just to break even if she had her children in day care, and more than $30,000 ($21,500 U.S.) if she used a live-out nanny. These figures would certainly be higher today. Table 4 shows calculations — also from *Chatelaine* — demonstrating that a woman earning $23,000 *after taxes* increases the family's disposable income by only $3,600 after expenses.

Table 4   The Cost of Working

Chatelaine *magazine took a look at what happens to the family budget when a couple expecting their second child decides to have mom stay home.*

	Both Working	*Mother at Home*
Net Income		
(after taxes and deductions)	*$62,300*	*$39,300*
Less:		
Housing	*$18,000*	*$18,000*
Transportation	*$9,200*	*$7,320*
Day care, two children	*$13,520*	Nil
Clothing	*$3,000*	*$1,500*
Breakfasts,lunches, dinners out	*$5,000*	*$2,500*
Food, utilities, insurance and		
other household expenses	*$8,580*	*$8,580*
Disposable income	*$5,000*	*$1,400*

Source: Homebase *magazine.*

A U.S. study found that, for middle-income earners, 56 percent of the second-wage earner's money is swallowed up by expenses. You might expect the picture to be very different for people earning a large second salary. Not so; the same survey found that, because high-income earners spend more lavishly, 68 percent of their second salaries never get in their pockets.

At this moment you may be saying, "That doesn't apply to me." Maybe you've worked hard, gained a foot in middle management, and with annual earnings in the high forties or low fifties, you're making a substantial contribution to the family budget. Or are you?

In *Two Incomes and Still Broke*, Linda Kelley explains exactly why so many two-income families have the feeling they're working harder all the time and yet just not getting ahead. The answer, which many working women would rather not hear, is basically the high cost of working: from child care (that costs typically $100 to $180 a week at a day-care center) to the never-ending birthday gifts and lunches needed for colleagues at the office. A nanny in Nebraska costs $250 a week; in New York, $500. No wonder researchers are saying that one reason the level of female employment in the U.S. has stopped climbing for the first time since 1948 is the high cost of child care.

Other job-related costs? It's hard to know where to begin. Commuting is one of the more obvious expenses, and it doesn't start and end with gasoline. If you need a second car mainly to get to work, you need to count in the cost of depreciation, interest on the car loan, repairs, insurance, a licence, maintenance, parking. . . . In Canada, even an inexpensive Ford Escort costs $10,000 CDN ($7,200 U.S.) a year, or about $192 ($138 U.S.) a week, to operate. In the United States, where gasoline and other car costs are lower, it costs close to $150 a week (about $120 U.S.) to operate a car. And there, and now increasingly in Canada, highway tolls are a frequently forgotten cost of our commuting.

Public transit, of course, is a better alternative, and traveling to work by bus and subway in Toronto, for instance, costs only $16 ($11.50 U.S.) a week. At the other end of the scale, a British Rail season ticket for outer suburb commuters in London typically costs $95 ($68 U.S.) a week.

Clothing is an open-ended item. Where you could get away with jeans and a top at home, for office work $10 or $15 for pantyhose plus $200-a-hit for suits are standard. For the professional who must make an impression in the courtroom or the boardroom, $600 is not out of line for a suit. But the real crunch comes with "opportunity spending." It's no coincidence that clothing stores are clustered around office buildings — lunchtime impulse buying constitutes a major portion of clothing sales. So although you may only list business suits, blouses, and shoes as the direct clothing cost of working, the truth is you would never have purchased that evening dress, earrings, and swimsuit last week if you hadn't been in the store on your lunch hour. Grooming is another part of the story — cosmetics, hairdressing, even the health club.

Look further, and you'll see a vast new army coming over the horizon: the hordes of convenience workers needed to fill in for busy double-income couples. They march by in their thousands — the dry cleaners and laundry people, the housecleaners, the pet groomers, the gardeners, window cleaners, caterers, tutors — there is no end to the procession.

Mention food and another army appears: the waiters and cooks at the restaurants where double-income couples lunch and dine, the people who prepare all the convenience foods that time-squeezed moms opt for on the way home from work. And because so much of the shopping is rushed, Linda Kelley estimates families sacrifice a minimum of $100 a month because they have no time for careful comparison shopping, whether for car repairs or Halloween candies.

And then there are the hardest categories of all to measure: guilt and reward spending. Count in the toys you bought your toddler to somehow compensate for not being there when he cries, the weekend ski trip to somehow make it up to your twelve-year-old that you have no time to help with her homework. And if your job takes you out of town a good deal, don't forget the expensive last-minute scramble at the airport to purchase some bauble that's supposed to make up for missing the football game.

Don't forget too the Friday night dinner (plus babysitter) that you both rewarded yourselves with at the end of a particularly hectic week at work. On this one we speak from experience; when Frank was a foreign correspondent based in London, it was our regular routine when he returned from a trip to walk across Putney Bridge for dinner at our favorite Indian restaurant. It was the civilized thing to do, but it didn't really make up for being apart.

Table 5, showing average expenses (in Canadian dollars) for one- and two-income earners in Canada, clearly shows that dual earners spend more in every category.

Table 5   Earning More, Spending More

Average household expenditures, Canada, 1992, couples with children under 14

	Two Full-Time Earners	One Full-Time Earner
Food	8,350	6,843
Shelter	11,678	9,128
Household operation	3,841	2,042
Furnishings, equipment	2,224	1,642
Clothing	4,030	2,405
Transportation	8,022	6,450
Health care	1,268	1,044
Personal care	1,316	987
Recreation	3,683	2,481
Reading, printed matter	352	245
Education	774	433
Tobacco and alcohol	1,587	1,199
Miscellaneous	1,852	1,191
Security, insurance, etc.	4,696	2,750
Gifts and contributions	1,207	898
Personal taxes	17,187	11,190
Total expenditures	**$72,067**	**$50,928**

Source: Statistics Canada.

Ray Loewe, the New Jersey financial adviser, told us he is frequently asked for advice on whether it's worth it for an at-home mother to return to work, to save for college for the children. By now you won't be too surprised to learn that he figures it only makes economic sense if the husband has an income of $20,000 or less. On the other hand, he adds, "We have other people who want to get out of the house and start their second careers, and that's fine too."

In their book *Your Money or Your Life* (Penguin, 1992), Vicki

Robin and Joe Dominguez take an even more radical view of the value — or non-value — of the job. "How much are you trading your life energy for?" they ask. They count, not just the hours we work, but the hours we spend commuting, the inferior food we eat away from home, the job-related illnesses, the vacations we need to recover from work stress, and the decompression time we need when we get home. Dominguez and Robin, who advocate a life of voluntary simplicity, add it all up and figure a typical worker, when all the costs are counted, is selling her "life energy" for a mere four dollars an hour. And they don't even try to assess the cost our children are paying for our twin addictions: work and money.

How much is it costing you to work? Try listing all the actual costs associated with your job as accurately as you can. Use the worksheet provided in Appendix II at the end of the book as a guide.

We don't want to be unnecessarily bleak. People, it's true, work for reasons other than money — for self-esteem, challenge, social contacts, and independence, among other things. But if you're both working your butts off and you're groaning that, if it weren't for the money you'd stay home, well, we think maybe you should come up with a better excuse. Because quite often the money just doesn't cut it.

You Learn the Value of Sharing

Five years ago, Nancy Devine was called into the boardroom and told she'd been "restructured" out of her $47,500 CDN ($34,200 U.S.) bank public relations job. She soon found she was not unique. Plenty more of her neighbors in the bedroom community of Aurora, an hour north of Toronto, where she and her newspaper-editor husband Doug live, were in the same boat. Nancy estimates there's a parent home in about half the homes in her immediate area. Like quite a few of her neighbors, she came home because she lost her job, and then stayed home by choice to be with Bonnie, eight, and Daniel, four.

All I ever wanted to be was a writer, a reporter. I wouldn't say I was the career woman extraordinaire because I had other interests.

I like to sew, and I love doing crafts. But my first job was feature writing for a funky little magazine, and I really, really loved my job. I went on to work for a community newspaper and then the bank, devoting as many hours as it took to get the job done. When a baby came along, I thought, well, it would just sort of fit in with everything else. I remember saying that to my mother, and I don't think she's stopped laughing yet.

But I found out what a baby is real fast. Bonnie was slow coming; at the end it was an emergency situation. It took me a year to get back on my feet physically and psychologically. Bonnie was six months when I went back to work. We had found Mary Poppins — an English woman named Carol — to look after her. She arrived with everything but the umbrella, and we shared the cost with a neighbor who had a little boy. Carol looked after them both, and she was wonderful. But the night before I went back I couldn't sleep. Next morning I got as far as the train and I met my manager. She said, "Hi, how are you doing?" And I burst into tears.

This was my day when I was working for the bank: I woke up at six-thirty, stumbled into the shower, and was at the train by seven-fifteen without seeing Bonnie or talking to Doug. If I had to work late at the bank, which was most nights, I'd miss the last train and get home at ten o'clock with Bonnie already in bed and my husband ticked off. Bonnie didn't have a clue she had another parent, except at weekends. She has asthma, and when she was sick in the night I'd say to Doug, "I know this isn't logical, but I think she's making this happen just so she'll see me in the night."

Once she was in hospital for a week for observation and I stayed with her. When I went back to work my boss called me in and asked me what my priorities were. It was one of those defining moments. I was so stunned I couldn't answer. I knew my priority was my child. And that meant I was stuck in the "mommy track."

At Christmas dinner, someone asked Bonnie, just to make conversation, "Do you live with your mommy and daddy?" She said, "I live with Daddy. Mommy works." I thought, it doesn't matter how much I try to cram into the forty-eight hours of the weekend, in her day-to-day life Bonnie has only one parent.

When I was working I let her get away with all sorts of things because I didn't want her to think I was the mean one. I can remember picking up a toy for her on my lunch hour for absolutely no reason. And that's guilt. When I came home I was like "Disney-Mom" — where can I take her out? I hated being jealous of our caregiver. I mean, Bonnie crawled for the first time for Carol, first stood up for her.

But even after admitting my child was really my first priority, my reaction at work was to try harder. I would ask for important work to do, and begged for extra training. I tried to be spot on, get to the train on time in the morning, and never leave early. In an organization that values "facetime" above everything, it didn't matter that your briefcase was stuffed with work you'd do at home.

When I was restructured, my first reaction was "I've got to get another job." But suddenly it dawned on me that if I worked at it I could freelance enough so that I wouldn't have to leave the house. So we talked about it, and Doug said, "Okay, well, keep looking for a job because we need reliable income." People I'd worked with were very supportive; I had freelance work to do literally the week after all this happened. As soon as the severance payment came in we paid off debts and upgraded our computer equipment. Now I have four or five regular freelance clients I work for.

Financially things improved too. When Doug and Nancy bought their $187,900 CDN ($135,300 U.S.) house, the mortgage payments were $1,500 ($1,080 U.S.), but after she came home interest rates dropped and the payments came down, to as low as $900 ($650 U.S.) at one point. Doug has also seen his pay increase. But with a combined income of about $55,000 ($39,500 U.S.), it's still sometimes a scramble to meet the monthly mortgage payment. A vacation now is buying a family pass for the week to Canada's Wonderland, a nearby theme park. Where they had two cars before, they now have one; if Nancy needs the car, she drives Doug to work. Their parents have also been "terrifically supportive."

We've changed our spending patterns, too. When I was working we often had meals out; now we don't. With my folks coming from the Maritimes, I had a good idea how to make things stretch. Chicken backs may look disgusting, but you can make a heck of a pot of soup with them, and on a winter's night that's nice to know.

The other big thing is what I call "the movement." There's quite a lot of at-home parents here now, and by staying home we're finding ways to develop a neighborhood. When I was working I hardly had a clue about the people who lived around here. Now, if I'm going to be late I'll call one of the neighbors and say, "Can you pick Bonnie up?" Or someone will call and say, "Hamburger's on sale at A & P, you know," and I'll say, "If I can't get out today can you pick me some up?"

In the summer we'll meet in the park, or in the winter call each other. Sometimes after we've walked the older ones to school we'll take the little ones and have a coffee or a juice at La Columba bakery. When you came to the door today I was on the phone with a friend telling her, I've just cleaned out Bonnie's closet and I've got a bag of things for her. One of my friends gave me a bag of pants her boys have worn the knees out of. Well, those are cut-offs for this summer, and the bottoms we're going to have some fun with and make patchwork vests.

If someone has a baby, everyone in the neighborhood makes or bakes something. If you see a stork on the lawn you know there's going to be some baking to do. When I had Daniel I don't think I baked or cooked for a month. Our freezer was stuffed. You learn the value of sharing.

I look back now at my time at the bank and I think it was such a hollow existence. You ask me "What was a good day at work?" and I have no recollection, none. But I remember every moment I've spent with my children. What changed it, I think, was walking Bonnie to kindergarten the first day. I'd always promised myself that when Bonnie started school I'd be sure and take the day off work. But that would have been just one day. And I thought to myself, walking her, this is nice, this is very, very nice.

And there have been so many special times. One day last summer my friend and I were sitting in the park with the children and it was getting hotter and hotter. It was time to get the girls from school and I said, "I'll go home and get the sprinkler out so they can play in it." And soon there were six or seven people there with their kids. Some had brought hot dogs, and I grabbed some lemonade, and we sat on the porch watching them run in and out of the sprinkler. It was one of those days you know you'd have missed if you'd never lived it.

If you'd said to me when I was at college that this is what I'd be doing, I'd have said, "Okay, how rich is the guy I'm going to marry?" We let money be so important, but there are more tangible things. Money gets in the way of what we want to do. On more than one occasion, seeing us sitting at the breakfast table as he goes off to work, Doug has said, "I don't know if we can afford this." But I think there's a certain calm in his life now, a certain order. When all this happened to me at work, I felt crushed, I felt a failure. Now I'll be able to say, where my kids are concerned, I did my best. God wraps his presents in very strange packages!

———————————

As a single-income family ourselves, we too have learned that it's what you get to keep that counts, and that sharing and making your own and handing down are the bywords for at-home success.

7

What About Dad?

*T*o the last generation it would have been unthinkable. But to you, as new parents wanting to be there for your child, the first question you need to answer is: who should stay home — dad or mom? Not only have attitudes toward fatherhood changed a lot in the past few decades, so have a lot of practical realities. It may be simply more practical and sensible for dad to stay home. Although it's far from the norm, in many homes today women are earning more than their partners.

In one out of four dual-income families in Canada, the woman is paid more than the man. With today's increase in at-home work and flexible schedules, a father may well have a career that can be put on hold or converted to part-time more easily than his wife's. And in an age where children are brought up in a more gender-neutral fashion, the male may simply be the more nurturing parent.

A case in point is George Ihnatowycz. When Annie, their first baby, was born, George and his wife, Sylvia, didn't even discuss who would stay home with her.

"I just didn't see myself doing it," says Sylvia, head of the art department at a Catholic high school. "I don't have the patience or the personality to be happy at home all day."

George adds: "When Annie came along we decided someone should stay at home. We just recognized that if we both worked it would be more hectic and everyone would suffer. And being with Annie was something I looked forward to, a challenge, enjoyable." Besides, Sylvia was earning around $40,000 CDN ($32,500 U.S.) while he was getting $30,000 ($21,500 U.S.). So he quit his job counseling troubled youth, and has been home now for ten years with Annie and Alex, who is now five.

How Many Dads at Home?

It's hard to put an exact figure on the number of dads at home, harder still to calculate how many are home with their children by choice. Many came home unwillingly, laid off in the downsizings of the early 1990s, and who could ever say how many actually came to enjoy the experience of being with their children? The U.S. Bureau of Labor Statistics estimates that 325,000 men between the ages of twenty-five and fifty-four were keeping house full-time in 1993 — up 26 percent from 1990. The figures don't show how many of these were caring for children, however. A 1993 U.S. study reported that 20 percent of preschoolers were being cared for primarily by their fathers.

Certainly the amount of interaction between at-home dads on the Internet and the success of several newsletters for fathers at home suggests that there are plenty out there. And even if their total number is small, fathers caring for children at home have a huge symbolic significance. When a woman stays home with her children, she risks being labeled a throwback to the fifties. When a dad stays home, he is seen as the wave of the future, the ultimate caring male. He's the guy who makes it respectable for men — and hence, more respectable for professional women — to put their children ahead of career. Some observers see dads at home as the best news yet for giving children the priority they need and deserve.

Says child psychologist Penelope Leach: "I don't think many people would want to reverse the situation where women are now playing an equal part in the traditional male world of work. That being so, I cannot see now, or in the future, any way of filling that gap at home except that men should be equal partners in the traditionally female world. I think there is still a clear assumption, bottom line, that children are women's responsibility, and I don't believe it. I think we have to believe that children are parents' responsibility."

Leach's view is still not a majority one. A 1996 Angus Reid poll found that over half of Canadians believe the mother is generally the better parent (see Figure 4). (Interestingly, the percentages were about the same among the men and women polled.) Overall, only 4 percent cited the father as the better parent.

Figure 4   ***Who's the Better Parent?***

Answers to "Who do you think is generally the better parent?"

Both/Neither 35%

The mother 56%

Don't know 5%

The father 4%

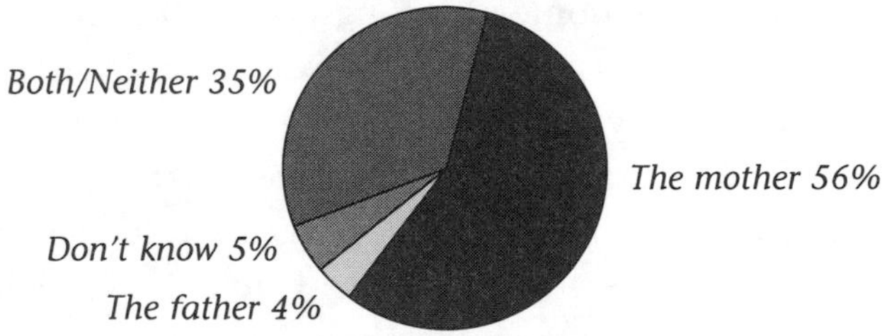

Source: Angus Reid survey, 1991.

George Ihnatowycz says: "I don't believe men and women should be categorized as parents. It comes down to the individual person. There's no such thing as a norm. Society puts expectations on women and, in spite of feminism, young girls are still brought up to be the caregivers. But breast-feeding is the only thing men can't do. You pick up the baby, hug it, burp it, change its diaper — that stuff is not in the genes, it's just technique. Men can learn techniques as well as women."

Is a dad as good as a mom? "No!" insists pediatrician Dr. Bill Sears. "But nobody's going to tell you the truth. Everybody is going to tell you what is politically correct. But there's no way the average father can replace the average mother. I think it's a question of biology, I think it's a question of nurturing and responsiveness. Now there are some fathers that come very close, but I still think mom wins."

Psychologist Brenda Hunter, author of *Home by Choice* (Multnomah, 1991), agrees. "Fathers and mothers are not interchangeable," she insists. In all cultures, she points out, "mothers are nurturers. Obviously it's better to have a nurturing father if you don't have a nurturing mother. But I think you get into some confusion there. If a child has a mother who is emotionally unavailable, then that child misses out. I see many woman patients who have what I call 'mother yearning' — one patient described it as 'a hole in the soul.' I generally find that depressed women have not had a comforting, emotionally available mother."

On the other hand, studies show that both parents are important attachment figures for babies. One found that, even where the mother was the primary caregiver, babies cried just as much when their fathers left them as when their mothers left them.

Still, psychiatrist Dr. T. Elliott Barker believes that women have an edge on attachment and nurturing, because the baby has been part of them for nine months. "If that sounds patriarchal," he says, "I don't apologize — it's biological fact. Women for two million years were biologically conditioned to rear babies, and you don't reverse millennia of biology. You can't convert men into women." Dr. Barker is concerned that if dads are seen as the primary caregivers, breast-feeding will be downplayed. "It's incredibly important, and only women can do it."

So why are some dads ready to buck two million years of conditioning and stay home with their kids? When Peter Baylies, the North Andover, Massachusetts, publisher of *At-Home Dad*, polled 1,000 of his readers, these are the reasons they gave, in order of importance:

1. Wanted to avoid putting children in day care.
2. The wife earned more money.
3. The wife was keener to work.
4. Dad was keen to stay home.

Interestingly, of those responding families where the father was the main caregiver, 51 percent of husbands and 43 percent of wives were "extremely satisfied" with the arrangement. Baylies, who is caring for John, aged four, and David, one, chose to stay home after being laid off from his computer job. Many of his subscribers, he says, are part of the "consultant" trend — men who are working from home with the help of fax machines, computers, and modems.

His poll also turned up one finding we found had come up anecdotally in our talks with at-home fathers: while feelings of isolation are a problem for many mothers at home, they are even more of a headache for full-time fathers. Even George Ihnatowycz admitted he was "a loner." In Baylies' survey, more than 60 percent of respondents reported feeling "somewhat isolated," while 6 percent said they were "totally isolated."

We'll generalize wildly here, and say that one reason for this is that men are simply not the social creatures women are, and find it harder making contacts. "It's kind of tough, really," Ron Wilson, a Buffalo, New York, at-home dad (father of Alex, aged three, and Jack, one), told us. "The only adult contact I have is my wife, and she's done a day's work when she gets home. I've not been very good about getting out and doing things."

Stephen Harris, the Cumberland, Maine, publisher of another newsletter, *Full-Time Dads*, suggests another reason: men can have a harder time feeling accepted in the mostly female world of at-home parents. "You go to the playground and you see lots of moms and babies, but rarely do you see dads and babies," he reports. "Some people see a man with a small child and their first reaction is, 'That's not right. What is that man doing?'" Harris was part of a "Moms and Tots" play group for a while, but found "there's something about being with your own gender." Now, he says, he has several men friends he sees fairly frequently.

Why did he choose to stay home with Ben, now eight, and Robin, five? "When we got pregnant we had just moved to Maine and I was looking for employment." His wife, editor of a computer services newspaper, was the bigger earner, anyway, "and she had always been career-oriented."

His eight years at home, he says, have changed him. "I know a lot more about kids, and I'm a lot more patient. No one has patience when they first have kids; you have to learn that."

Like other at-home fathers we spoke to, he's become used to other fathers saying, "I wish I could do that." Says Harris: "I think what they're really saying is, they wish they didn't have to put on a shirt and tie every day and go to work. I don't think they realize that this is probably harder work than what they're doing."

How do women react? "It's funny," he says. "A lot of the time they give me too much respect, make it a big deal. To my mind it doesn't make any difference which parent is home, but they say, 'Wow! It's wonderful that you're staying home, and so on.' Or: 'Gee, I wish my husband would get me supper when I get home.'"

"We're Not Substitute Mothers"

If there's one label at-home fathers bridle at, it's "Mr. Mom." Robert Frank, a thirty-nine-year-old Chicago father who completed his doctoral thesis while caring for his two children, told *USA Today*, "I think we've put an end to that Mr. Mom sensationalism. We're not substitute mothers, and we're not babysitting our children. We're here enjoying our children's lives." Frank argues that children cared for by their fathers get a double helping of love and caring: from their dads during the day, and from their mothers when they get home from work.

But dads at home still have a way to go before they are accepted as a normal phenomenon. Ron Wilson, the Buffalo dad, says when the young woman cutting his hair one day asked him what he did, and he replied that he was home with his kids, "she started laughing. I said, 'What are you laughing at?' She said, 'You should be working.' I said, 'No, someone should be home with the kids and I choose to do that, and my wife works.' She said, 'You mean you make your wife work all day and you stay home!'"

Such prejudices are just as damaging when applied to men as they are applied to women who choose to stay home. Only education about new roles for men can help there, and the signs are not all good.

Studies by Demos, the British think tank, show that more and more men *say* they want to play a bigger part in their children's upbringing. But saying isn't doing. Demos found that 69 percent of women take full responsibility for child care compared with 3 percent of men.

Many fathers now attend prenatal classes, and, in the British survey, the number present at the birth of their children has gone from 5 percent in the 1950s to 97 percent in the nineties. The proportion of men willing to take time off work to be with a sick child (self-reported) has gone from 18 percent in 1987 to 39 percent by 1991. In short, the surveys all show that young men are miles ahead of their fathers in showing a greater flexibility about gender roles. They're willing to bathe the baby and change a diaper. But for most dads the bottom line is still that they're "helping" their wives, not taking over child-care duties.

In Canada, under the parental leave program introduced in 1990, mothers get fifteen weeks of paid maternity leave, after which either the father or mother can take an extra ten weeks of paid leave. But in 1994, the last year for which figures are available, fewer than 4 percent of eligible fathers took up the offer. Even in enlightened Sweden, where parents are allowed to share fifteen months of parental leave with their partners, and since 1995 the government has dangled the additional carrot in front of fathers' noses of a month of parental leave of their very own, the government has advertised repeatedly to try to persuade men to take their paternity leaves. And it has met with little success.

Let George Do It

"Calm" was the word that struck us right away when George Ihnatowycz came to the door of his and Sylvia's eight-year-old house on the edge of Bolton, a town fifty kilometers north of Toronto. Of Ukrainian extraction, he talks quietly, and treats Annie and Alex as people who should be listened to. As we came in, Alex was tootling up and down the hall in a handsome blue Little Tikes bus borrowed from the community toy library that George has helped to run for several years as a volunteer.

George: When Annie was born we were debt-free and comfortable, so we sat down with the calculator to see if we could afford for me to be home. I didn't see it as anything out of the ordinary. Friends at work, especially women, thought it was a good idea. They liked the idea of men staying home with the kids. There's an understanding in the child-care field of the importance of family input. Since then, when I tell people what I do, I find men will say, "I could never do that," and women will say, "I wish my husband would think about that." But my father didn't understand it. He was very traditional, and even until the day he died he didn't understand what I was doing at home.

I knew being home with Annie would be time-consuming, I just didn't realize how time-consuming. I thought I was going to be able to sit down and read! Annie was a baby who loved movement. It was only when Alex came along later I realized Annie had been a very different baby. You could just put him down and he went to sleep. But she was fussy, and energetic; she was strong-willed and stubborn and she needed walking. To this day she's strong-willed and stubborn!

Most mornings I would take her for a walk in the park, take her to the grocery store. I didn't feel confined at all. I loved to do things with her. We started swimming lessons when she was six months old, and I would be in the pool with her. Later we went to a Gymboree toddler exercise program, and skating. My only focus was on value for Annie. If I had missed all that there would have been a lot of regret. Even now, as I get older, I have a feeling of not having enough time with my kids, especially on the weekends.

When Annie was three I had the chance to work two days a week, and I would take her to the YMCA day-care center. There was a little separation anxiety at first, but she got to love it. She was ready for it, and she felt comfortable. Then Alex came along and it started all over again. When it hits you a second time it's a bit of a shock. You've forgotten what it's like: the midnight feedings, the diapers. But there's the excitement too of seeing the different stages again, seeing a child learn to take the bottle, to roll over.

There was nobody else at home during the day on our street, but it wasn't a problem for me. I'm not a very social person. I keep to myself. It's funny, when I walk down to the school-bus stop it's all women. They start talking about their husbands, and then they realize there's a man there, and they stop. But it doesn't bother me. My field — child psychology — is dominated by women. I often see men come into our local parent-child center and you can see they're uncomfortable. I've never felt that. A lot of my friends are female. Originally I was the only male on the board at the center, but now there are three. The women would say, "George, tell us now from a man's point of view," and I'd say, "But my point of view is the same as yours!" Psychologically I was never worried for myself, but I worried sometimes what people would think about Sylvia — "Who is this woman who has left her children with her husband?" But she says that never bothers her.

Sylvia: It was George who showed me how to put a diaper on Annie. He could remember doing it for his little brother; he was twelve when his brother was born. George was fascinated with him right from the beginning. My dad's a lot like George. You know what they say, that when you're looking for someone, you often pick someone like your parents? Well, that was George. My mom worked and my dad always took care of us because he did a lot of shift work when they first came here from the Ukraine.

Lots of times when they were young and George was with them I felt left out. Oh yeah, it's no secret. Going to work in the morning and leaving them at home, and getting home and hearing that Annie did this and Annie did that, and not being there to see it — that hurt.

But I don't have the patience or the personality to be happy at home all day. Even when I'm home for a few days now, George will say, "Go back to work. Get outta here!" I wasn't going to be the one, but somebody had to stay home. If you're going to have kids you might as well give them some part of your life, because later on they're going to be on their own and they're not going to need you any more. Day care was something I was never crazy about. With me teaching and my husband involved with all kinds of learning-disabled kids, I guess we look at it from a different viewpoint. Kids are better if there's a parent at home, absolutely. Kids whose parents aren't home don't seem to have the social skills. They have a hard time settling down and concentrating, because, I think, so many of them have been thrown around since they were little. I think our children are different because George is at home.

I always made more money than he did. As a family unit, it made more sense that I went to work. But it wasn't just that. He's better with little kids than I am. He's more patient, much more patient. He's got that personality — he tries to figure a kid out, to see where the kid is and what he's thinking. I like working with older kids, but he's always been fascinated with early childhood education. I guess our kids are his experiment! He was never the macho type. He's really kind and considerate and often he thinks about other people before himself. He's a thinker, you know. He thinks about things before he ever says anything. Whereas me, I'm more emotional.

I think a lot of it comes back to the woman, too. If you want the man to play a part, you've got to say, "Hey, it's your kid too!" A lot of people think it's just a woman's thing having a child, but if you don't let your husband share in that experience you're losing something. You have to share. I hear women saying they're going to be the perfect mother, but I knew I was never going to be the perfect mother. I had a lot of doubts as to whether I could manage. So I just let George do whatever he wanted.

George: Alex and Annie have their own computer. It's amazing what they learn on their own if you just show them the basics. Since he was three Alex could operate a mouse. I knew nothing about computers, but Sylvia needed one, so I did a lot of reading and practice. Then I started helping other people with their computer problems, and then they began paying me for it. Now I have a little consulting business called Easy Computing. Had I been more driven professionally I might have missed work more, but being home has led me to a new career. I see working full-time again sometime in the future. Next year Alex will be at school full-time and I could increase my hours. But I think I would always like to be here when the kids get home.

We don't measure our lives by whether we've taken our kids to Disney World. We've never taken them on a plane. Sylvia and

I camp a lot. We stopped when Alex was born, but then started again. We bought a tent trailer and we've been as far as Prince Edward Island. Now we're planning a trip across the country. We love nature. Sylvia's parents have a cottage, and we go there, too.

Munching on a cookie, Annie says she hopes to be a vet. If she has children, she says, she will take them to work with her. Are there disadvantages to having a dad as an at-home parent? She can't think of any. "At school kids used to ask, 'What did your mom make for your lunch?' I'd say, 'My dad, you mean.' And teachers would always write notes and say, 'Give this to your mom.'"

George: Sylvia is quite used to other women asking me about my experiences at home. Unless you stay home, you don't really know. People picture you getting up late, having a coffee, turning on TV, and then making dinner just before your spouse gets home. It's not like that at all. There's so much more to do. When at-home parents get together they have so many stories to swap. You just have to go down to the bus stop and listen to them.

I don't take pride or enjoyment in housework. It's something that has to be done. It's important to have energy and good organizational skills and manage your time. You need to do several things at the same time, like starting the laundry, making dinner, and cutting out newspaper coupons. You want quick and easy. I got a wok for my birthday — great! You can cut up and prepare things ahead of time, then five minutes and it's all ready. I find in keeping house it helps having physical strength. Vacuum cleaners are heavy, especially on the stairs. Annie weighed ten pounds as a baby — that's heavy to turn over. My cooking? Just enough to get by. I was not afraid of the kitchen, but I was a basic meat-and-potatoes kind of cook. Sylvia makes the birthday cakes. Annie likes my quiche; she thinks I make it from scratch!

Brought Up to Be a House-Spouse

George and Sylvia have an entirely traditional set-up, with the one difference that Sylvia is the parent who goes out to work all day and George is the parent who stays home. We suspect, though, that another couple we met, Keith Nunn and Beth Baskin, represent the wave of the future. Beth and Keith, who live in a tiny, two-bedroom 1860s terrace house in downtown Toronto, blend their home and work lives so that they share the upbringing of Morgan, their eleven-month-old daughter. Keith is a freelance graphic artist and also sings in a band, while Beth is a church outreach worker who earns about $42,000 CDN ($30,000 U.S.) a year.

Beth: I think most people looking at us would think we're pretty alternative, whatever that word means. I'm sure, with Keith being a very active father, that we cause all kinds of folks amusement. They wouldn't think of us as traditional. But in the sense of wanting to give Morgan a real strong sense of family and a stable home base, we're fairly traditional. But certainly in the roles we've chosen for ourselves, we're not traditional at all. Early on, when I had just met Keith, one of the things he told me was that his mother had brought him up to be a house spouse.

Keith: I don't think it was a conscious choice on my mother's part. My parents were divorced, and from the time I was nine until about fourteen, when she remarried, my only experience was seeing one parent at home looking after us. I was the oldest of four at that stage. I made lunches for my siblings, and then, when I was fifteen, my mother had another child and I was around a baby on a pretty regular basis.

My mother also did some home care for other people's children, and what I noticed was that they formed quite a strong bond with my mother. It didn't bother me at the time, but reflecting back on it I would far rather Morgan have this primary relationship with me or with Beth than with someone we pay. Why me at home rather than Beth? That's easy — she has a shorter fuse!

Beth: It's true. It really came down to temperament. I am a people person who enjoys being out and immersed in things, and Keith in a lot of ways likes to have control over a limited amount of space so that he can be more focused. I love our daughter very much, and enjoy spending time with her, but after being on maternity leave for four months I was quite glad to go back to work. In some ways I would enjoy best only working half-time, but I'm not sure I could keep it to that because I get so immersed in things.

Keith: Part of it was the financial thing too. I tried to develop a business at home so that I could work from home, however many children we had. But I must say my expectation of how much work I would really get done was pretty unrealistic. If we didn't have a loan to pay for some of the equipment I bought to work from home, I'd chuck it for a while and just service my two major clients. I don't really make a serious living by any means, just enough for our entertainment and to pay for car rentals when we want to go somewhere for the weekend (we don't see the need to own a car).

Beth: And I'm easier to employ. I have a diploma in pastoral work and most of my job right now is social work.

Keith: We didn't think it through very carefully. We decided before Morgan was born that I would stay home with her, but it was quite nebulous. Somehow I thought she would play quietly and I would go and work. Once she's awake, as you can see, she requires a fair bit of attention. It's fun most of the time, but sometimes it's a bit frustrating when I have a deadline to meet. But there are good times, too. For example, I'll be playing with her and she'll be just a little bit sleepy, and she'll come over and put her head on my chest and put her fingers in her mouth and maybe nap for a bit. You know, pretty wonderful sort of moments.

Living downtown makes it possible for us to get together during the day, too. I'll pack Morgan up and we'll go and meet Beth for lunch. We often go to church at Wednesday lunchtime, so that becomes one of our family times. And if I have to go to a meeting or meet a client, if I'm stuck for an alternative I'll drop Morgan off at Beth's office.

We have friends with children who have moved to the suburbs and basically they just seem to hide out with their kids. I mean, their children become the sole focus of their lives. We play on a baseball team, and we take her along to games. We take her to pubs — nonsmoking ones. We've even taken her to outdoor concerts and the odd club concert. I was lucky growing up: I was involved in adult things from the start. I learned not to hassle adults when they're doing things, and I learned how adults interact. That's why we involve Morgan in these activities.

Beth: We're trying to bring her up vegetarian, too. The more I read, the more I realize it's just a healthier way of life. We're not health-food nuts by any means, but I try to buy foods that are healthy and less processed. Raising a baby completely vegan, without any meat, dairy products, or fish, is a daunting task. Making sure they're getting all the nutrients and vitamins they need out of the vegetables they're eating is a bit of a stretch. So we're giving her some dairy products. But definitely she'll get smaller amounts of eggs and dairy products than most children do. It's just a healthier way of life. Anyway, I can't help believing that nursing and having a grain-based diet has gone a long way toward keeping her healthy. And even if she decides against it when she's older she will have had these years meat-free.

What sort of parent is Keith? In lots of ways he's more patient than I am, although in terms of being woken up, I'm more able to deal with that — no grumbling and telling her to put a sock in it! It's funny, when we're at home, Keith is the primary parent, and I'm what dads are. I get to have the fun, and Keith comes into the kitchen and tells me, "I don't let her play in that cupboard!"

Keith: It does seem like a reversal of roles. At home I deal with things — I feed her, change her, put her to bed, get her up. But when we're out, it's the other way, I let Beth do it. I'm sure people think I'm useless, but it gives me a bit of a break.

Beth: The other day, though, she and I were upstairs and Keith was going out to a meeting, and just as he was going out of the door she started crying. He said, "Thank you, Morgan!"

Keith: I must say that before Morgan was born I used to wonder, what the hell will I do if Beth changes her mind and wants to stay home with the baby? Then I've got to go out and find a friggin' job! Which I don't want to do. I want to stay home with my daughter. I was looking forward to it, not that I was prepared. You just lunge into these things and deal with the consequences later.

———————

While George wasn't bothered by the isolation that men at home seem to feel to an even greater extent than women, and Keith didn't mention it, we learned a great deal about it when we arrived at a nameless hamlet on the highway outside Buffalo, New York, and met Ron Wilson.

Ron, a thirty-one-year-old engineer, is a great dad, no doubt about it. But you could hear the frustration coming through as we talked in the neat-as-a-pin home he and his wife, Denise, rent on a street where no one else seemed to be home. They moved to the Buffalo area from Los Angeles when Denise, also an engineer, was offered a good job in quality control at the Fisher-Price toy factory. Ron had been in aerospace and there was no aerospace industry nearby. But with Denise earning $55,000 U.S. ($76,000 CDN), they decided they had enough for Ron to stay home and look after their two small boys, Alex and Jack.

Some fathers Ron meets seem jealous of his being able to be home. "They ask me, 'What do you do all day? Sit around and read magazines?' If you've never done it, you don't realize how much it takes. You can write out a schedule of what you do and it doesn't sound much, but it's the constant attention they need. At Jack's age, kids are learning to walk, and everything is a hazard. You don't like to say no too many times, but you don't want them opening up the oven door. So you follow them around all the time. You can't sit down and read a magazine while your toddler's heading for the stairway."

There are regrets, too: "When I was working and I would get home at night I would play with Alex all the time until he went to bed, because it was a nice change. But now I'm home with the two of them all day, I don't play with them as much. It's more of a job. It gets more tedious. When Jack came along, Alex didn't like the fact I didn't play as much with him as before. Unfortunately the TV became more of a companion for Alex than playing with Daddy all the time. I try to limit that as much as possible, but it's kind of difficult when Jack's asleep upstairs and Alex wants to go for a bike ride. I have to tell him to wait until Mommy comes home."

Does Denise feel any jealousy? "Yeah, I think the kids are more attached to me. Alex has grown out of it, but Jack is very attached to me. He comes to me for sympathy, and he doesn't like when I leave. Mom can leave and it's no big deal. I think it bothers her, but she's secure enough she doesn't let it get under her skin."

During his typical day, he hardly sees anyone. "There are lots of kids living here, but I think the parents all work. I've not been very good about getting out and doing other things." There's a community college across the street, and Denise has urged him to take evening classes, "but I guess I'm kind of an introvert, like my dad. In a way, though, I miss the day-to-day interaction with my coworkers. There's been times when it's been a real rough day and I need to get out of here and do something, and then I wonder, 'What do I do?' A lot of the adult friends I have here are my wife's coworkers, and we'll go out and do something with them. But as for adult friends who share, say, my interest in old cars, I don't really have one.

"I try not to unload my baggage when Denise comes home, tell her how bad it is. Because then she can say, 'Well, you don't know what kind of a day I had.' But when you're on your own, who do you complain to? You can only keep it bottled up so long. I think Denise can read me well enough to know when I've had a bad day."

Ron admits he's frustrated that he's expected to do the traditional male chores — like cutting the grass — as well as all the indoor chores like preparing dinner. "Denise works, and I do everything else," he says. "I know she goes to work and it's stress and she needs to come home and relax. But when she comes home and I need some release and she doesn't want to do anything, things are really tough. It's one of those times when I suppress things again. I guess I bottle too much up."

But: "There are good times too — when they laugh and have fun. We feel lucky, and we're talking about having another baby. She wants a girl, and sure, I'd stay home with her. I'll stay home until they go to school. Maybe longer. I remember my mom always came to school functions that were in the day, and I thought that was great. So I would kind of like to work at home and make my own hours and participate more in my kids' lives."

So, can a father be as good as a mother? Judging by George, Keith, and Ron, the answer is yes. Although, in the context of a society where two-thirds of children are in surrogate care, the question may not be that important. Lucky the child who has a parent home, whether mother or father.

We salute the fathers home with their children. It would be nice to see Dads at Home Day celebrated internationally; you can't have too much of a good dad.

If you didn't know before, we suspect you're under no illusions now: Deciding to stay home with your children is an infinitely complicated decision. And it doesn't get easier as the two-income family becomes more and more the norm and the social and economic pressures put on parents to entrust the care of their children to others become irresistible.

There are no easy answers to the conundrums of career, economic well-being, and emotional survival at home. You'll have to confront these questions with your partner and in your own heart. But it all has to start with the question we addressed at the beginning of this section: What's best for your child? No one brings children into the world with the intention of giving them a second-best or a third-best start in life. So the trick is to begin with the very best start imaginable — and see how you can make adjustments and compromises in your lives to achieve that ideal to the greatest possible degree.

Being at Home

8

Finding Community

"**Y**ou're alone at last. Your mother, who was here to look after things while you were in hospital, has gone home. Your husband walks out of that door," says Heidi Brennan, a management consultant now home with her five children, "and the isolation of the entire house folds in on you."

Almost every parent who chooses to stay home has had a similar experience. "Unquestionably I felt isolated at first," says Brennan, who lives with her lawyer husband, John, in an older suburb of Washington, D.C. "I think the mistake many of us make when we stay home is that we don't realize we are going to need a community. I would go out with my baby and I couldn't wait to see another mother; I just lived for those moments. I would wait for my husband to come home just to have company."

Fighting the Isolation

The truth is that, just as you planned financially to be home, you need to plan as much as you can to meet the challenge of the isolation. And your spouse needs to be part of those plans. Talk about the need to be home together as much as possible — working spouses shouldn't get the idea that having their better halves at home lets them off the hook. Talk about the impact long hours or work trips are likely to have on you, and discuss how they can be avoided or minimized. This was always a sore point for us: Frank could never understand why Ayesha would fly off the handle when he'd phone at five to say he had to work overtime. It's hard for the spouses who go off to work to realize the importance their at-home partners attach to their being home.

Try to adapt to the at-home lifestyle even before you're at home. You may both want to disentangle yourselves from work-connected activities like the lunchtime squash game, and discover the pleasures of an evening stroll together. You need to find more time for each other, because from now on you will be more dependent on each other. It may be a time for discovering new, more economical, foods and pastimes, and to examine where you live with new eyes. Are there at-home parents with their children in the park? Introduce yourselves and get to know them — you can't believe how much you'll need them later.

Some mothers we spoke to felt it would be a mistake to work until the last minute before your baby's born. The process of childbirth will take so much out of you that you need time to rest and gather your strength beforehand, so you can make a better adjustment afterwards. Nearly all of them spoke, too, of the shock they felt when they discovered the amount of work there is looking after a baby. When you quit work, you may wonder how you are going to fill your days, but you'll soon find the problem instead is how you are going to get it all done. It's a good idea to make priority lists for each day, especially at the start, so that you have somewhere to begin.

Hardest to plan for is the emotional impact of staying home: the loneliness, the fear of your new situation, the hormones, and the pure exhaustion of caring for a newborn. . . . A few weeks ago you may have been handling a million-dollar budget with a dozen people answering to you; today a broken dish can reduce you to tears. "I don't think I realized how depressed and overwhelmed I was," says Diane Fisher of her time at home with her first child. "You'd think as a psychologist that's what I'd be good at. But I was so cranked up about being a good mother that I wasn't paying attention to myself."

A working woman who is suddenly at home often has a lot of difficulty adjusting to her new identity. Heidi Brennan found herself asking, "Who am I, now that I'm a mother?" She had grown up in a culture that told her, "Don't base your identity on motherhood."

Brennan, who is now public policy director for Mothers at Home, has written, "I could not avoid feeling sad at the loss of my work identity." Yet it didn't feel right when she introduced herself by saying, "I *used* to be a management consultant." It took her, she says, two years before she really felt at home saying she was a mother.

On the other hand, that emotional period when you're first home can also be a time when lifelong friendships are forged. Listen to Mary Ellen McCormick, once a high-flying advertising woman, now a mom at home:

"I really had a hard time adjusting at first because at that stage all my friends were working and no one was home. We were living in a condominium apartment and I kept looking around for new moms, but I didn't see any. Then I pulled out a flyer I'd received inviting me to join a new mother support group at the hospital. I got on the hospital elevator with Lindsay, who was only a few weeks old, in the baby carrier, and there were two other moms with little babies. I said, 'Oh, are you going to the support group?' They had been roommates in the hospital.

"One of them had a daughter who had been born the same day as Lindsay. The other one had a baby born the day after, and she had named her daughter Lindsay, too. After that, the three of us started meeting weekly in one of our homes and became a mini moms' group. Then another friend joined and we would sit around and nurse our babies and eat stupid things like peanut butter and jelly sandwiches or tuna sandwiches, because nobody had any money. We not only shared stories about the babies, but advice on how to cope with our husbands, ideas on how to get through the day. We became very, very close.

"This is ten years later and to this day we are the tightest group. There are five of us now and we have dinners with our husbands quarterly. When the children were smaller, we would have Valentine parties, Easter parties — we'd get together for any holiday. We went through hard times together, too. One of my friends had a two-year-old that died. My son Tommy was born in Fairfax Hospital half an hour after her daughter, Jane, was declared dead in the same hospital. They didn't tell me right away, and afterwards I went into a depression. I felt terribly guilty. It took my friend six or eight months before she could even come and see my baby, even though we were so close. But we're still very close."

Nearly every community has parents' groups, formal and informal, and you owe it to yourself to go looking for them. Here are some tips:

- Check your local library for programs for parents-at-home and preschoolers.
- Early on, make contact with the local La Leche League, not just for breast-feeding advice, but for contact with other mothers.
- Scan local supermarket and church notice boards for news of moms and tots programs.
- Consider joining a church or synagogue, but check first with the minister to find out if there's a high ratio of young families attending. And even if you don't join, churches are places that often house parent groups.
- Even if your baby is still small, find the local preschool, because mothers tend to congregate around them.

If your neighborhood lacks facilities and groups for parents at home, consider starting your own play group, babysitting co-op, or mothers' club: all it needs is a few new parents gathering, usually at the start in each others' homes, to share knowledge about the hundred-and-one questions that confront the novice mom. When Katie Williams Hoepke, of San Carlos, California, started a mothers' club, it led to her helping to start thirty-five other clubs! "You find ten people, and a few weeks later there are a hundred," she says. "Soon people are saying it's too large, so you split off clubs."

If you're very lucky, your neighborhood will have a parent resource center, professionally run, with a toy library attached. These centers are the ultimate answer to the needs of the at-home parent, providing advice for novice parents and social contact for moms and dads, as well as for their children.

We visited a wonderful one, The Children's Place, which occupies three former classrooms in a school in a multi-ethnic neighborhood in the West end of Toronto. Sarah Garner, who is now on the board of the center, tells us, "I was on my own at home for nineteen months before a friend told me about this place. We were busy, we did a lot of things, but it was time for us to get out and about." Sarah is holding her two-and-a-half-year-old daughter Claudia (she also has an infant, Monica). She is surrounded by children, moms and dads, single parents, and child minders of all colors and nationalities.

"Getting out and seeing people and just breaking up my day is really important," she says. "Coming here has made an incredible difference to my parenting skills. You pick up tips from other parents on things like how to get a child into a car seat, and how to control anger."

"This is my other home," Precy Uy, who is from the Philippines, chips in. She has been bringing her son, Gabriel, here for two years, and now also brings an infant she looks after. She makes good use of the center's toy library, and she has taken courses at the center in parenting and first aid. The center's director, Angela Otelino, says that when parents discover the resource center, they nearly always have the same reaction: "This is too good to be true! Wow, I didn't know something like this existed."

There are parent resource centers across Canada and the United States — although not nearly enough. They attract little publicity, but they should, because they are the parent at home's best friend. They provide an ideal destination for an outing whatever the weather, and the chance to share and talk that every parent needs. They are a source of expert help on health, nutrition, and parenting. If you're home with a child, check with your local town or city hall to see if there's one near you.

For an earlier generation of mothers, these formal support

centers weren't as necessary, as there were any number of neighbors who could be called on for advice. The much-maligned coffee klatch was a forum for the exchange of information and a way of preventing isolation as much as it was a chance to chat.

Today's mom at home must find her own ways to combat feelings of isolation. There are no marching orders in this daily battle. For her, it's a life to invent. Ayesha, for example, says being alone inspired her to learn to bake and sew and find dozens of ways we could live better and more economically.

The mother at home with a child or children must make every day opportunity day. She didn't, after all, stay home so the kids could watch television. Maybe one day is special because the leaves start falling from the tree out front, and rustly, dry leaves are things of wonder even for an eight-month-old. Another day it could be the first snowfall that amazes, with baby feeling the flakes on her tongue for the first time. Every mother (and elementary schoolteacher) has thanked goodness for the seasonal events, like Valentine's Day, Thanksgiving, Halloween, Hanukkah, and, most of all, Christmas, that allow for a whirlwind of stories and coloring, cutting out, pasting, decorating, and baking.

In our family, we sometimes laugh at our daughter-in-law, Kim, who has the house ablaze with Christmas decorations almost before the Halloween masks and the scary spiderwebs have gone from the trees out front. But listen to her two little boys, Atlee and Evan, tell about it all, and you know that thirty years from now they'll be telling *their* kids about all the remembered excitement and fun.

If all this sounds like a lot of work — it is. And that's another price at-home moms pay: no one gives them credit for all they do. Mary Ellen McCormick says she used to be totally frustrated when her husband, Peter, would come home to their apartment and say, "Well, what did you do all day?"

"I don't know what I did all day, but I was busy," she'd reply. She felt he wasn't understanding her, so, she told us, "one Saturday morning I got up at eight and got dressed. He said, 'Where are you going?' I said, 'I'm going out.' I left enough breast milk in the fridge, and everything to take care of the baby, and said I'd be back at six. I went to the mall and to the library — such freedom!

Well, when I walked back in the door, even now I can see him standing in the hallway wearing nothing but a pair of shorts, his hair standing on end, the baby wearing nothing but a diaper, and everywhere were baby's spit-up towels and pieces of three or four outfits, and in the kitchen all the stuff he'd eaten all day was in the sink. The place was a disaster. I said, 'Please don't ask me what I do all day.' After that I felt my husband was in touch. I mean, you can't describe being alone with a new infant. You have to experience it."

Making Time for You

The freedom Mary Ellen talks of experiencing that day is also something mothers bring up often, and longingly. If isolation is the biggest problem for moms at home, the lack of time to oneself comes not far behind. We recommend finding a regular way to create a little pool of sanity and peace in a busy life. It may involve having your husband look after the children for an hour or two on the weekend so you can visit a friend, or signing up for an evening aquafit class at the local pool, or setting aside a regular "mom's night out."

Lis Fyles-Foly, who quit her job as an editor in employee communications with a large bank after her third child was born, wrote us: "While my family is extremely important to me, I treat myself well. It's hard to be good to everyone else if you are not good to yourself. I work out regularly, take piano lessons, do volunteer work at my sons' schools, and always have a stack of library books to read."

Deborah Fallows, who worked as an academic before coming home, told us, "I decided from the beginning that it would be really important for me to have some element of my former working life left intact. So whenever it happened that they were asleep and I had some time to myself — which was rare at the beginning — I was extremely strict with myself about not doing household stuff." Instead, she devoted the time, however short, to researching or writing the book that took her five years, *A Mother's Work*. "It was my intellectual time."

It's important, says Arlene Rossen Cardozo, author of *Sequencing*, not to confuse staying home with doing housework. If the vacuuming doesn't get done, who cares? You're there because you want to be with your child, not because you want to have a spotless house.

Even the routines of looking after your baby can get in the way of your enjoyment if you let them. Nancy Seid, a freelance writer from Saratoga Springs, New York, described in *Parents* magazine how she was actually jealous of her husband, Matt, who would come home at the end of the day, pick up their son, Zachary, and start playing with him. She'd been so busy attending to chores and Zack's basic needs — feeding, washing, and so on — that she hadn't found time in the day to play with him. "My solution," she wrote, "was to do what my husband did: take some time every day to play with Zack." Soon she and the baby were dancing around the living room, playing "choo-choo" games, and singing.

Vivian Rothermel, who lives in a condominium apartment on the outskirts of Washington, enjoys writing, too. Mostly she writes about her life looking after Graham, aged six and a half, and Candace, four. But with Graham in school now, she is at her happiest alone with Candace, building what Cardozo calls "a joint bank account of stored memories." Says Vivian: "We have a late breakfast, an unhurried morning. We play lots of memory games and have stories. It's really a lovely way to spend our days."

It's the little secret of mothers at home: that it really is possible to take time and enjoy your children. Psychologist Diane Fisher says, "I've had women friends in the fast lane who dropped out tell me in a kind of whisper, 'You know, I'm really enjoying being with my kids,' like they wanted me not to tell anybody."

Mentor Moms

We learned another secret, too, in the course of our research: that what new moms are looking for even more than other mothers with children their own age is mothers with children a little older. Heidi Brennan recalls, "I liked to see my neighbors who had older children. I looked on their word as law. They were wise people."

There is even a term for this phenomenon: "mentor moms." We think they're such a great idea we wish every neighborhood had at least one. With their own mothers often living far away, many young moms told us how important it was to find more experienced parents they could turn to for advice and support. Even before we met her, we'd been told about one outstanding mentor mom, Luanne Johnston.

We met her at her front door as she arrived home from her local parent resource center with the youngest of her four children, Susan, aged eleven months, in a baby carrier. She's at the center just about every day, advising on breast-feeding, sleep habits, and so on. Other times she'll pick up a few groceries for a mother with a sick baby, or do some baking for a mother just home from hospital. Luanne, who is thirty-eight and grew up in rural Wisconsin, met her millwright husband, Larry, when they were both doing community work for the Catholic Church in British Columbia. In a sense, she says, the missionary work she was doing for the church has never really stopped.

Aside from down-to-earth advice on bringing up baby, Luanne and Larry offer young couples in their part of Mississauga, Ontario, an example of communal values and sharing that can make life for the parent at home much more enriching, even on one modest salary. The Johnstons get by on an income of less than $30,000 CDN ($21,500 U.S.) a year. It helps that they live in a co-operative townhouse development where the residents pay moderate rents and share out duties. Larry is on the maintenance committee, and Luanne is in charge of youth activities, organizing parties and, for instance, helping children plant a vegetable garden every summer.

They have one car (a 1990 Buick they bought secondhand), and Luanne does her grocery shopping at a nearby discount supermarket that is within easy walking distance.

What would she recommend for new parents? "Take parenting classes. Go to meetings of the La Leche League to learn about breast-feeding; you can get a basic idea in just four meetings. Perhaps someone having a baby should live for a couple of days with a family with a baby so they get a better idea of what it's going to be like. The biggest thing I find with mothers is lack of confidence. They think other mothers have it easier, smoother. They are surprised when I tell them I have had problems. The more we talk the more we realize we are the same. We go through the same struggles. It's part of life.

"When you meet a mother who has gone through it she can give you the strength to carry on, maybe even laugh. I think a lot go back to work because they don't have anyone to tell them they are doing a great job. You need someone to pat you on the back, to cry with you through the rough times. They don't realize the struggle they have to go through is part of their growing up, that they need to go through this with their children. The tiredness that comes with two toddlers and a baby! That's when you need friends. I don't think a mother was ever meant to raise children on her own. You look at societies around the world and you see so much more communal effort and support for the mother."

That, of course, is where our Western societies are missing out. Motherhood in the past was a communal affair, with relatives and friends always on hand with advice and help. Isolation may actually be a greater obstacle today to the parent wanting to stay home than money. The parent planning to stay home, as we've seen, is wise to build all the community support possible.

9

Picking Your Neighborhood

Wwhat does your choice of neighborhood have to do with being home with your children? We say, a great deal. It has a powerful impact on how isolated you feel, how much you see of your spouse, and on your transportation needs. The kind of home you choose, including whether, for instance, you decide to rent or buy, also has a bearing on the financial aspects of staying at home; this issue is discussed in detail in the next chapter.

It may be that you already live in a neighborhood with terrific facilities and the best sort of neighbors. Or maybe you can't afford to move, so the point is moot. But if you're choosing now where to live, or if a huge mortgage is the obstacle holding you back from staying at home, consider the points we raise in these two chapters when you make your final choice.

Moving to an entirely different sort of neighborhood was a choice we made when our children were young, and in retrospect we didn't handle it too well. Our oldest son, Frank Jr., was eleven when we sold our colonial two-story house in the suburbs and moved into the city. We had lost our hearts to a three-story house, all dark original wood inside, built in 1913 in a quiet downtown neighborhood. Since he's grown up, our son has told us that at the time he thought we had experienced a terrible financial setback and had been forced to move into the slums!

Frank Jr. was a product of the suburbs, a kid who had grown up seeing only wide streets and new houses. What we should have explained to him and his sisters and brothers was that now dad would be able to get home from work in ten minutes, and that mom, in blizzard or heat wave, would get part of her daily exercise walking across the nearby bridge to some great stores where she would soon have dozens of friends. We should have told them that, all through their growing years, they would be able to use the subway, just a ten-minute walk away, instead of relying on us to drive them; that, in their teens, the excitements of the city (the legal ones!) would be close at hand, allowing them to get home in some sort of reasonable time on public transit.

We should have pointed out that, with its many small rooms, the downtown house provided privacy, if not total quiet, for a growing tribe, that there were plenty of at-home parents nearby to keep an eye on things, and that the street teemed with children so they'd never go short of someone with whom to play street hockey or catch.

Although our children were always free to follow their interests — our youngest daughter went to an arts-oriented private school — we never, ever signed them up for organized activities simply to keep them busy. Today, a generation later, there are still lots of children on our street, although the at-home parents are fewer and organized activities are on the increase.

The Suburbs vs. the City

We'll come clean right away about a prejudice we bring to this project: we believe that the dormitory suburb has serious drawbacks for the at-home parent. Suburbs are the domain of the car, and most of them offer little chance for face-to-face human contact and a good deal of isolation. And worst of all, they are so far-flung that the working parent is forced to spend hours on the road — hours that would be better spent at home. In today's long-hours culture, the longest hour of the day can be the one that drags between six and seven, when the at-home parent is tired, the children are feeling rambunctious, and the working spouse still hasn't walked through the door.

We don't deny the allure of the suburbs. For many young couples, moving to the suburbs is a nostalgic return to their own childhoods, to green grass and swings in the yard, to mom having coffee with Doris from next door and pollywogs in the creek in springtime. But that's not the way it is any more. Today's Doris has a job in the city and leaves at seven, the streets are empty because everyone's working; and if there are pollywogs still in the creek, kids aren't allowed down there because you never know if there may be weirdos around. Parents at home can find friends in the suburbs, but it will mean a lot more driving than it used to. And when their children want to play with other kids, they have to be driven to friends' houses. Suburbs also tend to be one-generational; all the families are about the same age, having moved in when the houses were built, so kids rarely get to see older folk or even the middle-aged.

We see another, even more important, drawback. If you're going to be home with your baby, the most important other person in your life is your mate. And the suburbs, it seems to us, couldn't be better designed to keep couples apart. To make it to far-away jobs, parents often leave before their kids are up, and arrive home late and tired from the stress of the road. In addition, errands take longer, all needing to be done by car and requiring one parent or the other to spend more time behind the wheel.

In making our housing choices we tend to put too easily all the emphasis on how much bricks and mortar we're getting for our money, and set no value at all on a much more important commodity, time spent with our families.

Build attractive housing right down the street from where people work — and they will buy a house twenty miles away across town because it has one more fancy bathroom for the same money. Early in the century builders actually showed their developments surrounded by smoking chimney stacks, to reassure people that they would be within walking distance of work. In the century since we've swung entirely the other way — believing apparently that work should be as far as possible from home (even though there are few smoking chimneys these days).

Heidi Brennan, public policy director for Mothers at Home, says that buying a relatively modest house very near to downtown Washington has been a factor in helping to keep her busy lawyer husband, John, involved with their five children. "It means John can commute in twenty minutes and spend time with the family instead of driving forty minutes to a much larger house where he wouldn't see as much of the kids," she says. "Sometimes he works long hours, and then the short commute is even more important. Or if I really have to do an errand, John will come home or I will drop the kids at his office."

For working couples, a close-in or downtown neighborhood is the icing on the cake. Nothing could be more chic than walking to a sidewalk cafe in Georgetown or to Starbucks on Vancouver's Robson Street for a cappuccino and the Sunday paper. But for the parent at home the advantages last all week long.

It was New York writer Jane Jacobs who, in her 1961 classic, *The Death and Life of Great American Cities*, first drew attention to the vitality of the city, to the virtues of its density and diversity, and to the human scale of its neighborhoods. Jacobs is a great believer in the importance of sidewalks and the life they engender. Planners in this century have favored a total separation of business and residential functions. The result: streets of houses, usually fronted by garages, where there is no life, and shopping restricted to distant and sterile shopping plazas.

Jacobs favors a more traditional model mixing homes and stores, ensuring the survival of busy streets lined with merchants. The payoff, in her view, is "eyes on the street." You don't have to be as concerned about the safety of your children because merchants and many others are there to see what goes on. And in preserving neighborhoods, instead of allowing them to be destroyed by high-rise developers, argues Jacobs, we're keeping human-scale settlements in which people know each other.

We are lucky enough to live in Toronto (where Jacobs also now makes her home), a city that has had more success than most in preserving its neighborhoods. "I know all the shopkeepers on

Bloor Street," says Angela Otelino, director of a lively parent resource center in a modest West-end neighborhood where people still sit on verandas watching the world go by — and keeping an eye on the local kids. "I don't have a car so I will go to Longo's grocery on the corner and he will say, 'Hi, Angela, how's the kids?'"

Contrast that with Linda and Steve Ryan and their typical sub-urban street with high fences around the backyards, a long way from downtown and a long commute from Steve's job. "It's not ideal for Emily and Alex [the two oldest kids, aged ten and nine]," says Linda. "The kids don't have anywhere to play. The parks are wide open, and there's no trees, no shade, no ravines to hang out. We're always driving them to their friends' houses. The library is in a local mall, so they're not able to go there themselves because it's too far to walk."

It's true that, since Jacobs wrote her book in 1961, life in the city has become more difficult. More couples are both working, so it's harder to know your neighbors — although the city still has a mix of old and young, so there are retired people around. And the center cores of many large American cities have deteriorated to the point where few middle-class families would choose to live there.

We spoke to a young couple who had spent the first six years of their married lives living in the Capitol Hill district of Washington, D.C., enjoying the mix of rich and poor, black and white, old and young in their pedestrian-friendly environment. The wife particularly enjoyed meeting other moms when she went walking in the park with her stroller.

But with their third child expected, fear of crime finally persuaded them to move to a suburb forty kilometers (twenty-five miles) out of town. On a good day it takes the husband forty-five minutes to get to work, and they still regret leaving behind their many friends, the moms in the park, the elderly neighbors they'd have in for Thanksgiving. Now, they say, their kids are growing up knowing only people "just like us."

A sense of personal danger (frequently unwarranted) and a concern about "poor" schools (for which read schools containing a large number of nonwhite or immigrant kids) are fears that drive many young families to the suburbs. In late 1996, *Personal Money*, a *Wall Street Journal* publication, highlighted two almost identical houses only ten minutes from each other in Essex County, New Jersey, one selling for $212,000 U.S. ($295,000 CDN) and the other for $404,000 ($561,000 CDN). The only difference is that the more expensive house is in a district served by what is perceived as a better high school. Our advice: while your children are small, forget about high school. You can always move later — if you still see the need. Concentrate instead on what will make your children's lives better now: the proximity of their parents and the parks, libraries, and other services that will make their lives at home rich and stimulating.

So we say, you don't have to move to the far-out suburbs to find a "nice" neighborhood. Many North American cities, especially the smaller ones, still have downtown neighborhoods that demonstrate the same lively qualities that Jane Jacobs celebrated. You just have to search them out.

Unfortunately, a mistaken counter-view has taken hold. "It's a great place to raise kids!" the real-estate salesperson will declare, with an airy wave at a treeless subdivision. Says who? Not kids, if you ask them. Kids don't really care about Jacuzzis or big yards. They prefer a sidewalk on which to rollerblade over a useless lawn. Grass, for them, belongs in the neighborhood park, where they can play soccer or T-ball. Surrounding their house, it's just one more distraction that keeps dad busy with the lawn mower on weekends instead of spending time with them.

When kids are small, what they want most is you, and as much of you as they can possibly get. As they grow older, the homogeneity, the blandness of the suburbs is the last thing they want; inevitably, as soon as they can get wheels, they will head for the lights of the city. And what goes for kids goes twice as much for the parent at home, who, more than anything, needs human contact of the broadest kind, stores with style, the best libraries — not empty driveways and the long wait for the spouse to come home.

"I would take two steps down the promotional ladder in order to be five minutes from work," Penelope Leach says. "I'd do almost anything not to have to commute." In *Children First* she writes: "Commuting is everywhere taken for granted, its basic wastefulness and inhumanity accepted without question."

"Fine for her," you say. "She lives in wealthy Hampstead in London; most people move to the suburbs because that's all they can afford." For some, that may be true. It is true that the down payment for a new house is generally lower than the one for a resale house — though not always. And the further out from a city center you go, the cheaper the prices.

But most people are not moving out further simply to afford a house; they are going further in order to buy bigger houses, fancier houses with wastefully large backyards, grand entrance halls, and Scarlett O'Hara staircases, and shiny, big kitchens — all gimmicks that in no way improve the quality of your family life.

Buying a city house, or one close to the city, usually means settling for one with a smaller yard and less space. It involves a different set of priorities. Instead of asking, "Does it have a two- or three-car garage?" you should wonder, "Is there a public swimming pool and a library within walking distance?" Rather than "How close is the highway on-ramp?" ask, "Is there a bus stop at the corner?"

New "Old-Style" Communities

Another alternative to "traditional" suburbs is appearing on the horizon. Some developers, reacting to bland, spread-out, car-oriented suburbs, are now building new communities that derive their inspiration from the small towns of the past — Seaside, a new town in Florida, was the first. In these new settlements, street fronts are not dominated by garages; the garages are often tucked around the back, reached by back laneways. The best of the new schemes involve a mix of housing — row houses, low-rise apartments, detached houses — with narrower streets that invite play rather than drag racing, neighborhood stores, and employment opportunities built right into the community so that people can walk to work.

Certainly these neighborhoods are better for families than

conventional suburban developments that completely segregate residential uses from everything else. But we remain skeptical. We suspect the most famous of these new small-town solutions, Walt Disney's Celebration, now being built near Orlando, Florida, will be an ersatz caricature of small-town living. How could it be otherwise with Disney's name attached to it?

Are the more modest new "old-style" developments just as good as old-fashioned city neighborhoods? We don't want to go overboard in idealizing downtown neighborhoods. You could say of the new developments that just because you build a milk store at the corner, that won't stop people jumping in their cars and driving to one ten minutes away on the highway. But it's true downtown, too — people in our neighborhood use their cars to go to the store when they could easily walk. And, to be fair, there are many downtown neighborhoods where couples both work and the homes are empty all day.

On the positive side, the new-old towns may offer you and your neighbors the chance of employment, especially part-time employment, right in your own neighborhood, making possible all sorts of flexible, cooperative child-care arrangements, and so make staying home with your children an easier choice. The density of the development — like the best of today's townhouse schemes — makes interaction between parents at home easier. If people are prepared, for instance, to do without a second car and make more use of bicycles and walking shoes, then these streets really could come alive.

But we still have an important reservation. These communities are being built on the fringes of the urban sprawl, as far away from the city center — the place where people are likeliest to work — as any other form of new development. Taking an hour or more to get home to a gingerbread row house with a back lane is really little better than taking the same time to get home to a tract house.

So, What Do You Want?

What should you be looking for? Obviously, the kind of place where it will be good to be home with the kids. Unfortunately, such neighborhoods aren't marked by road signs; you have to do your own research. What makes it more difficult is that, as we learned from our encounter with the Withrow Park mothers, one neighborhood can teem with at-home parents and programs, while only a few blocks away the streets are empty and deserted from one weekend to the next.

Weekday Liveliness

The first piece of advice we have for your search for a neighborhood is not to buy or rent on a Sunday afternoon. "It's only a twenty-minute drive to downtown," the salesperson will say; and it is — on a Sunday. But during the week the highway will be clogged and it could take a good hour. A place that looks darned enticing on the weekend, with dads pushing tots on the swings in the playground, moms chatting with each other out front, and kids playing ball in the street, may have a very different aspect on Monday morning with the cars and the kids all gone.

Heidi Brennan suggests, "Drive up and down on a weekday to see who's at home. Look for minivans or station wagons and tricycles on the sidewalk."

Don't be shy about knocking on doors where there seem to be children, and buttonhole parents at the local park to find out what goes on in the neighborhood. Check the walkability of the neighborhood; if cutting back means the parent at home will have no car, it may be important to have shopping, doctors' and dentists' offices, libraries, churches, and schools within walking distance. And even if you do have transportation available, it's still a big plus when you're home with a baby to have a neighborhood that's lively and interesting to walk through. We kept a big, old English pram, which wasn't much use when we went in the car, but was great for walking expeditions, with lots of room for diapers, shopping, and what-have-you in the basket underneath. These days some of the newer, more substantial strollers serve the same purpose.

Cultural Affinity

Another element you might want to bear in mind is something a little hard to define that we'll call cultural affinity. Look for signs that you feel your family will fit in, in whatever ways are important to you. We're not talking here about the bland sameness of some neighborhoods. But, for example, one couple we interviewed, Alexandra Jenkins and her physician husband, David, live with his parents in a large, old house not far from Withrow Park. Not only do the Jenkinses appreciate the number of parents at home nearby, but as vegetarians they're glad to live only a few steps from The Big Carrot, a large organic-produce supermarket where they're likely to run into like-thinking parents. It's also good to be close to a church or community center with activities for you and your children.

Economic Opportunities

Hard-headed concerns can also enter into the choice of where to live. Buying a modest home close to a fancy area, for instance, gives you extra opportunities for many kinds of home businesses. Better-off people are always on the lookout for services others can provide, whether it's caring for their children or grooming their poodles. Especially if you have only one car, look out for a budget-priced supermarket nearby.

Proximity to Family

The final factor that came up time and time again when people talked about where they lived was family. Many mothers at home said they'd found it invaluable having a sister or sister-in-law — preferably several — or parents or in-laws within easy distance, not only for social contact but as a source of help when those inevitable emergencies arise.

You Don't Even Need a Car Here

Ann and Erich Frank used to dream of living on a farm in the country. Today they have a ground floor apartment in a grand, old wooden house on a leafy street on the upper West side of Buffalo. And they're not sure they'll ever move to the country.

We found Ann, a qualified teacher, in the midst of a happy bedlam on the concrete parking pad out back, surrounded by half a dozen children she cares for, including her own two, Leo, aged four, and Nora, nine months. She and Erich got together when she was working in the props department in a Buffalo theater where Erich was the carpenter. When children came along, the couple's income was meager and unreliable. Going into teaching full-time seemed the best, maybe the only answer, for Ann. In between blowing bubbles, tightening up roller blades, and comforting occasional childish tears, she explained why it was a solution she resisted.

We just assumed we would have to have two jobs to survive. Leo was born in the summer, which is when you're generally laid off in the theater, so that worked well for us. I was going to go back to work and study for my teaching certificate at the same time. I was switching to teaching because we thought it would be a more family-oriented schedule than the theater. I took Leo to work with me for a while.

At first he would sleep a lot, and I would carry him everywhere. He was adorable. But then he would be awake more and need attention, and it was a little disruptive for the other people at work. So I had him with a child-care provider. I liked her, she was really good. But I didn't like leaving him. I hated it. When I was studying I would come back at lunchtime to nurse him, but when I started student-teaching I couldn't do that. The day was shorter, but it seemed longer because I couldn't see him.

Once I finished my schooling, I knew I had to find a job, but I didn't really want to. I went to some interviews and came really close to getting a job. And I think that was what shocked me. I had been looking forward so much to finishing school and being home with Leo for the summer. And I just started to know going back out to work was not the right thing for me. I knew we needed two incomes, and I didn't want to leave him, even though we had fabulous child care. I thought about teaching: I'd be spending the day with everyone else's children, but I'd be thinking all the time about my child.

And then my child-care provider said one day, "You should try this." So I took an adult education course in home child care. At that point we were living in a third-floor apartment with balconies that wouldn't have been suitable for child care. So I tried other things: I worked freelance for a while from home as an artist and worked on furniture while I tried to stay with Leo. But I ended up leaving him with people or with Erich so I could get the work done. That wasn't great, and I wasn't making much money.

That was a really scary period when we didn't have much money. We both have student loans, my own in deferment. We were doing things like not paying the utility bills until they threatened to cut us off, and we borrowed from our parents a couple of times. We argued a lot. His parents were actually really upset and appalled when they learned I was going to continue to work after having Leo. I don't think they ever understood our financial situation. But Erich understood how I felt. I was really emotional and angry sometimes and irrational, but he knew the real situation.

And at that point I started to talk about doing child care. Erich was so afraid he couldn't even think about it. It takes him a long time to get used to big changes in life. Then he was a little more receptive. And about that time we moved here. It was a three-bedroom, ground-floor apartment. And all of a sudden we had a neighborhood and a more child-friendly home and a really agreeable landlord. So we decided to try it.

We had to do some safety things to put the place in order, and we bought $150 worth of first-aid equipment. It's worked out great! I really enjoy it. Not being a business person before, I learned the hard way about the need for contracts and policies. In one case the person was not paying on time and then got crusty when I asked about it; then someone else treated me as if I was a menial. So I learned.

The day I got my first client I found out I was pregnant again, so I decided I would not take any more beyond the one child until the baby was born. I was off two weeks after her birth, and then I started building up slowly because Leo was a little possessive. But he's an easygoing kid and he's pretty good now.

It's always tough when Erich is laid off in the summer, but with me doing child care we at least have enough money to buy groceries. We went to see a financial consultant, and we're getting better at juggling money. When we would have an emergency we would put things on the credit card, and that's the worst thing you can do. Now we're whacking away at it, trying very hard to pay off our credit card. We can look ahead, see future patterns. We're trying to work out a situation where we can save and do things the way other grown-ups in the United States are doing them! Last year our total income was $34,000 U.S. ($47,000 CDN). It will be more this year because I have more kids; the parents pay $125 ($175 CDN) a week for full-time care. That's the high end of the scale because I'm really good at it!

I know a lot about child development, and I do my best to help parents prepare their kids for school. I think every child-care situation is different. I try to figure out how things are at home for the child so that I can do things the same way here. That way it's not so stressful for them.

Winters, though, are hard. It's a little crazy, and cabin fever sets in. I called my husband a lot at first. We get out as much as possible just to keep ourselves sane. I've been forced to learn more patience than I ever thought I had. What keeps me sane is knowing that right now this is what I want to do.

You need to see other adults during the day, too. I'm lucky in having two at-home moms as neighbors, and I've become active in the Family Child Care Association. I started taking their courses, and I've just been elected secretary.

I keep hearing from parents that they are very happy going to work knowing their kids are somewhere they feel good about. But it's clear to me I'm not a person to do that. I don't think I would ever be entirely happy leaving my children with a care provider. It's just a personal thing.

I know a lot of moms feel they don't have a choice. One

woman called me the day she gave birth. She had to go back to work in two weeks and she was desperate. I had one mom recently whose child I was watching who was trying to finish her graduate work, but it wasn't working out for her. I said maybe she should do child care. It's not for everyone, though. I had a friend try it for nine months, and she decided it wasn't for her.

I walk a lot with the children. We're very near Delaware Park, which is wonderful, and we go to the playground. If I can fit them in the car I take them places. This week, because I don't have a baby to look after right now, we went to the zoo. And when Erich is off we go to the nature preserve nearby.

We didn't think about it when we came to live here, but we have so much. We're within walking distance of a library, and there's a little grocery. I think I am convenient for parents working downtown — I get more clients that way. And Erich, who works a lot of late nights as a stage hand, can get home quickly after work. You don't even need a car here; there's a woman around the corner who does child care and she doesn't have one. We've ended up living here a lot longer than we thought because this is working out so nicely and because Buffalo is such a nice place. It's a good neighborhood and there are plenty of things to do. I just wish we had a bigger yard so we could set up a swing set.

When I started doing child care I thought it would be a temporary thing and I would go back to teaching at some point. Only I really like this and I feel it's really important work — perhaps more important than teaching. Now we're thinking about home-schooling Leo and Nora. I've been reading about it and meeting people who are doing it. It sounds like it might be just an extension of what we're doing already. Erich is all for what I'm doing now; it seems to be the answer for us.

Ann and Erich are a perfect example of why picking the right neighborhood isn't simply a matter of looking in the weekend newspaper and seeing which builder is offering the fanciest home for the least money. They made the right choice through luck, only realizing later how many advantages their area offered. You can get lucky too — with some careful forethought.

10

Picking Your House

Picking the right neighborhood, as we saw in the last chapter, is a vital factor in determining the kind of life you'll lead at home with your kids and the amount of time you'll get to see your spouse. Picking the right house is important first and foremost because it will determine to a great extent whether you can *afford* to stay home.

We are, let's face it, a society of house gluttons. Especially in the booming 1980s, all too many couples bit off more than they could chew, buying the most expensive house for the least possible down payment, blithely expecting that rising house prices and inflation would allow them to afford it eventually and confirm the wisdom of their investment. We were no exceptions. When we bought our present house in 1968 (for $47,500 CDN) we hadn't sold our previous house, and we committed ourselves to payments we could barely afford. Inflation (and a convenient overseas posting that allowed us to rent out our house for a few years) came to our rescue, but it could easily have been otherwise. Couples who went over their heads in the early 1990s frequently saw the value of their houses tumble, and many lost their homes.

But win or lose, one consequence of house gluttony — signing up for a huge mortgage — is that it preempts your choices. If it takes two incomes to pay the mortgage, then you don't really have the option of staying home with your children.

So this chapter, in addition to looking at what kind of house is best if you're staying home, will discuss when it makes sense to unload the house you have if it's standing between you and staying home. We'll also look at questions such as:

- Should we rent or buy?
- If the decision is to buy, how can we keep costs down?
- Does it pay to move?
- Are there other forms of housing that offer better options for single-income families?

Rent or Buy?

Is it best to buy? If you bought a house in the last five or ten years you may well have lost money on it. Economist David Foot, co-author of *Boom, Bust & Echo* (Macfarlane Walter & Ross, 1996), a look at our future in demographic terms, says that with the baby boomers all stocked up with houses, and fewer young house buyers on the horizon, the real-estate market is not likely to see big gains until after 2010. There may be all sorts of psychological reasons for buying a house, but as an investment, it's not as sure-fire as it once was.

The truth is that buying a house is a good form of forced saving, and if the prognostications of the demographers turn out not to be true (experts have been wrong before) there's still the chance that, when you finally want to sell, house prices will have jumped. But where a parent wants to stay home with a child, other lifestyle issues are involved. A mortgage can be a huge drain on family finances, and a down payment can wipe out years of saving, sometimes making it impossible for homeowners to live on one income. Remembering that in most cases surviving on one income to be home with the kids is not a forty-year commitment but a question of two or three years, maybe five, and that these are not years that can be put off until later, "when we can afford it," we think staying at home may sometimes tilt the balance in favor of renting.

For many families that notion goes right against the grain. We've been conditioned to believe that owning a house is not only the rock on which family life is built but also, in the long run, our best assurance of long-term financial security. Governments have reinforced that idea — in Canada by making a principal residence exempt from capital gains tax, and in the United States by making mortgage interest tax-deductible (in the 1996 election, President Bill Clinton promised to provide a capital gains tax exemption for American homeowners, too). But times have changed. Owning a home may no longer be the path to modest fortune it was in the past.

It's also worth remembering that renting frequently allows a more central location, cutting out the need for a second car and providing access to facilities that can make life at home fuller and happier. We think of the young woman with two children to whom we rented a city home we owned that was close to the subway and every sort of amenity. In the twelve years she and her elderly mother were our tenants, she got her engineering degree, found an aerospace job (we brought down the rent when she was laid off for a period), saw her mother move to a seniors' residence, and finally, last year, bought a place of her own. The modest rent in this case gave her the freedom to build her life, concentrating on the things that were important to her. The same principle can work for parents who want to be home with their kids.

Financial adviser John Clode, who has a number of times advised couples to sell their homes and rent instead, finds his clients, understandably, a little shaken. They respond, "If I rent, I'll have nothing to show at the end for all that money I've spent." His answer is that it's often better to separate housing costs from savings. If you rent, especially in jurisdictions where there are rent controls, you have predictable housing costs that are likely to be less than the costs of owning a mortgaged house, and if you're wise you'll put your savings into mutual funds or some other investment vehicle to take care of you later.

In fact, in 1996 Sean Hennessey, an associate professor who

teaches personal finance at the University of Prince Edward Island, figured out that a judicious renter, over a forty-year period, could come out $5 million ahead of a homeowner in Canada ($2 million in the United States because of those tax-deductible mortgages). He compared a family buying a $140,000 CDN ($100,000 U.S.) home and paying off their 8 percent mortgage over twenty years to a family renting at an initial $950 CDN ($684 U.S.) a month, with the rent rising by 3 percent annually. Hennessey is perhaps optimistic in his view of human nature. He assumes that the renter will take the $35,000 ($25,000 U.S.) that would have been the house down payment and invest it in a mutual fund that returns 14 percent a year (a not unreasonable figure based on historic returns), as well as investing all the savings in costs a renter enjoys compared with a homeowner. Nevertheless, his findings are impressive.

Some couples today who got themselves in too deeply are making the tough decision to sell and move downmarket. Alan Silverstein, a real-estate lawyer and author of a string of books on housing, including *Home Buying Strategies for Resale Homes* (Stoddart, 1997), explains that while people have traditionally moved up to bigger homes, recently there's been a trend for people to "buy down" to cheaper houses or move laterally to houses of equal value. In many markets, yesterday's monster homes sit unsold. There are no figures showing how many people are downsizing to be home with their children, but it's obvious that in general a more rational housing ethos has replaced the insanity of the crazy eighties.

How Much House Do You Need?

Is it worth selling an expensive house and buying a cheaper one? It certainly worked for magazine editor Paula Brook and her husband. When she decided to quit and stay home with their two children, aged thirteen and ten, they sold their expensive home in the swank Kerrisdale neighborhood in Vancouver and bought a cheaper one.

"As it turned out," Brook wrote in a *Saturday Night* magazine article about her experience, "the decision was good for everyone. We found a charming if quirky house on the North Shore, close to good schools." They ended up with a smaller mortgage and solved their other problem — paying for a cottage they owned — by going partners in the project with Brook's sister and her family. "It was definitely a downshift," Brook admits. "But it's a way better neighborhood, with young families, much closer to schools, so there's less carpooling. Everything has changed for our daughters. I think they feel their lives are just easier, more relaxed. They can come home any time and not worry whether they have a key or not, because mom's always home."

You can err by buying too much house. It's much less likely you'll err buying too little house. We met another couple who originally felt they had made a mistake and bought too little when they bought their first home. But it turned out to be a lucky stroke.

"We bought this condo for $89,000 when I was pregnant with Graham," says Vivian Rothermel, who, with her husband, Brad, lives in an attractive low-rise apartment development in Washington. "We walked in here and fell in love with it, and we thought, oh, we'll live here for a year or two, then move into a house. Well, that didn't happen because the bottom fell out of the real-estate market and now you can't give these condos away."

Brad, who sells insurance, and Vivian, who is home with Graham, now aged six, and Candace, four, kicked themselves afterward for not thinking ahead when they bought a two-bedroom unit, which is a bit of a squeeze with their two little ones. But it couldn't, in fact, have been a luckier move.

Early on Brad and Vivian's skills with money, they admit, were nonexistent. They were married right out of college at twenty-two and, says Vivian, "we were just so happy to be together we didn't plan anything. We were kind of live-for-the-moment people." They overspent on their credit cards, were behind with their income tax, were being chased for debt. They even had to borrow from their families to survive at one period when Brad had no regular salary and they were living on his meager commissions. They might have gone under financially if Brad hadn't got a salaried job and if they hadn't signed up for a budgeting course.

They threw away their credit cards, refinanced their mortgage at a lower interest rate for a saving of $60 monthly, and stopped eating out. Now they're eating better because Vivian has become a careful shopper, spending only $200 to $250 a month on groceries, and enjoys making inventive meals.

And the apartment that seemed too small has turned out to be a godsend. It's right near Brad's office, so he can come home for lunch, and although there aren't many moms at home around during the day, Vivian has three sisters living nearby, all at home with their children. She doesn't hanker for a big yard of her own any more; friends with houses tell her they have to drive their kids everywhere. Meanwhile, her nieces and nephews are always saying they want to live with Auntie Vivian and Uncle Brad because they have the biggest yard (the grounds around their apartment building) and a pool that's hardly used.

Vivian admits she used to envy friends who had big careers and high-earning husbands and bought fancy houses. She used to tell friends, "I wish Brad was more ambitious." They told her, "Forget it, he's so kind, and he spends so much time with you." She doesn't even dream of having a state-of-the-art kitchen any more.

If You Choose to Buy

One factor that changed in the mid-1990s, making owning more attractive, is the cost of borrowing. Interest rates dropped, and in both Canada and the United States it frequently became as cheap to own as to rent for many people. In Canada, if you are a first-time buyer, you can withdraw money from your Registered Retirement Savings Plan for a down payment, providing you replace the money in the fund within fifteen years. If that path is not open to you, you can still buy a home for 5 percent down, although you'll then need mortgage insurance amounting to $2\frac{1}{2}$ percent of the amount borrowed.

To keep the costs of buying and owning down, Alan Silverstein tells first-time buyers they must do their homework first. Making an offer on a house is only the last step in the chain. It's a good idea, he says, to get a pre-authorized mortgage from the bank or credit union so that you know exactly what you can afford.

If you're both still working, it will be a temptation to use both salaries to qualify for the maximum mortgage. But John Clode points out that if one of you is planning on staying home, that's not such a good idea: "If you're pouring all your resources into the mortgage, you only need one setback and you've got a problem." The more equity you have in your home — especially if you're planning on being at home — the better. "If you can't make it on one income, I definitely don't think you should be looking at buying a house. The higher the mortgage payment," he warns, "the tighter a stranglehold the house has on you." That's why so many couples believe that, when children come along, they have little option but to keep working.

If rates are moderate, Silverstein advises young couples to take out a long-term mortgage — say, five years — for stability. That's doubly recommended for couples making do on less than two incomes, who can do without mortgage-interest shocks along the way. "You know exactly where you stand," he says.

If you don't already know the neighborhood where you're buying, then, as we suggested in the previous chapter, make a point of walking it, talking to people, looking for clues about the type of people who live there and the quality of neighborhood life. If you're going to be home, this information is not merely academic; it's what's going to make your life happy or otherwise.

When you're buying a resale house, in addition to a lawyer and a real-estate person, you need a good home inspector on your side, suggests Silverstein. Again, if you're just getting by financially, you can't afford surprises, so the two or three hundred dollars a thorough inspection costs before is money well spent. A good home inspector (don't use your brother-in-law, or a renovator who wants to get your business) is also your best ally when it comes to checking out a fixer-upper — be sure the house is basically sound and just needs some tender loving care. Remember, if you're going to have a business at home, check on the wiring and telephone lines to make sure they're computer-friendly.

Silverstein also says it's useful to get to know as much as possible about the seller of the home. Sellers fall into three categories, he says: willing, anxious, and desperate. "If it's a marriage breakup or a relocation, they're not going to quibble over the last dollar or the appliances," he says. In our experience in home buying, we found it never did any harm to congratulate the owners on their lovely home and give them the feeling their "baby" would be in safe hands. That way they'll want you to have it.

Banks, on the other hand, have no hearts to appeal to. But, says Silverstein, if it's a power of sale or a repossession, they won't bargain to the last dollar, either. The best time to buy? In his view, in the weeks before Christmas, when there are few people looking. Keep away from two-bedroom houses — they're harder to sell later — and opt if possible for the most traditional sort of house; people are notoriously conservative when it comes to buying homes. In an older neighborhood, a two-story traditional would probably be a four-square house with dining room to one side and living room to the other side of the front door. In older suburbs, a split-level or ranch bungalow fits the bill. Just be wary of any house that seems to be an architect's folly or sticks out from its neighbors in any way.

Silverstein also warns about apparent pluses that can turn out to be negatives. Being near the school is great — but not too near the school. Being near the highway may seem a good idea on Sunday afternoon, but beware on Monday when the traffic noise builds up. And while a swimming pool may be an asset on a large, suburban lot, on a city lot it can be a real liability when you come to resell because downtowners tend to have other priorities.

Your Home as a Business

Often a couple can make use of a purchased home to bring in some income, too. But if you want to use your house for anything besides your home, be it starting a bed and breakfast, renting out the basement, or conducting a home business, be sure to check the zoning status with the town or city. Basement apartments, for instance, even if they're already extant and currently tenanted, are often illegal, and you could lose that income if there's a complaint.

If part of the building is rented out, make sure the rent is legal — under rent control in some jurisdictions, improperly high rents can later be rolled back retroactively, forcing you to come up with a hefty refund.

That's not to say that, even if you've bought your house simply as a single family residence, it isn't worth considering renting a room to a student if there's a college nearby (he or she may even be willing to babysit as part of the deal) or to an elderly person. The extra money all helps to make staying home affordable for you.

Still hard pressed to find the money for that house? Parents, as we mentioned in Chapter 6, can sometimes be an ace in the hole. Many members of the last generation made pots of money on their homes. Now many of those older parents see their kids struggling and can help out with a gift or an interest-free loan. If you've got a solid relationship, it's usually sufficient for the son or daughter to sign a note acknowledging the debt. If you want to be sure the capital is secured, especially in the case of a marriage breakup, Silverstein says it's worth registering the loan as a second mortgage against the property, although no interest is paid and so there is no tax due. Some parents actually take a mortgage out on their homes to make money available to their kids, but Silverstein doesn't advise it. If the deal, or the relationship, turns sour, the parents could end up losing their house.

Even if you've got, say, a 5 percent down payment, such a loan can be useful. If it tops up your down payment to 25 percent, you won't need mortgage insurance, and that's a big saving.

Some families go even further in providing housing security by creating family compounds. If that sounds like an option open only to the rich — along the lines of the famous Kennedy family compound at Hyannisport — it doesn't have to be.

Other Housing Possibilities

Living Among Family
In the small Ontario town of Shelburne we visited the Berry family compound. It consists of an 1860 red-brick farmhouse, originally occupied by Tuck and Marion Berry, with a modern addition on

the back and a bungalow off to one side. It represents a creative solution to many of the problems plaguing parents who want their children to grow up surrounded by family.

This is how it happened: In 1975 the Berrys' daughter, Susan, and her husband, Leslie McKenzie, were looking to buy a home. Tuck and Marion said they could have a quarter acre to build, and with Tuck supervising, Susan and Leslie had raised a new bungalow sixteen weeks later.

Living right next to their folks is not everyone's idea of a perfect arrangement, and Susan, who is now clerk-treasurer of Shelburne, says it was meant to be only a short-term answer. But they've been there now more than twenty years "and have never had a row."

In the mid-1980s, Marion and Tuck's other daughter, Sharon, and her husband, George Meunier, were also looking to move, while Marion was feeling the old house was getting awfully big for just the two of them. The upshot: Tuck built a large, self-contained addition, he and Marion moved into it, and Sharon and George moved into the main part of the house.

The arrangement involves a lot more than inexpensive housing. All the time the two Meunier boys and the three McKenzie boys were growing up, they were surrounded by family. They had their cousins, their grandparents, and, because Sharon was an at-home mom who has also been a home-care provider, there was always someone there when they came home. "They were never latchkey kids," says Susan.

Now Tuck is eighty; Marion, a retired nurse, is a year younger. When Marion was ill with pneumonia for a time, Sharon was always able to nip through the door that still connects their otherwise separate living quarters. "It's kind of neat I'm here, because I can do for her," she told us recently.

Tuck's only complaint about all those years when his five grandsons were growing up is that "The peas disappeared awful quick from the garden."

Child psychologist Penelope Leach's family ran a three-generation family compound for twenty-five years. It centered around a large building in rural Gloucestershire where her mother, herself, her two sisters, and their families each had their own quarters. "It was a wonderful way for the children to grow up," she says, and now she and her husband have bought a sprawling old farmhouse on England's south coast, hoping to establish a similar compound for the next generation.

People in the city are often looking for family of some kind, too. Psychiatrist Dr. Elliott Barker cites the African proverb "It takes a village to raise a child"; in poorer countries around the world you see community effort and support for the parents raising their children. Only in the wealthy countries are a parent and children at home left to their own resources.

Co-ops

Co-ops are another way to capture communal feeling. They are a way of life for millions in Europe, and Canada has a total of 70,000 co-op housing units, mostly in Ontario and British Columbia. Unfortunately, few are being built now, and those that are generally are not subsidized. In the United States, co-operative housing — and we're not talking about the fancy co-op apartments in New York City — has received even less public support. Nevertheless, Jim Stockard, a town planner in private practice in Cambridge, Massachusetts, told us how a number of years ago he and his wife, Susan, teamed up with seven other families to buy a three-story apartment building and create a co-op they ran themselves.

Says Stockard, "We led very conventional lives — the men went off to work, and the women stayed home with the children. But I think if you were to poll the women you would find they felt very much less isolated. And they all got started on second careers, I would say earlier than they otherwise would have, because they could trade off day-care arrangements with other people in the group." Susan stayed home until the youngest of their two children was four.

"I believe the more connections we create between people, the better," he continues, "and we've touched each others' lives more meaningfully. It's unfortunate that there is virtually nothing in our national ethic that suggests that sharing your life with other families is a valuable or appreciated way of life. Everything concentrates on the individual, on putting your own stamp on your land, on your children."

In the 1950s and even the 1960s, when more moms were at home, a sense of community was far more apparent, even in new suburban neighborhoods. Now you have to make a bigger effort to connect. Alexandra and David Jenkins bought a large, old house in the east end of Toronto, which they shared initially with David's brother and sister, and which they now share with his parents. "It was wonderful when Wendy and Amy [now aged five and six, respectively] could go up and see their Aunt Caroline and Uncle Mark," remembers Alexandra, who is home with the girls.

Part of a House

Forms of housing that break away from the traditional single-family home offer one-income families the chance not only to have more contact with others but, frequently, to live more cheaply. In many cities, duplexes and triplexes have traditionally given young couples and immigrant families a start in the housing market. Often a couple can buy the building, live in one apartment, and use the rent from the other(s) to help pay the mortgage. Margaret De Melo, of Brampton, Ontario, writes that in order for her to stay home with her fifteen-month-old son, Daniel, she and her husband, Gustavo, not only "run vehicles that would be collecting pensions if they were people" but rent out the basement of their older home, which Gustavo converted into an apartment.

"The New Home"

An architectural team at McGill University, in Montreal, has refined an old idea to produce what they call "The New Home." A narrow, three-story building — just like the houses in many of our older cities — it is totally adaptable inside, so that walls and even plumbing can be moved and stairs added without much trouble. In Montreal, the house costs about $50,000 including land, and can be bought initially as a triplex, with the owners taking over more of the building as their needs expand. When their children eventually leave, the couple could once again revert to living on one or two floors and renting the rest. It's a house for life — something both new and old in the North American experience — but its biggest advantage may be that it is economical and offers parents the financial flexibility they need in order to spend more time with their children.

Should You Move?

Don't let us alarm you into thinking you *have* to find some new, innovative housing form or communal style of living in order to be home with your children. The fact is, many of the people we interviewed stayed exactly where they were when they decided to stay home, and often with good reason. Moving entails a lot of expense. If you sell your home, real-estate commissions and other expenses may swallow up a good portion of your equity. Not to mention the trauma associated with moving, which, especially if you've just had or are about to have a baby, is one hassle you'd probably rather avoid.

So the first step is to examine your present situation. It may be far from ideal; your spouse may have to spend hours on the road commuting. But if, for example, you have a neighbor who is a good friend and who is there all day, you may want to look no further. Says Penelope Leach: "We all know of cases where life has been totally altered by the chance of a perfect neighbor. Maybe the perfect neighbor moves in, the kids get on together, the husbands play golf together, and these families become inseparable. That's very important."

And even if you don't start with that advantage, we still say to try to look at where you're living now with new eyes. See if there are moms or dads with children at the park on weekday mornings, and, as we suggested in Chapter 8, thoroughly check out local facilities for parents and children. And if you need more space, consider adding on to your present house or renovating.

As for that dream of the perfect house, you may have to let it go for a while. "I used to dream of having a house filled with beautiful things," Jullian R. Ambroz, at home with her three children, wrote recently in *Welcome Home*, the magazine published by

Mothers at Home. "Now I live with my husband, kids, Doberman, and cats in a small, ranch-style home in the South. It is filled with sturdy furniture that we bought at an Army post closing sale. There is brown indoor-outdoor carpet in the dining room, which is ugly, but easy to clean. We have a mauve-colored couch that is great for bouncing on and for making into tents. . . . It is a far cry from the house of my dreams. But it is a house that reflects the happy mother that I have become. And when I see my two-year-old and her dad snuggled up on the worn sofa, one thing becomes crystal clear. I am living in a home that, despite its somewhat shabby furnishings, is really filled with extremely beautiful things."

This is About Family

An example of how a couple who ended up with more house and more costs than they could cope with sorted themselves out, not without difficult choices, is Sandy Lubert and Andrew Campbell, a couple of schoolteachers in their early thirties. When we met them, they were in a state of shock, contemplating a "Sold" sign that had just gone up on the lawn of their attractive, three-bedroom house. They had put it on the market not really expecting to sell it, and within four days they had two offers.

It had been their dream home when they'd bought it two years earlier for $183,000 CDN ($132,000 U.S.) — a modestly priced house hidden away in a valley in an area of much higher-priced homes in the West end of Toronto, and bordering on miles of parkland.

But Sandy and Andrew, after months of hesitating, had decided selling the house was the only way they could afford for Sandy to stay home with Kevin, who is nearly two, and the baby she was expecting in a few months.

Sandy: The kids next door were waiting on the driveway as we pulled up with our moving van asking if they could take our dog for a walk. It was that kind of neighborhood. When the "For Sale" sign went up, a neighbor across the street called, "Don't move, don't leave us!" It's really an emotional time for us. We only sold the house on Sunday and everyone is saying "congratulations," but we're saying, "Why? We really don't want to move."

Andrew: I think we're still a little bit shocked by it. But when it came right down to which was more important, our kids or our house, it was no contest.

We had debated for a couple of years whether buying a house was the smart thing to do, and had put it off, saying renting would probably be a wiser decision. I guess there was an element of impulse. It was a nesting thing. Sandy was expecting Kevin and we wanted to create a nice place for our child to grow up.

Sandy: We were living in an apartment infested with mice and we had neighbors below who played their music all the time, and suddenly not being able to control our environment, and having a child in that environment, didn't mesh too well. Also there was some pretty subtle but definite pressure from family: my mom saying, "Well, I can lend you the money for the down payment," and my brother had just purchased a house. Suddenly it seemed really easy and very attractive. And then we found this valley and fell in love with it. The neighbors are supportive, Kevin has been involved in Kindercamp and programs at the library, and the park system is so great — we're big walkers and there are miles of trails right at our doorstep. And the school where I've been teaching part-time is right at the top of the hill, just a few minutes away.

Andrew: We don't want to do it. It feels like necessary medicine. But the house was owning us. We were constantly battling to get it under control. It's the battle that wears you down.

Sandy: We decided long before we had children that it would be important for one of us to stay home with the kids. I've always felt just as long as I can remember that that was the most important job I would ever do. I come from a family of six, and my parents did a wonderful job of raising us. But it's funny — our mom stayed home with my older siblings, but then she went through the feminist movement and by the time I came along she'd had it with domesticity and she was raring to go back to work. So she was working full-time as a nurse when I was growing up, and I always wished she had been home for me.

Andrew: I think professionally, too, we see the importance of it. We're both teachers and before that we worked with young offenders, and when you're in that sort of job you're confronted with the effects of bad parenting.

Sandy: Although I don't think making a choice to work is necessarily bad parenting. I think having a parent raising the kids who doesn't want to be home is worse than a good nanny or a good day care provider. But if you're a parent like me who more than anything wants to raise her children herself, then how can you do it if you're away eight hours? Other people make different choices, but I came to the point where I realized very clearly that if you're paying for day care you're paying someone else to raise your kids, you're having very little input.

Andrew: Sandy was home for a year and then, as a sort of stop-gap — until we could solve our financial problems — she went back to work part-time last September. We thought, "$1,000 [CDN; $720 U.S.] a month — our problems are solved!" — forgetting we now had child-care costs of about $500 [$360 U.S.]!

Sandy: We hired a nanny for half a day, and certainly it worked out very well. She was very good, an articulate person and extremely loving. I mean, it got to the point where we were almost convinced she loved Kevin almost as much as we did. And then, something extremely telling, I switched to working full-time in April, May, and June. They needed someone and I teach French immersion and it's hard to find someone. Kevin had this wonderful nanny, but still he was a little sad to see me go in the morning. But by the middle of May, if he woke up in the night, he was calling out for her, and he was calling me Tammy — her name. I'd say, "Mommy, not Tammy!" I just worked up the hill, so I came home at lunch, and I was home at three-thirty, so I was present for him more, I think, than most parents would be, and still he bonded to her and she was basically the mom.

Andrew: I talked about it to people at my school, and their reaction was, "Yeah, I remember the first time that happened to me." They felt it was great he had this person he had bonded with. When Kevin was born I took five days off work, but then every week I was away from him I would slip back in terms of my relationship with him. At the weekend I'd gain a bit of ground, and then slip back.

Sandy: We always knew parenting was something we would value, but nobody can ever prepare you for the bonding that takes place. If anybody had told me I would love him this much I would never have believed it.

Andrew: It's such a short time. It's just the blink of an eye and he's two years old and you've missed a lot of time with him. We were making decisions based on keeping the house, and that's not right.

Sandy: When we bought the house, we said to ourselves, "We know it will be tough, but we'll make out somehow." We were close to making it work each month, but we weren't quite making it, so what happened the last couple of years is we've borrowed a bit here and a bit there. I said, "You know, we borrow money to buy a car, why don't we borrow money so I can stay home?" So we actually did it. We took a loan. It didn't last very long. What we'd planned was that I would do tutoring or supply-teach one day a week, but none of those options really panned out for us. And suddenly we realized this year that if I'm going to stay home until the children go to school, that's going to put us in an awful lot of debt.

I think we also realized that if I did tutor or teach — or, like a friend of mine, take in children for day care or start a business at home — they're all compromises, because, although you're staying home, you're still not spending the time with your children. If you're doing day care at home, your child is one of several.

Andrew: I think we were very naive. This was the first home we ever bought, and we severely underestimated all the costs that were involved. We've struggled with it for two years and we've given it a good try, but it just hasn't worked out.

Sandy: We were able to afford it on two incomes, and that's what happened initially. But when my maternity benefits ran out we really agonized, saying, okay, we can keep this house and have both of us work, or we can keep this house and have me teach night school. But then Andrew and I wouldn't spend any time together. And this is about family, this is about children and parents. If it's a question of raising children who are going to be happy and confident, there's no question — we'll move tomorrow. We'll never, let's face it, live in the lap of luxury. We don't eat out, we don't smoke, we don't party, we rarely buy clothes for ourselves, and Andrew's parents provide most of Kevin's clothes. We were willing to make all these sacrifices, and it didn't bother us because we liked being home. But when you do all these things and you're still not able to make it work, then something's got to change.

I think our big mistake was that we borrowed our down payment to buy the house, so we've been paying that off as well as our regular mortgage payments. We've also got our student loans and the loans we've taken in the last couple of years. So it's not just the mortgage and taxes that are killing us. Andrew makes $48,000 [$34,500 U.S.], and our monthly costs include mortgage, $960 [$690 U.S.]; down payment, $350 [$250 U.S.]; taxes, $200 [$145 U.S.]; student loans, $200; and a bank loan, $250 [$180 U.S.].

We figured when I was working full-time we were just making it. Other times it's fluctuated from being a couple of hundred dollars behind to eight hundred dollars a month behind. And then we had to have a new $2,000 [$1,450 U.S.] roof put on last year, and that came as a shock. And the car cost us $500 [$360 U.S.] in repairs yesterday. There's always the wear and tear on the house with children, and now the appliances are getting to the point where they need to be replaced. You forget that these are things you don't have to worry about when you're renting.

Andrew: When the roof went we realized we were so close to the bone that if anything unforeseen happened — like the car dying — then we would be in big trouble.

Sandy: That's a second reason for moving. It takes Andrew half an hour to get to work in the morning, but, because of traffic, it takes an hour or more getting home. After that stress he's not in very good shape when he gets home. This morning we went to the area around his school looking at rental places. If we could rent cheaply we could cut down on all those unforeseen costs, Andrew would be able to take the bus or ride his bike to work, and I would have the car. It's such an expense owning a vehicle; having a second one would be crazy.

Andrew has virtually no time during the week now with Kevin because of the travel, and on the weekend he has to cut the grass or fix things. Everyone thinks of gardening as a nice hobby, and I'm sure it's lovely, but in these time-intensive years with your children you begin to resent it when you'd rather be spending time in the park with the kids. People say that as teachers we have the perfect situation, because we can be home summers with our children, right? But it's not enough.

Andrew: My dad has said that to me a few times. I think he feels our expectations are too high. He's said, "You've got two weeks at Christmas, you've got March break, and you've got two months in the summer. How much more could you possibly ask for when the average person gets two weeks' holiday a year?"

Sandy: The plan now is that I'll go back to work eventually. At some point we have to start thinking about us, and Andrew is very sensitive to the idea of us not losing ourselves and each other for the kids. We're committed to this change for the next four years, but we've also learned enough to know we really don't know what we're doing in terms of parenting. I'm a teacher now, but, as I was only saying today, I'm so excited about settling into this role as mom. I just can't wait for the moment when I can say proudly, "I'm a mom."

We smile when people say they have no choice about being able to stay home. They say, "Well, we would lose our house if we were to live on one income." Well, we have lost our house. But you always have a choice.

Choices, in fact, are what it's all about. Too many of us allow others to dictate our choices, egging us on to buy a too-expensive house or more car than we need. And that's why, ultimately, so many children see so little of their parents. In the next part of the book we'll explain how we and many of the parents we met have found ways to spend less, freeing up money for the things that really count.

11

Living Better, Spending Less

*T*he frugal lifestyle, or voluntary simplicity, is suddenly the lifestyle of choice. Some are embracing it for global reasons — because they realize our Western consumer society is astonishingly wasteful of the earth's limited resources. Others are opting for frugality for purely personal reasons — because they find their quality of life is actually improved when they spend less. And many of the parents we've spoken to are finding that living more simply leads to a richer life for themselves and their children, and gives them the time to enjoy it.

When she's making a salad, for instance, Karen Buckley will send Melissa, who is six, to fetch a green pepper from the vegetable garden just outside the back door. The pepper is free, and Melissa learns that food isn't simply something that comes from the supermarket. Other summer days the Buckley house is filled with the delicious aroma of raspberry jam cooking. Karen, who is home with her three children, reckons she saves $60 CDN ($43 U.S.) a month using cloth diapers, and even more money growing her own vegetables, getting the kids' toys at garage sales, and buying meat when it's on special and throwing it into her freezer.

"If I didn't do these things, we wouldn't be able to live the way we do," she says. On the other hand, says Karen, who lives with her husband, John, an auditor with the Ministry of Finance in Ottawa, in the small town of Carp, Ontario, "I do really enjoy it." Finding new ways to save money is fun, as well as allowing her to stay home with Melissa, Robert (aged four), and Julia (one), she says.

Frugality isn't for everyone. Some parents, seeing their time at home with their children as a temporary interruption in their careers — the sequencers — may want to put more emphasis on activities that keep them abreast of their fields than on clipping coupons to save a few dollars. As we said at the start of the book, some options suit some folks and some suit others.

But whatever your feelings about embracing frugality, getting control of your finances is the first priority. Taking care of debt, making sure you're not paying out too much for your mortgage, your insurance, and your car costs, and avoiding extravagances like regular eating out will go a long way toward making you a viable one-income family. And with a little part-time work on the side or a small business you could be about as well off as when you were both working full-time.

Karen, for instance, used to be a system product manager for Harlequin Books, the multinational romance publisher. She'd planned on returning to work after having her first baby, but after a few months with Melissa she found she simply couldn't leave her. Now she drives a school bus two hours a day, taking along her children ("They pay me to drive my two oldest to school," she says, laughing). Recently she and John figured that, when you count in day care, taxes, and commuting costs, they're bringing home about the same amount of money with her earning $6,000 CDN ($4,300 U.S.) from the driving job as they would be if she still had her $30,000 ($21,500 U.S.) job with the book company. Their total family income: about $58,000 ($42,000 U.S.). And then, of course, there are all the savings from the jams and pickles she makes, the vegetable garden, and the bargains she hunts down in supermarkets and clothing stores.

Like any parent at home, though, her real payoff, she says, comes with the time she and John have to help Melissa with her reading, prepare meals, and work with the children in the garden.

"I don't think a house can function properly when two people are working full-time," she says.

The advantages of a one-income lifestyle, as we say, are not purely dependent on reading the grocery store flyers or scouting rummage sales. But it helps!

Like Karen and John, we opted for the frugal lifestyle originally out of necessity. We simply couldn't have survived otherwise. Our kids — grown now — still make faces when they think about all the powdered milk they consumed! But then, as we learned more about money and ways to save it, living cheaply became a game. We read everything we could on how to be thrifty, not because we wanted to lead a pinch-penny, joyless existence, but because we wanted to spend what money we had on the things we really enjoyed. Necessary economies turned into pleasures. We started out camping with a tiny nine-by-nine-foot (three-by-three-meter) tourist tent because we couldn't afford anything fancier, and eventually had some of the greatest holidays imaginable under canvas.

Frugality became a lifelong habit. We still case garage sales Saturday mornings — generally to buy things for our kids and their kids — and now, after giving up camping for several years, we're back at it again, these days with our grandchildren. We're still playing the thrift game and it's set the pattern of our whole lives, allowing Frank to retire at fifty-five and permitting us to split our time between homes in Toronto and in Wales (where we avoid the need for packing by keeping full wardrobes of clothing bought at charity stores). And frugality can ultimately give you the choice of staying home with your children as long as you feel they need you.

There really is no secret to how it's done. Linda Ryan, whose budget we examined in Chapter 4, is quite typical of the parents we met. It goes without saying that she buys clothing at garage and rummage sales. Hand-me-downs are such a tradition in the Ryan house that Christmas wouldn't seem right if each of their three girls wasn't wearing the dress her sister wore when she was that age. Son Alex has been playing soccer for five years, and they haven't had to buy a new pair of soccer shoes for him yet. They save all their coins in a jar for their annual camping vacation.

A family outing is going to a local $1.50 cut-rate movie theater, taking their own snacks with them. They rarely eat out, but every Friday night is pizza night, when they all have fun making their own pizzas. Linda has also caught on to the idea that one of the best investments you can make is buying groceries in bulk when they're on special — from cases of apple juice to chicken nuggets — and keeping them for when they're needed.

We were fascinated by the number of families we interviewed that had become vegetarian, or partly so. They hadn't started with that idea, but suddenly, with a parent at home, they were more conscious of food issues and the opportunity was there to seek out or grow their own vegetables and prepare these healthful foods — at a lower cost.

There are all sorts of books out there on living frugally; we recommend *The Tightwad Gazettes*, I and II (Villard Books), by Amy Dacyczyn, for money-saving tips, and *Your Money or Your Life*, by Joe Dominguez and Vicki Robin, for a more radical approach to the idea of money and work. But don't feel overwhelmed; nobody learns frugality overnight. It starts with a few small gestures in the direction of living leaner, then slowly becomes a sport and a challenge. As we write this, Linda Ryan just dropped us a line to tell us of her latest money-saver: "We gave up cable television. This saves us $38 [CDN; $27 U.S.] a month," she writes. "It cost us only $200 [$145 U.S.] for an antenna and we've found we absolutely don't miss the cable."

We devote the rest of the chapter to tips from our own experience and what others have passed along:

Appliances

Utility companies are on an energy-efficiency kick these days, offering lots of little tips, but don't expect them to tell you serious ways to save energy. A little research can save you a lot.

First of all, wherever possible, choose gas over electric. *The Tightwad Gazette II* has printed interesting figures from the Baltimore Gas and Electric Company showing that monthly operating costs for a gas range were $1.85 compared with $10.98 U.S.

for an electric range ($2.57 and $15.26 CDN). The point: using electricity for heating is nearly always the most expensive route.

For your guidance, here are some figures — from the Canadian electrical power industry, it must be admitted — on how much bang you get for a buck's worth of power from different appliances:

Refrigerator-freezer, 500W, automatic defrost	*70 hours*
Refrigerator-freezer, 300W, automatic defrost	*117 hours*
Electric oven, 800W	*3 hours*
Dishwasher, 1300W	*3 loads*
Central vacuum, 1600W	*8 hours*
Portable vacuum, 800W	*15 hours*
Clothes dryer, 500W, medium temperature	*3 loads*
Clothes washer, 500W, with electric water heater	*4 loads*
Window air conditioner, 1050W	*12 hours*
Central air conditioner, 3500W	*3.5 hours*
Electric water heater	*210 liters (46 gallons)*
Iron, 1000W, medium temperature	*12 hours*
Single lamp, 60W	*203 hours*
Compact fluorescent, 15W, equals regular 60W	*813 hours*

The Furnace

Be friends with your furnace. Ayesha's advice is to get to know this forgotten appliance, read up on how it works, learn about things like efficiency ratings, buy a maintenance contract with your public utility, and make sure the furnace is cleaned regularly. Always be there with the service person — you'll learn more, you're less likely to be cheated, and the end result will be a more efficient furnace that saves you on fuel bills.

Dryers

If you live in a house, think about getting rid of the clothes dryer, one of the most energy-wasteful appliances. In summer a clothesline leaves the clothes with that outdoorsy smell no detergent can match. In winter, basement clotheslines help to provide needed humidity for circulating through the home.

Dishwashers

Traditionally, this has been a wasteful appliance that steals energy twice over: in addition to the power these devices used, you had to keep the thermostat on your hot water tank at a wastefully high level to provide the exceptionally hot water required. Now they have their own water heaters, and operate more economically. The most efficient will add $1.60 a week to most power bills, less if you heat your water with gas. More to the point, without a dishwasher, dishwashing becomes a social opportunity, an activity children, at least while they're small, are happy to share. With or without a dishwasher, consider turning down the thermostat on your water heater — you'll save money and kids won't get scalded.

Freezers

Here's one appliance we wouldn't be without. If you've got the space, an economical chest freezer (not too big or you'll find yourself with stuff in there you put down three years ago) is a great idea for storing supermarket specials and freezing your own fruits and vegetables in season. Ayesha freezes raspberries and other fruits in large ice-cream containers so she can make fresh batches of jam throughout the year. Fancy side-by-side fridge-freezers just don't provide the space needed for these serious tasks.

Small Appliances

You know what we mean: all those little gadgets cluttering our kitchens and bathrooms. Individually they may not be power gluttons, but we remember mornings when the fuses blew because there were so many hair dryers, radios, toasters, and what-have-you in use at the same time. As always, less is best. Casual clothing styles today mean little or no ironing; microwaves are a wasteful way to reheat coffee, and encourage you to use processed foods. Try to find economical compact fluorescent light bulbs on sale, and install dimmers, light-timers, and motion-detector lights.

Air-Conditioning

Unless you live in a scorcher climate, we'd say pass up central air-conditioning — a wasteful and expensive luxury. Just keep one room air conditioner for emergency standby on those few days in summer when the temperature really soars. Avoid homes with large expanses of glass, and keep your house cool by closing the drapes during the day (good advice for winter, too, to keep heating costs down).

Before winter, insulate and draft-proof, then, over a period of months, see how low you can turn the thermostat and still be comfortable (with a sweater, if necessary). Turning the thermostat down at night should be a habit if you don't already have a timer.

Buying Appliances

Check back issues of *Consumer Reports* to find what they had to say about the item you're looking for. You'd be surprised how often they discover best buys — appliances that perform as well or better than products costing a lot more.

Where to buy? We recently replaced the fridge we'd owned for thirty years. Frank spent the morning on the phone to big stores hunting down the non-freon model recommended in *Consumer Reports* and looking for the best price. He ended up talking to our daughter's landlord, who operates a small appliance store. Result: we got the best price and a no-fuss service call when the refrigerator door needed adjusting.

Get booklets on energy-efficiency ratings from your local electricity or gas supplier, and let the efficiency rating labels (called "EnerGuide" in Canada) guide your choice. You'd be surprised, too, if you check your newspaper want ads, how often almost unused appliances, especially fridges and stoves, are sold for half the new price. Remember, though, that many electrical appliances have been dramatically improved in efficiency in recent years, so an older model may be a power guzzler.

Extended warranties are not there to help you; they're a device stores use to boost prices and profits. If you've done your homework, you're buying a reliable product and shouldn't need the warranty. You'll only really need it if you're buying something likely to break down, in which case why buy it? But make sure to keep all receipts and regular warranty cards. (Dishwashers, microwaves, washers, and VCRs are, according to the sadly departed newsletter *The Frugal Bugle*, the appliances most often needing repair.)

Baby Needs

It's true that cloth diapers cost less. Amy Dacyczyn, founder of the *Tightwad Gazette* newsletter, says she used cloth diapers, which, some claim, cause fewer rashes, and figures she saved about a dollar a day. Ayesha used them too, but says if she were making the decision today, she'd probably use disposables because of the amount of time involved in washing and folding diapers. It's a value judgement.

Baby foods are shockingly expensive for what you're getting, and are apparently designed for people who have difficulty mashing a banana. We have to ask ourselves how babies survived before Mr. Heinz came along. The answer was — and still is in many parts of the world — that with a little care, babies can eat many of the same foods we adults eat. This may not appeal to you, but parents in many countries take a little food in their mouth, chew it, and give it to their babies with their fingers. (This is another slant on "eating like a bird!") Otherwise, mash or puree a little of your vegetables with gravy, or cut up pasta along with hard-boiled egg, and you have a meal. Potatoes, sweet potatoes, and carrots are good candidates for baby food, but avoid broccoli, Brussels sprouts, or other high-fiber vegetables that can cause gas. Your own applesauce is fine, and you can even give the baby fresh apple if you cut it in half and mush each mouthful with a spoon. Freshly squeezed orange juice is fine too, diluted with a little water.

Food

The supermarket is the front line in the battle to save bucks. The enemy is highly organized and sophisticated. Without a keen eye for small print and a steel-trap memory for prices you don't stand a chance. Look out for deceptive words like "lite," which may mean nothing at all, or "cholesterol-free" when the product patently isn't. Manufacturers have a habit of concealing price increases by shrinking the amount of product in the package. Supermarkets often shove the expensive, processed products in your face, and, if they even stock it, hide the cheaper, basic stuff away where you have to look for it. The good news is that, as millions of frugal shoppers know, the keen-eyed consumer who knows her prices and products can come out the winner in this battle of wits.

Supermarket Savvy

Coupons: to the uninitiated they seem like an awful lot of bother for a few cents off. Not so! You don't rush in and use your coupon the day it arrives in the mail. You add it to your coupon wallet, keeping a careful eye on its expiry date, and wait for the product to go on special. By combining coupons, specials, and special offers on the package, you can sometimes get the product for next to nothing — perfectly legally. If you have a like-minded frugal neighbor, swap coupons so you end up with coupons for the products you prefer. But don't let coupons become an obsession or they'll use up more of your time than they're worth. And don't buy products you don't need or want just because you have a coupon — that's what the manufacturers want you to do.

Get to know the supermarket price cycles. You may, for instance, see your regular instant coffee on sale for a dollar off. But if you've watched prices over a period, you'll know it's likely to be two dollars off next week. Supermarkets are funny that way.

Let the weekend grocery flyers be your battle plans. If the specials are outstanding at two or more chains, it may really be worthwhile to visit several to stock up. If you don't have the time for two trips, or don't want to waste the gas, just go to the store where you can pick up the best deals this week. It's a new game next week.

An alternative to scouting the flyers and driving all over town for the bargains is to locate near a good discount supermarket —

within walking distance ideally — and rely on the weekly rotation of specials to give you the chance to stock up.

We have little time for the big warehouse chains like Price Club. After comparing warehouse prices with supermarket prices, we're convinced you can do far better by stocking up at supermarkets when the items you need are on special. In addition, you often have no choice in the warehouses except to buy amounts that are far beyond your needs. And those huge, truck-sized shopping buggies — gross! Our final objection: the warehouse chains are putting neighborhood supermarkets out of business, leaving the elderly and the car-less to fend for themselves.

In Europe people still shop every day for their groceries because they want everything fresh. It's not a bad idea here, either. If you're out walking the baby anyway, drop by your supermarket on a daily basis (we're assuming you're not an impulse shopper who grabs up everything whether you need it or not). You'll find all sorts of in-store specials, especially on the reduced produce stand, and meats too are often marked down. If you get to know the produce and meat managers, there's a good chance they'll even mark items down for you if you ask. This way, too, you can carry your groceries home under the stroller a bit at a time, and never have to use the car. And watch the screen at the checkout like an eagle: you'd be surprised how often they have the wrong price in the computer, nearly always in the store's favor.

Finally, need we say it? Don't shop when you're hungry; don't take older children along with you; buy what's in season; make a list and stick to it; and bring your own shopping bags — some stores will pay you to use them if you ask.

Buying from the Farmer

Bulk-ordering with your neighbors from a food co-operative that delivers to the door can be a good alternative, especially if you're into vegetarian eating and need organic lentils and grains you don't find in your local store in bulk. But again, you need to know your prices. Just because it's trendy doesn't mean it's competitive. The same applies to "farmers' markets." The produce may or may not be fresher, but the prices are quite likely to be higher than those in the much more cutthroat competitive ethnic markets you find near city centers.

The Garden

We're big on gardens — they have so many stories to tell. We're not thinking of big expanses of grass that you have to waste the weekend cutting, but gardens to grow with. Where worms abound and butterflies flutter just out of reach of small hands, and cardinals feed their young right there at the feeder. Gardens can be made almost anywhere — on a balcony, behind apartments, on tiny city lots, and in distant suburbs. Size is not important; variety is.

Our ideal garden has some grass for playing, some hideaway spots, maybe a tree for climbing, and some space for flowers and vegetables. The rush-rush instant gardener "puts in" annuals — such as petunias and impatiens — that dutifully flower until first frost and are then pulled out. For the at-home parent, a garden is a classroom, a painter's canvas, a nature playground where you experience growth and the seasons with your child. And it needn't cost a lot.

True gardeners share their bounty. Befriend a gardener and, if you're lucky, you'll be rewarded with cuttings and roots for your perennial bed that would cost a fortune to buy. Then be patient; perennials take time, so use bulbs and annuals to fill in the empty spaces the first year or two. Start a wild woodland garden on a north wall or fence and see the wild ginger and trilliums bloom almost before the snow has gone. Eventually your flower bed will be a clock marking the seasons, from the tossing jonquils of spring through the fat buds and exotic fragrances of June irises, to August's towering sunflowers and the purple majesty of fall's Michaelmas daisies. And when the time comes, don't forget to share your bounty with another gardening beginner.

Even if you've only got a small garden, there's likely room for rhubarb, a growing experience in itself for young observers. Its fat, red buds are up through the ground almost before the snow has gone, it grows like Jack's beanstalk, it's fun to pick and slice up, and, combined with apples in a pie, it's the earliest tasty treat from the garden.

On vegetables, we won't say you'll save money growing your own, because when yours are in season they're at their cheapest in the store. But again, being home gives you the chance to share with your child the thrill of the first seeds sprouting on a windowsill, to run fingers through the black earth, and to crunch a carrot that was in the ground only a few minutes ago. And you'll know for sure what, if any, pesticides were used.

One other thing: once you start, you could quite easily find yourself under the garden spell for the rest of your life. You've been warned.

Picking It Yourself

Even if you have no garden or don't grow your own vegetables, you can certainly pick your own vegetables, and fruit, too. Some of our happiest summer memories are of taking children — today, grandchildren — to pick-it-yourself farms. There's a delightful slowing down of life, a sense of returning to calmer earlier times in the strawberry or raspberry patch with the sun overhead and the gentle murmur of pickers' voices. Toddlers, of course, can be a problem, bumbling through the rows, but as soon as they're old enough to help children love to pick — popping the odd one in their mouths, of course. And in the fall, there's no more fun to be had than picking apples and pears at farms where they have tractor rides and other thrills for the children. Having no room for a vegetable garden on our small city lot, we don't limit ourselves to raspberries and strawberries. As they come in season, we pick beans and snow peas, as well as sour cherries and red and black currants. Of all the fruits, black currants, we find, yield the most flavorful jams and jellies for often quite a modest amount of fruit. (A tip: always get down on your knees to find the biggest, juiciest black currants in the heart of the bush.)

Making It

It doesn't make sense — we know that! Why sew clothes for yourself and your children when the world is bulging at the seams with cast-off clothing? Why bake bread and muffins and brownies when you can buy the stuff cheaper day-old at the bakery? Why make jams and jellies and pickles and preserves when whole industries exist to do it for you?

And we'd agree: on a pure dollars-and-cents basis, sewing and baking and preserving often don't add up. Certainly many parents at home, especially when babies are small, say, "Forget about baking a cake — I don't even have time to go to the bathroom!"

True enough. But, we'd suggest, there's a dimension to the frugal life that goes beyond simply living cheaply. Ask a mother who has made a Christmas dress for her toddler why she didn't buy one at the store. You probably wouldn't dare! Because it was the love she put into the dress that gave her the pleasure and the dress its value. Tell a grandfather making a wooden train set for his granddaughter that they make the same thing cheaper in Taiwan, and you'd be missing the point. We do things to show our love for people.

This book is not about getting rich. It's for people who are prepared to make sacrifices to be with small people they love more than anything in the world. Every parent brings something different to that experience; it may be a passion for books, a knack for handicrafts, or simply their love. In each case, it's enough. But making things is another expression of that love, whether it's a batch of brownies on the counter when the kids come home or a white woolen jacket knitted for the coming of a winter baby.

And, surprise! Making things *can* end up saving you money, too. Bread is the great example in our house. The weekly baking day was always a joy to come home to, the house filled with that never-to-be-forgotten smell. Ayesha baked eight loaves at a time. For her, kneading the dough is almost a spiritual exercise, and for the family, the flavor of fresh, homemade bread will always be associated with home. One son, grown now, of course, still comes around for his favorite — the one loaf that always somehow gets burned.

Several times down the years we compared the cost of home-made with the store product; invariably the homemade loaf cost only a fraction of what the store bread did. One reason: super-markets regularly discount large bags of flour, and if a bag leaks, it ends up on the reduced shelf at a giveaway price. With cakes, muffins, and other baked goods, the price comparison is even more telling — and you know only good stuff went into the home-baked goods.

You can pick up preserving jars for a song these days at garage sales — with everyone working, there's no one home to make pre-serves or jams any more. Tomatoes, peaches, strawberries come into season, we buy a few at the store, maybe even gather a few strawberries or raspberries at the pick-it-yourself farm — and then they're gone until next year. Children who grow up in a house where the seasons are given their due — where marmalade bub-bles on the stove in January, and strawberry jam in June — learn about the world and where things come from.

Meanwhile, in the basement storeroom, there's a whole year's supply of cranberry sauce for the turkey, red-currant jelly or applesauce for the roast pork, pears and peaches and marmalade for breakfast, frozen blueberries for the pies and muffins, and tomatoes for the spaghetti sauce. Believe us when we say that the contents of our storeroom and the freezer have turned out to be a far more successful investment than any stock certificates in our safety deposit box.

If you need advice on how to preserve, just contact your local agriculture department — they'll have recipes as well as directions to pick-it-yourself places in your region.

Beating the Bank

Bank charges, once a harmless little pup, have turned into a rag-ing pit bull in recent years. Whole bank departments, we're convinced, exist for no other reason than to come up with new charges, and if you're living on less you'll need to beat them at their own game. The simplest approach is not to do business with banks; use a credit union instead, if possible. We've belonged to a credit union for twenty-five years (Frank was on the board of directors for a number of years), and it's helped us with low-interest loans, mortgages that were always open, and a host of other services.

Credit unions are nonprofit, and any surplus they make is plowed back into providing cheaper services. Traditionally they limited their membership to the employees of a single firm or government department, but in recent years they have opened their doors to all comers. Late in 1996 the U.S. banking lobby succeeded in a court action against a credit union that welcomed outsiders, and that could have implications for the whole movement. The credits unions are currently appealing; the issue bears watching.

But even with credit unions you still need to compare fees and look out for yourself. We have our no-charge credit card with another institution, and although the credit union offers debit cards we've said a polite "no, thank you" because we don't want to be charged every time we use one to pay.

Talk to your bank or credit union about having the best sort of account for your needs, and check out the fine print to avoid charges. Some banks offer free checking if you keep a minimum balance — usually $1,000 — in the account. If you're using a credit card, put all your monthly bills on it to save writing checks — and make sure to pay it off at the end of the month.

Vacations

Keep two words in mind: "sharing" and "camping." A number of the couples we spoke to make use of cottages belonging to parents or other family members, while others rented cottages with other families to keep down the cost.

Camping has always been our answer. We camped the first time when our oldest daughter was only a few weeks old (although we wouldn't recommend that as a good way to start camping). There's magic for a kid to toasting marshmallows around a campfire and then sleeping under a canvas roof. Advantages: you get to enjoy some of North America's most magnificent scenery in provincial, state, and national parks, and kids usually seem to take about three minutes to find friends at the campsite, disappearing forthwith to play with them.

Oh yes, it rains, and there are bugs. We'd recommend a dining tent and board games for rainy days. In Britain, where frequent rainy skies make tent camping a dubious proposition, we found renting a caravan or house trailer already on a site was a reasonable alternative — although still considerably more expensive than camping.

If you are considering camping, it's a good idea to rent or borrow gear for your first trip — then you get an idea if it's your kind of vacation. If it is — and your kids, once they've tasted it, will probably be emphatically in favor — it's best to ease into camping purchases rather than buying the whole lot at once.

The first year you'll want your sleeping tent, of course, and that may cost $300 or $400 CDN. And of course you'll need sleeping bags, a camp stove, a lantern, and a cooler. But your dining tent (around $230) can wait until the second year, along with many other items you'll enjoy adding as the years go by. The total cost for family camping gear, depending on how elaborate you get, is around $1,500 to $2,000, and you may eventually want a small trailer or roof rack to carry it all. Maybe that sounds like a lot — except that the expenditures are spread over several years, and the equipment will last you for many years.

If you divide that cost over just eight years, you have a two-week vacation each year for about $500 plus food and gas. Those two weeks at a cottage are likely to cost $1,500.

If you're tempted to try it, here are two suggestions from our own experience: First, set up your new tent in the backyard the day before you go, so you won't be trying to read the directions while everyone's crabby and wanting dinner. Second, for similar reasons, book your campsite ahead of time, and make sure to arrive in early or mid-afternoon so you have plenty of time to set up while there's daylight and everyone's in a good mood.

Shopping

Don't do it. To be discovered in a shopping mall without a clear purpose can be extremely dangerous to the health of the budget.

Vices

Quitting smoking, of course, is the very best thing you can do for your health (and your children's health), and is mighty good for the budget too. But you don't need to give up all your little pleasures. Alcohol, in moderation, especially a glass or two of red wine daily, has been found to be beneficial to your heart, so watch out for sales at your wine or liquor store.

And it's good to have a little splurge. Our pet vice is going to the movies. We had the habit when we met, and it's carried us through the decades. Oh, we know we could save more by waiting for the movie to come out on video, but that's not the same. So for years we've arranged our affairs to take in the lower-priced afternoon matinees, when we even have the theater mostly to ourselves. And don't, for goodness' sake, deny yourself those little meals out together that every parent, especially the parent at home, needs occasionally for the sake of sanity.

What we've been talking about here is a whole new philosophy of spending. In *Your Money or Your Life*, Joe Dominguez and Vicki Robin say we shouldn't regard expenditures in a neutral way, as if they were inevitable and unavoidable. Instead of lumping together "clothing," for instance, they suggest you break down clothing expenditures into what is necessary and what is simply vanity. How many of the shoes we buy, they ask, do we wear regularly? Instead of lumping food expenditures together, they suggest separating the food you need from snack foods or foods bought for entertaining. You get the picture? The idea is to separate simply living from simply consuming. It's not enough, say Robin and Dominguez, to simply record the money spent on gasoline and repairs and loan payments for a second car; you also need to examine the need for the car at all.

Frugality often starts with expediency — the need to cut back spending in order to live without that second income. But getting control of spending frees up time and money for the better things.

Where's the Rest of Your House?

Laura Clatterbuck, her husband, Mark, and their three children (Martha, aged eleven, Joe, eight, and Bill, five) live in a very modest bungalow in an area of suburban Fairfax County, Virginia, noted for its super-luxury homes. Mark, in addition to his daytime job as manager of a car repair shop, earns money evenings cutting his time-pressed neighbors' lawns, while Laura pays for the groceries by caring for their children.

We've been married seventeen years this fall, and we waited five years before I got pregnant. You could say we had our retirement at the start. In those first years we traveled, we ate out, we even got to stay up late. There are seasons in a marriage, there are times that are good and times that are bad. And I think you need several years' perspective before you see the picture. I'm very glad we waited five years because it gave us time to get to know each other and time to buy a townhouse. Then we were ready to be parents.

But three kids in five years — that was a little overwhelming. I don't think we were looking for that. There were some intense years there where I was in such a fog I would just barely get through the day. The physical demands are so strong when they're little! We didn't have much time for each other, and I had no resources left at the end of the day for Mark. But time passes; now they're bigger, more independent, and really fun to be with. So I guess it's summer again.

I worked from the time I left high school, and I was earning more than my husband when our first child came. I tried really hard to get them to set up an on-site day-care center at my work — I thought that would be the answer. I intended to go back to work, but when my three months' leave were up, I found I couldn't.

I couldn't have left that baby any more than I could have left my right arm at home. It didn't feel like the decision was up to me; this was biology working. I knew I was in trouble the first time I tried to leave her. She was just a few weeks old and I had a dentist's appointment. I was leaving her with her grandma, and it was physically painful for me to leave her behind. I couldn't wait to get back home. I needed her as much as she needed me. She was a very needy child; she nourished all night, and she cried. She's a lovely person now — one of my best friends. But she was a horrendous baby!

It was a hard call for my husband. He was terrified we weren't going to be able to pay the bills. What I did was do some typing at home. Cottage labor, they called it. How I kept it up I really don't know. I'd make a pot of coffee after dinner and my husband would take over the baby and I'd work until one or two in the morning. I'd try to catch a nap in the day. It was always a big decision when I put the baby down to sleep — do I clean the house, sleep, or do my work?

Then she and I got a job. We went to someone else's house and took care of her little boy two or three days a week. One thing led to another, and after my little boy was born I started taking care of another little boy. I cover the cost of the groceries — that's always my aim. In this area you can pay $125 or $150 a week [U.S.; about $170 to $210 CDN] for full-time care for an infant, and the licencing rules say I could have as many as five children here. But we have no family room and no basement; my house is not really set up for it. We live in each others' pockets here. Besides, the last thing my kids want to see when they get off the school bus is a house full of toddlers. When I got a few more kids than I was really comfortable with, it really started to show on them, so I cut back.

We bought this house when I was pregnant with Joe because we wanted to be closer to my husband's work. We wanted to be in the sort of neighborhood where every house is different, not a cookie-cutter neighborhood. We could have gone farther out and got a nicer house, but we got a fixer-upper. In 1987 it cost $135,000 [$188,000 CDN] and we had big plans for it. We figured we could put an addition on it. My husband even drew up the plans, but it would cost about $50,000 [$69,000 CDN]. By the time we can afford it, the kids will be gone and we won't need it any more. Joe has friends over in the next neighborhood where there are big palatial homes. We had a friend of his over, and he looked around, went in Joe's room, and then said, "Mrs. Clatterbuck, where's the rest of your house?"

We have the house half paid for now and we're hoping by the time the kids are ready to go to college we can refinance it again. We weren't really looking at school districts at the time, but this has turned out to be one of the best — the next best thing to a private school.

Now it takes my husband only twenty minutes to get home, but most evenings we don't see much of him because he's working at two jobs. He kind of fell into having his own landscaping and lawn service. We bought a big mower to cut our grass and it turns out so many people here have more money than time that they're prepared to pay what I think of as a king's ransom for someone to cut their grass. I would love it if he could switch over to the business full-time — he's cut out to be his own boss. What's stopping us are his benefits at work, especially the health benefits. We can't take risks. We pray for rainy nights because then Daddy comes home because he can't cut grass in the rain!

I think fatherhood hit him unawares. His own dad died when he was eight, so he basically grew up without a father. He was surprised at the depth of feeling you have for this little creature that you made. He still wishes he could be home with them, although I don't think he has the same threshold as me. He would tire more easily. Often when he gets home from working the two jobs he gets just the leftovers — they're tired and grumpy and ready for bed. He doesn't get to see the best of them. But he tries to make up for it at weekends. He bought a boat — much against my better judgment — but it's turned out to be wonderful. The Potomac River is only thirty minutes away, and every weekend we're gone. The boat is our family room.

We used to go camping on vacations, but we're too many for our little camper now. So lately we've been taking the boat, going to a lake, and renting a house with another family. We went last year for a week. There were seven children, and it was a squeeze. I think we ate out only once. We make a big pot of chili and find ways to do it real inexpensive.

Most of the kids around here go to summer camp, but we can't afford to send ours. So the last two years I've volunteered at the Girl Scout camp, where there's a program for the girls' younger siblings. That meant last year I could take the three children for ten days and it cost only $110 [$153 CDN]. I put in a lot of hours, but we had a wild old time.

As far as clothes are concerned, I virtually never buy new clothes. There's a great stream of children's clothing out there, and if you let people know you're not too proud to take hand-me-downs, you tap into that stream. A woman I used to sit for phoned me one day and asked me if I wanted some children's clothes. She brought over ten trash bags of kids' clothes some fancy relatives of hers had given her. I passed on clothes to a low-income day-care center and to a neighbor. We have so many clothes they don't fit into my kids' drawers. I'm the yard sale queen, too. Sometimes I come home with the car filled from stuff I find.

My mother is the coupon queen. She knows what I like and clips the coupons for me. She doesn't mind going in three or four grocery stores to buy the kinds of coffee and cereal we like.

Cars we don't have to worry about since my husband is a mechanic. Everyone has a minivan, but we drive that '78 wagon out there. My criteria was eight seatbelts: we have three kids and they all want to bring a friend when we go some place. And that wagon has eight belts. It may look a beater, but my husband built a new engine and put it into it. He drives a '72 pickup to work.

A lot of people by this time would have gone back to work, especially next year with my youngest in elementary school. But I'm beginning to realize it's even more important to be home now than it was when they were babies. I can't see having them come home to an empty house. You planted the seeds when they were little, and now you have to decide which way the plant will grow. Now is when the outside influences, the media, and their friends come into play.

My daughter is eleven and the hormones are starting to kick in. She's flapping around, trying to find out where she fits. She's not a little kid, but she's not a grownup yet. I try to figure out my Joe. He's either going to be the world's biggest con man or a diplomat — he can charm the birds out of the trees. He's going to need us. Our youngest dressed up as a question mark at Halloween, because he's always asking questions. He'll ask me if it's fun to drive, what do lightning bugs eat, and why does the skin on your fingers get wrinkled? Good questions — and if I'm not here, who's he going to ask?

They had career day at my daughter's school the other day and she wanted to go as a mother. I was very flattered. She had a baby doll in a carrier and she wanted to put curlers in her hair. I said, "Have you ever seen me in curlers?" She said she'd carry a coffee cup instead because I always have a coffee cup. I said, "How about a steering wheel, because I'm always driving you?"

I wouldn't want her to get married as young as I was. That's my one big regret: that I never lived by myself. But I think she will feel the same way about her babies as I do — unless I'm here to babysit. And that can be worked out!

The trick is to keep your marriage going. If you're throwing yourself into work and kids, you've got to remember that guy you married and hope there's something left at the end of it.

Mark's family health history is not real great. His father died in his early forties and his brother had his first heart attack in his early forties too. My husband turned forty last year. So I say every year is precious for these kids. You don't want to miss anything. Is it risky? Yes. I often say I'm one man away from welfare. I'm very vulnerable. My husband is working two jobs for us and I couldn't replace his income. It's a risky way to live, but we made our choice: the choice to have three children.

———————

Perhaps there are risks in the way the Clatterbucks live. They don't have the financial backups that many dual-income families have. They can't offer their children the extravagant lifestyles their friends at school may be enjoying. They can't allow for every eventuality, every possible mishap. But our experience tells us they are right to be daring, that by living frugally they will be able to cope with setbacks. And that their children will learn a measure of self-sufficiency that will be entirely foreign to their well-to-do neighborhood friends, and that will stay with them for life.

12

Cars:
Less Is Best

Cars and kids: what's the connection? How did this chapter on
automobiles sneak into a book about staying home with your
children? The answer is that many people buy a car in order to get
to work, then work in order to pay for the car. In the end, that
seductive chunk of metal and plastic in the driveway helps to keep
people chained to their jobs — and so unavailable to their children.

It's a vicious circle from which it's difficult to escape. Many of
us build our lives around the car, living and working in places
accessible only by automobile. We live in a constant cycle of loan
payments, insurance and repair costs, and so on. Taming that alli-
gator in the garage can be a big step toward getting a budget
under control.

It is, believe it or not, even possible to live without a car. Laurie
Feldman, a former criminal prosecutor living in Wallingford,
Connecticut, doesn't have one. In her case poor eyesight prevents
her from driving, so she and her four children are quite used to
walking or cycling where they want to go.

Not having her own car has, if anything, been a plus for
Laurie. When we spoke to her, the whole family had just walked
the half-mile (just under a kilometer) to the town center for an

ice-cream treat. She walks with the children to the doctor's office, to school, to the synagogue, and to do regular shopping. Her husband, Steve Gilles, fetches home the heavy groceries in his car.

Her children, she reported in a recent issue of *Welcome Home* magazine, love being out all seasons. A trip to a used-clothing store two miles from the last house where they lived would turn into a full-scale expedition, with bikes, stroller, a visit to a baker, and a picnic in a nearby park. With a car, the whole trip could have been wrapped up in an hour — with a lot less fun. As Laurie's seventy-four-year-old neighbor told them, "The children of mothers who do not drive have special adventures."

Laurie has no choice because she can't drive, but some other parents we met who are home with their children have chosen to get by with one car or none at all. Keith Nunn and Beth Baskin, happy Toronto downtowners, for instance, took their '84 Honda to the wrecker's when it needed $3,000 worth of repairs. Now they walk to the St. Lawrence Market in downtown Toronto, bring their produce home in the stroller, and rent a car when they need one on the weekends. They are not anti-car people; "Growing up in the suburbs of Vancouver, I really enjoyed driving," says Beth. But getting another car was going to cost a lot, and now, says Beth, "Not having a car is a factor in being able to live the way we do."

Where both parents are working, it's often surprising what a large portion of the second income is swallowed up by car expenses. And when a baby arrives, things often get worse, not better. Today, it's our observation, the arrival of a tiny mite weighing in at around seven pounds is enough to convince some parents they need a vehicle capable of carrying a good portion of the Chicago Bears football team. So if you're planning on staying home, take a hard look at your car costs.

Some general principles:

- Where vehicles are concerned, less is best.
- Buying secondhand is generally a better idea than buying new.
- Buying, in the long run, is a better proposition than leasing.

The Cost of a Car

The fact is, most of us are in servitude to the big car companies, to the insurance industry, to the repair people, to governments that rely on motorists' taxes and tolls, fees and fines, and to the banks with their merry-go-round of loans and lease payments. And all for a shiny set of wheels that sit immobile in traffic jams a good bit of the time!

Dollar Costs

The economics of car ownership are crazy. A car with a starting price of $25,000 will end up costing around $40,000 when you count in various taxes, charges, and financing costs. And that's not even including insurance, which typically adds another $800 to $1,000 U.S. a year to the bill. In Canada (where gas and other costs are higher), running even a compact costs 40.9¢ CDN a kilometer (18¢ U.S. a mile). In the United States the meter ticks over at 13.8¢ U.S. a mile and 16.7¢ for a minivan (30.6¢ and 37¢ CDN per kilometer respectively).

Environmental Costs

Then there's the toll cars take on the air quality and oil supply, which is actually increasing as oversized vehicles such as minivans and sport-utility trucks herald the return of the gas guzzler.

The New York Times reported in July 1996 that the average gas mileage achieved by American motorists is on the decline. From 1973, at the time of the Middle East oil crisis, to 1985, the figure improved by an amazing 54 percent as, under pressure from the federal government, manufacturers improved engine efficiency and concentrated on smaller cars. But from 1985 to 1994, thanks to growing sales of vans and trucks, it dropped back about 5 percent. With the truck and van trend accelerating, the figure is likely still going down.

Not only are people driving bigger cars, but, because people now work and shop farther from home, the average distance driven by Americans annually rose 48 percent between 1973 and 1994. That's bad news for family budgets and bad news for the environment. While gasoline continues to be sold at giveaway prices in North America — less than half of what it costs in Europe — that wasteful situation is not likely to change.

How can we break free from our servitude to the automobile? There are some radical answers around. In Edinburgh, Scotland, there are plans to build a car-free community where residents would have to sign a covenant promising not to buy a car as a condition of moving in. Who would ever sign? With housing cheaper because space doesn't have to be set aside for cars, and children free to play in a car-free environment, you might be surprised. For anyone who has visited Venice, one of the lasting memories is of a city without cars, of giant St. Mark's Square with no sounds but those of human feet and human voices.

The Less Car, the Better

Coming back to the noisy, polluted, expensive reality of most North American cities, what can parents planning on staying home do? First of all, they can make the car as small a part of their lives as possible, in every way: own fewer cars; make each car smaller; get small cars that are cheaper; and use them less.

How Many Cars?

We've already discussed the savings of owning one car rather than two. What about less than one? Car sharing, where two or more families share in the ownership of a single vehicle, is one option some are trying, although it's not practical for most families. But how about car-sharing in your family? Just as Debbie Kusturin, whose story appears at the end of this chapter, keeps the car one day a week when she needs it for chores, other families could probably work out arrangements to split up car-use as needed. Carpooling and using public transit, if only for part of the time, can also free up the family car.

How Big a Car?

If you commute, the money you'll save on gas with a small car will more than make up for the occasional inconvenience of not being able to transport a couch or a little-league team. When your needs grow, we'd suggest looking at a station wagon. When our kids were smaller we bought a Volvo station wagon — then replaced it with another one after ten years. With a humongous roof rack up top we managed to take everyone camping, even managing to pack in the six children and a good part of our earthly belongings when we returned by ship from Britain after living there for three years.

Trucks, sports-utility vehicles, and even minivans — the auto trend of the nineties — are impractical vanity vehicles no different from the over-powered Stealths and Mustangs favored by wild young males.

Minivans impractical? Indeed. Families have fallen in love with the minivan, and in Canada they account now for one in three auto sales. But their size, which is well beyond the needs of most families, comes at a high price. Minivans and, to an even greater extent, sports-utility vehicles, cost more to start with, and, because they are more costly to repair and are the favored target of car thieves, are more expensive to insure. Because they are in so much demand, manufacturers can charge a premium for them when setting list prices, and you're less likely to cut a good deal with the dealer than you are buying a conventional sedan.

We'd add that, in spite of their rugged appearance, several sports-utility vehicles performed badly in insurance industry crash tests in 1996, and *Consumer Reports* has faulted some models for a tendency to tip over on turns.

Compact cars typically get about 30 miles to the U.S. gallon, minivans about 24, and sports-utility vehicles about 17, some as low as 13. (In Canadian terms, compacts burn about 7 or 8 liters of gasoline per hundred kilometers, minivans, 10 or 11, and sports-utility vehicles a dismal 14 or 15, with some as high as 18.

What to Buy?

Our first advice would be that holding on to the vehicle you already own for as long as possible, even if it's a gas guzzler, is probably the cheapest option for most families. If you sell you take a drubbing both ways — in what you get for your car and what you pay for the next one. If you must buy, Mohammed

Bouchahma of the Automobile Protection Association, who drives an '86 Toyota Cressida, suggests you look at a two- or three-year-old car that has already lost 30 to 35 percent of its value through depreciation. If you possibly can, pay cash for the car; if you can't, borrow the money from your credit union or bank.

Which kind to choose? Instead of going for the glamor names or the car your brother-in-law bought, we suggest sitting down with your partner and carefully analyzing your car needs. Remember, less is best.

Do Your Homework

When you've decided the least amount of car you can get by with, we'd suggest you head for your library or newsstand for the latest April automobile issue of *Consumer Reports*, which contains frequency of repair records for all models and recommendations on the best new and used cars to buy. Canadians who join the Automobile Protection Association (in Toronto, call 416-964-6774; in Montreal, 514-272-5555) also receive *Lemon-Aid*, the outfit's very thorough run-down on cars to pick and cars to avoid. Phil Edmonston's annual books, also called *Lemon-Aid* (Stoddart), are similarly invaluable. For new-car buyers, both the Automobile Protection Association and *Consumer Reports* provide details on the actual dealer cost of vehicles to give you a basis for bargaining. *The Used Car Book*, by Jack Gillis (HarperCollins), published every spring in the United States, also contains good info on the car to buy.

Once you've finished reading up and have a model or two in mind, it's a good idea to check with your insurance agent to find out how much it will cost to insure it. Rates can vary enormously, depending on repair costs and the popularity of that model with car thieves.

None of this, of course, protects you from the unscrupulous seller, and buying a used car will always have its risks. Get all the documentation you can about maintenance and previous ownership (in Ontario now, sellers are required to provide a used-car information package containing much of this information), study old repair bills for clues as to whether the odometer has been changed, and don't be afraid to phone previous owners for further information. If they're not forthcoming, beware. Finally, and most important, cultivate a good mechanic who can check the vehicle before you buy.

Buying vs. Leasing

If you want a new car, should you buy or lease? In Canada, 40 percent of new vehicles now are leased, but we think it's mostly a mug's game. Many of those who lease are lured by low monthly payments into leasing a fancy car they couldn't afford to buy. Both in Europe (where leasing is a new trend) and North America, lease agreements are often so complicated that most customers have no idea what they're really getting for their old car or what interest rate they're paying in the lease agreement. Using figures published in a Canadian Ford advertisement, for example, it's possible to see that a Windstar GL Special Edition originally costing $25,000 would, if leased, then purchased at the end of two years, eventually cost $36,276. The same vehicle purchased over twenty-four months, financed at 9.5 percent, would cost $31,168.

According to Robert Lo Presti of Orangesoft, an Ontario software firm that has developed a program called CarCalculator to compare leasing costs, over fifteen years a person who buys a car every five years and finances it will be ahead about $35,000 CDN ($25,000 U.S.) of someone who leases a car every three years. Our advice: if you can't afford to buy a certain car, you can't afford to lease it.

Some sample figures (all in Canadian dollars):

John leases his car		Jane buys her car	
Years 1–3		**Years 1–5**	
Car price (inc. taxes)	$21,774	Car price	$25,547
Down payment (inc. taxes)	$2,875	Down payment	$2,875
3-year monthly payments	$412	5-year monthly loan payments	$488
Total outlay	**$17,707**	**Total outlay**	**$32,156**

Years 4–6		Years 6–10	
Car price	$24,493	Car price	$31,114
Down payment, taxes	$3,234	Trade-in (inc. tax credit)	$9,750
3-year monthly payments	$464	5-year monthly loan payments	$459
Total outlay	**$19,938**	**Total outlay**	**$27,540**

Repeating this exercise over a fifteen-year period, with John leasing a new car every three years, and Jane buying one and financing it every five years, the fifteen-year outlay for John is $113,626 CDN (about $82,000 U.S.), and for Jane, $78,835 (about $57,000 U.S.).

Other Hints

Buying or leasing the car, of course, is only the beginning. Once you get it home, there are plenty of ways you can keep driving costs down.

Don't be afraid to lift the hood. With more and more self-service gas stations, cars are not checked the way they used to be, which can mean big bills when something goes really wrong. Check oil, coolant, windshield washers, and tire pressure (using your own pressure gauge) regularly. A short night course can equip you to change the oil and tune up your own car.

Save on insurance by increasing the deductibles from a typical $50 to $250 or even $1,000, depending on your pain threshold. It's only really worth claiming on your insurance for a major accident. Shop around for the best rate — they can vary enormously. Sometimes, by doing all your insurance business — car, life, and home — with one company, you can get a preferential rate.

Another obvious way to save is simply to use your car as little as possible. You'll not only save on gas, but on insurance — the lower the annual mileage the lower the rate — and you'll run less risk of getting traffic tickets, which are expensive and can boost your insurance rate through the roof. And keep an eye on the declining value of your car; as we mentioned earlier, it doesn't take long for it to reach the point where it won't pay to buy collision insurance because, following even a moderate accident, the company will write it off and pay you the miserable depreciated value.

Think of your car as an enormously expensive luxury — which it is. Scheme like mad to get it out of your life as much as possible — by carpooling, bicycling, using your computer or even the phone to work from home, or cutting back to a four-day week.

And we'd put in a final word for a means of transportation that predates Henry Ford by several million years: walking. For families especially, the social advantages of walking together can't be compared to being cooped up together in a car. Do the kids want to run ahead? Let them. It gives the two of you a break to talk on your own. Does one of the children have a problem to talk over with dad? He can drop back and they can talk all they want. Does mom want to explain to Teddy about how clouds form? She won't be interrupted. Or you can just be quiet without anyone feeling they have to fill the silence. Call it free-flow family interaction. There's nothing like it.

It Ended Up Being a Wonderful Street

Debbie and David Kusturin live deep in car country. Their comfortable, three-bedroom home is on a little street named Hood Crescent on the very fringes of development in Brampton, outside Toronto. David has a forty-five-minute (minimum) drive to his job downtown as a construction manager, and Debbie is home without a car most of the time with Victoria, aged four, John, one, and Jennifer, her fifteen-year-old daughter from her first marriage. With no shopping or other facilities within walking distance, you'd think she'd be stranded. Think again.

David: We'd been looking for a place to buy for four months without any luck. Everywhere you needed a 25 percent down payment, and we didn't have it. Then we found this place. There were just three houses on the street, and this was still a vacant lot. The house was $177,000 [CDN; $127,500 U.S.], but the down payment was only $10,000 [$7,200 U.S.]. We just signed for it — then I phoned my parents to see if they could help. We bought the place in half an hour. We weren't thinking too carefully. Three years later, when the mortgages came up for renewal, property values had dropped and financing was hard to get. Some people around here lost their homes. But at the time we bought, it seemed like a window had opened for us, so we jumped at the chance. We were just wondering how we would manage.

Debbie: We both worked at the same construction company; that was how we met. I was a secretary earning about $32,000 [$23,000 U.S.]. We talked about having children even before we got married. But I didn't want to go the day-care route. I'd done that when Jennifer, my first one, was little. After Jennifer's father left, I was basically a single mother living in a twelfth-floor apartment with nowhere for her to play. I would get up in the morning, take her to the day care on the bus, then take another bus to work. I was trying to do everything. I would pick Jennifer up, come home, make the dinner, do eighteen different things. I would always try to comb Jennifer's hair and tell her a story before she went to sleep, but I felt I just never had time to spend with her. It's so much pressure. You feel so guilty. I still regret those lost times with Jennifer. I didn't want that to happen again with my next child.

But we figured we could never afford for me to stay home at that time. We talked about me working part-time so I could be home some of the time. Another option was looking after children in my home, so I took a course in that even before we moved in here. We put flyers up everywhere offering to look after children. But we were just too far away from everything, and I got no response at all. So I signed up as a child-care provider with the regional government. I was looking after children of disadvantaged parents, mostly single mothers going to school. The trouble was it was just like a revolving door; they were always sending me different children. Then there were government cutbacks, and the children just sort of petered out.

It was the lowest point of all for the Kusturins. Using severance pay Debbie had received when she'd quit work, they had bought a computer which, they had thought, would allow her to work at home, but that didn't work out, either. Then, when Victoria was eighteen months old, they made a tough decision: Debbie would go back to work as a temporary office worker. Only one thing had turned out right — the street.

David: It ended up being a wonderful street.

Debbie: There are so many families with children, and there are a lot of young moms at home. I got to know Linda, Marie, and Elizabeth, and when I went back to work I left Victoria with my neighbor, Josie. Then, if I was working, Jennifer would pick her up from Josie's when she got home from school. We were really lucky having Josie so close, and Victoria was pretty good going to her. The first time we had a problem was when we'd been on holidays and she didn't want to go. She cried and cried, and that was pretty tough. I temped for two years.

David: Then John came along and we didn't know what we were going to do. Perhaps Debbie would have to work part-time. Luckily, I got a bit more money at work, and Debbie was able to stay home.

Debbie: We just watched our spending. I nursed them both until they were about eight months — that saved a lot of money. I was just shocked when I saw the price of formula. It's about $37 [$27 U.S.] a case, and that comes to about $80 [$58 U.S.] a month. I used cloth diapers, too, with Victoria, although by the time John came along they were falling apart. It's quite an investment getting a new set, so I've been using disposables with John.

And the cars! When my '87 Plymouth Horizon finally went, we figured we were lucky to get $200 [$144 U.S.] for it. And we knew we couldn't afford to replace it.

When David's car finally broke down, we got practically nothing for it. He bought an '87 Audi from a guy at work. He drives it to work four days a week, and the other day I drop him at the station, then I have the car for chores. That's all I need it, really. My friend Linda has a car, and she has always told me any time I need a drive to call her. The funny thing is, every time I get the car it needs work done. Last time I had it I spent most of the day in the muffler shop with the kids. It was only ready just in time for me to meet the train!

When I first came home with Victoria I felt a bit isolated. Now she's older and she's easier to talk to, and I can do so many things with her. Mornings are kind of busy. It's ten o'clock by the time I have everything done, and then there's an hour before it's time for her to get ready for junior kindergarten. We sit and color or paint and do puzzles and read books, and we have a lot of conversations. With Jennifer I feel we both missed out a lot. I feel we could have had a better relationship if I'd been home with her. We didn't talk the way I do with Victoria.

I don't have to say to Victoria, "What did you do at school today?" She tells me all these things when she gets home, and she goes on and on. We're around each other so much we talk and talk. I love it.

Bad days? When John won't go to sleep all day and he's cranky by late afternoon and I'm frazzled. Right now John is very clingy. But Victoria — as soon as the front door is open, she's out and looking for her friends. She knows everyone on the street.

David: It takes a lot of creativity to keep kids amused. It's harder to stay home than go to work. Debbie sometimes has classes and I watch the kids for the whole day and by the end I'm exhausted. When I get them to sleep I have to lie down.

Debbie: He makes supper most of the time, so he tells me on the car phone what to get ready for him. Often we're still talking on the phone when he's walking through the door. My cooking is just ho-hum, but he enjoys cooking.

David: I like to experiment. Chicken teriyaki, curry, Singapore noodles, that sort of thing.

Debbie: Sometimes I worry that our kids don't have the things other kids do. But Victoria has swimming lessons, and we found the money for her to have dance lessons. It's harder with Jennifer. Most of her friends' parents are in a better position than we are. She says, "I want this or that," and she can't have it. We say, "Go babysitting to get the money." But we feel kind of bad.

The little ones wear hand-me-down clothing. We get boxes given us, and I just took a bag of clothes to my friend across the street. When they're babies they don't care. Luckily the grungy look is fashionable, and Jennifer and her friends love going to the Goodwill store to buy second-hand things.

David: I honestly thought we would be struggling a lot more than we are. We look at furniture stores and cars and say, "Some day!"

Debbie: Eventually I want to go back to work. I'm taking courses in interior design, and this September I will get my certificate. This time I want a career, not just a job. Right now, though, I feel a lot better being home with them. I know their moods. I feel so much better knowing what is happening and I think they feel better too.

My sister's little girl is four months old now, and my sister phoned me one day and said, "I want to go back to work." I said, "No, you don't. Just relax, that's the thing." Most people resign themselves to the fact they can't afford to do it. I hear women who are working say, "I'm tired of feeling guilty." When I say I'm home with my kids they say, "That's the best way." I say, "Yes, it is."

Debbie and David managed to unchain themselves from two-car dependency, even though they live in a neighborhood where most people would say you couldn't survive without two cars. Once again, creativity, luck, and mutual support — the at-home parent's three pillars — made the impossible possible.

13

Your Business
at Home

*D*o you have what it takes to join the fastest-growing work
trend of this generation? We're talking of course about working
from home or having your own home business.

The figures are little short of astonishing. It seemed like a
slightly harebrained idea when media guru Marshall McLuhan
predicted in the 1970s that soon more and more people would go
to work by getting up from the breakfast table and strolling over
to the computer. But by the early 1990s, when Faith Popcorn, in
The Popcorn Report, named this the "cocooning decade," with people focusing their work and leisure lives on the home, the tidal
wave was already forming. And today it's in full flood, with an
estimated 25 million Americans and 2.1 million Canadians (about
a tenth of each country's population) now working for themselves,
mostly at home. The latest Canadian figures show an explosive
growth rate for this trend, especially among women, with a 9.5
percent annual increase in the numbers of self-employed women.

As we've seen, some have started businesses at home after being
"downsized," while others work from home as a way of keeping up
in their field, later returning to an outside job when their children
are older. Whatever the motivation behind it, staying home has

become a real option for many parents who might not have considered it before, largely because of the growth of opportunities brought about by the arrival of the personal computer.

Really, it's a return to the past. Long ago, nearly all work was done at home, and children were part of it. Now once again, the barriers between home and work, and even, for some families, school, are tumbling, and once again the home is becoming the hub of many people's lives. The best news is that working at home removes the need for a long commute to work, freeing up people to spend more time with their children.

At its simplest, the home business can be simply a computer in the corner of the basement. To see the other extreme, we visited the pleasant old country house of Wendy and Rolf Priesnitz in St. George, a small town in southwest Ontario. A discreet sign at the end of the driveway announces *Natural Life*, the name of the ecology magazine they publish. Coming through the front door, you're in for a surprise. Inside it's sunny and bright, with lots of artwork, but most of the ground floor is given over to desks, work tables, computers, fax machines — all the machinery of the modern office. With their two daughters grown, the Priesnitz couple use this floor for producing books and newsletters on home business, home-schooling, and other topics, while their living quarters are now relegated to the second floor.

"I don't resent it," says Wendy of the electronic invasion of her home. "It's our office. I love it." Instead of traffic and skyscrapers, their office looks out on flowers and birds and, in winter, scenes of snowy beauty. And working at home, she says, "means we can stop identifying ourselves by what we do, and start looking at ourselves as whole people. That's the wonderful part of it."

Where do you begin to get a home business going? In Wendy and Rolf's case, they were keen on the environment and a number of ecological issues, and had always had a problem finding information. They decided there was a need for a magazine, and thus *Natural Life* was born.

For many people, though, the home business notion begins even before the particular business idea is found — with a wish for a certain kind of life. You want to be home with your child, for instance, and you see working at home as a way to make up for some of the income you'll be losing by quitting your job.

Juggling Work and Children

The first thing you need to know is that if you have a newborn or, even more so, a one- or two-year-old, there are limits to how much work you can expect to do.

Says Wendy: "You can't run a full-time business with a baby around, unless it's a very flexible kind of business." Anyone who's worked from home can tell you there will be times when you'll get an important phone call and the moment you answer it the baby, sensing competition for your attention, will start to yell. And if you don't respond, the shouting will only get louder, until you tell your party, "I'm sorry, I'll have to call you back."

By "flexible," Wendy means a business where you're not dealing with the corporate sector all the time, one where a crying baby in the background doesn't matter, and where, perhaps, you can take your baby or child along without objections being raised. "I think, to some extent," she says, "it's our responsibility to educate the world that this is a good way of doing things, that there's a positive environment for the children here."

Child psychologist Penelope Leach worked for years from home. "I think it would be quite wrong," she says "to assume you can work at home with a small child and have *no* child care. But there's a huge difference between the sort of child care you need if you're catching the train in the morning and what you need when you are there in a supervisory, emergency role. Basically what you need is someone to entertain and divert your child."

Parents working at home told us the ideal person to care for your child while you're trying to work at home is a take-charge type who will involve your child in activities and outings without having to interrupt you to settle every little problem that arises. Your child will soon learn, too, that when you're working you're not available. Alternatively, you may want to consider out-of-home care for a few hours a day if you can find the right person nearby to look after your child while you get down to work.

Another answer might be to swap time with other parents working at home, or, if both you and your spouse are working at home, to schedule your day to share the child-care chores. Psychologist Brenda Hunter told us she did much of her work as an editorial consultant when her family was young either late at night or in the early morning, while her daughters were still sleeping.

It's a good idea, too, to do your most concentrated work in the time you have to yourself. Use an answering machine to screen calls and leave casual business matters for later. If someone else is in the house looking after the baby, it's not the best thing to run every time she cries or makes a noise. Instead, schedule regular play-time breaks so she'll know when to expect you.

Leach sees one big advantage to working at home that's rarely mentioned: "People in offices are lucky if they do six hours of concentrated work, even if they're out of the house from seven-thirty a.m. until six p.m. If you're home, it is not hard — and believe me, I've done it for years — to fit in more work than you would ever do in an office, with minimal child care."

Telecommuting

The first thing to decide is whether you want to work at home for yourself or for an employer.

Telecommuting — working for a company, but staying at home and connecting by phone, computer, and fax — has in this decade become just as big a trend as home businesses. It's one way you may be able to continue to work for your present employer and still be home. That way you retain your benefits and seniority.

If performing your present work at home seems like a practical idea, try presenting a professional-sounding and well-researched proposal to your employer. If you do work something out, be sure to start modestly; whether you're telecommuting or working for yourself at home, it's easy to take on more work than you have time for — and then you've defeated the whole purpose of being home.

Telecommuting is marvelous for employers: it means they don't have to provide you with office or parking space, and studies show people working at home are markedly more productive. It's marvelous for the environment, because it results in fewer people driving cars. But is it marvelous for you? It's easy to feel cut off working at home, and for sure you're likely to be forgotten when promotions come along — out of sight, out of mind. Weigh that against not having to commute, saving all that money on lunches and office clothes, being able to get your work done in a shorter time because you're not hampered by meetings (although children have been known to cause interruptions too!), and the pleasure of being home. For many people, the telecommute wins out.

Your Own Business

Is It for You?

Feel you'd really like the challenge of having your own business? In her book *Bringing It Home* (Alternate Press, 1995), a guide to starting your business at home, Wendy Priesnitz says you need to begin with some hard-headed self-evaluation. You need to discover whether you have the temperament to work on your own and make decisions alone without getting flustered. You need to ask yourself serious questions about your organizational abilities and your get-up-and-go quotient. Will you be able to come back fighting even on those days when everything goes wrong?

You also need the support of your spouse, and the understanding of your children if they're old enough. Be realistic about how much time you can give your business and about how much you'll make (you can't expect to have a full-time income if you're working part-time).

You also need to consider whether your house is suited for it — and that includes checking zoning and condominium bylaws to see if you're permitted to have a business at home. In our own experience, we found work surroundings to be of the first importance. We've set aside two of the nicest little rooms in the house as our two offices, both with agreeable views of the garden, and when Frank gave up his downtown office and came home to work we bought an attractive desk, an ergonomically sensible desk chair, and a whimsical yet comfortable armchair for his third-floor eyrie. Result: he has an office away from the noise of the house, comfortable and well-lit, that he looks forward to going to every single morning.

Unless you're the sort of person who can work in the midst of bedlam you must find a private space to work, and then make it as attractive as possible. Apart from anything else, you need a separate work area so that you can charge a portion of your mortgage, taxes, and other expenses against your income taxes.

Choosing a Business

What kind of business should it be? "It must relate to your own interests and skills," says Wendy, "because obviously you're going to be doing this for a lot of hours, so it should be something you're good at, even passionate about." Study trends and brainstorm with friends and family members to come up with ideas, she says. Beware of getting so enamored of an idea that you're blinded to its drawbacks. Wendy once wanted to open a bookstore in the cute little town where they were living. But when she checked the details she found rents were so high she'd never make a profit. Subsequently she saw three book stores open in the town — and later close down.

Some areas to consider:

- *Mail order:* If you have an area of special interest, and a product or line of products in mind, you may already have the ingredients for a successful direct-mail business. Catalogues are expensive to print, so knowing your market and directing your pitch at the right people is essential.
- *Consulting:* Everyone's doing it, but that doesn't mean there isn't still a demand, especially if you have special expertise, or are prepared to develop it, in a new and expanding area.
- *Arts and crafts:* It may sound old hat, but if you have the vision to develop an item there's a demand for — whether quilts or patriotic tea towels — you'll find your customers.

- *The Internet:* The possibilities are only beginning. Companies need skilled people to help them develop their Websites and to think of new ways to reach the millions who now have access to the Internet.
- *Newsletter publishing:* Newsletters are proliferating, and there may be a market for yours if you have special knowledge and access to the right audience. Layout and writing skills are important, but what will really sell your product is information your clients can use.
- *Mobile services:* People have less time these days, which means they're willing to pay a premium if they can get someone to come to them with a service. It may be a personal trainer, a mechanic, or a pet groomer. In fact, pet owners and seniors are two groups likely to need at-home services no big firm can provide.
- *Franchising:* Take extra care if you're thinking of buying a franchise. The advantage is that you get expertise, advertising, and a product ready-made. But a substantial investment is often needed, and people who buy franchises often end up losing their money. Research just as thoroughly as if you were starting your own business from scratch, and talk to as many of the firm's franchisees, and their competitors, as possible.

The list of businesses you might get into is limited only by your imagination. Here are just a few Wendy mentions in *Bringing It Home*: interior designing, computer programming, party services, proofreading, child/elderly care, property management, book-keeping/accounting, freelance photography, translation, tutoring, cosmetic sales, nanny agency, catering, plant care, gardening, on-line research, tailoring, landscape design, calligraphy, house/pet sitting, housecleaning, and hairstyling.

For many men and women, a business at home has provided a wonderful opportunity to take up the career they were really cut out for — even if it means a few years of study. We've seen it in our family. As a little girl, Ayesha was fascinated with growing plants, but when it came time to pick a career, nursing seemed a more practical choice. Now, with her family grown, she's gone back to her first love, is well into her university horticulture course, and already has several clients for her gardening services.

What it comes down to, says Wendy, is finding a need and filling it. "You need to be out there talking to people in your field, finding out what's not being done well or not being done at all."

The Nitty-Gritty

The simplest sort of home business is probably one that flows from what you were doing before. You will have only one or two clients, usually one of them your former employer, and this kind of freelancing involves a minimum of marketing, planning, and bookkeeping.

These are the bugbears of the home businessperson. We all like being creative and enterprising — it's just the bookkeeping, the tax returns, the call-backs that get us down. "For many people," says Wendy, "it's a rude awakening, but you realize sooner or later this sort of thing has to be taken care of — whether it's having your spouse doing the collections or hiring someone to do it — or your business will fail."

It starts with having a thoroughly researched business plan, including a realistic assessment of who your customers are likely to be, how you plan to reach them, and what capital costs are involved. You don't need to earn as much from your business as you did from your job because, thanks to income-tax deductions, you'll probably get to keep more of the money for yourself. But you'll need to brief yourself about depreciating equipment (your computer, your car, your office furniture), figure out what child-care costs you can charge, and be strict about paying your income tax on a regular basis.

And you need to be professional, especially if you're dealing with the business world. That means dressing appropriately and, if clients come to your home, having a presentable office. It means having a separate business line if you have phone-age children, and returning calls promptly.

Integrating Business and Family Life

There are countless books and courses, newsletters, and Internet sources that will introduce you to the joys of researching your business idea, drawing up a business plan, advertising, and all the other essentials that can't be ignored. But for the parent at home some of the key issues will be emotional ones, of which none is more important than keeping a balance between your business and your spouse and children.

Wendy says she's known women who stayed home to be with their children, started a home business, and saw it grow to such an extent that they had no time to be with their children. She counsels, "You have to know what your priorities are and control the growth of your business so that it will do what you want it to do."

It takes a family commitment for a parent at home to start a business, she continues. "There's a degree of seriousness that your spouse has to understand. You really need emotional support because it's a roller coaster — one day you're up because you got a new customer, the next you're down because something goes wrong. Your spouse has to understand you are not necessarily going to get the meals made or have the laundry done. You've got to be able to say, okay, I've got some hours, and these are the hours I'm going to be working on the business and nothing else. And if the dusting doesn't get done, the world's not going to fall apart."

Is it easier when husband and wife work together at home? Not necessarily. "I always tell couples," says Wendy, "that they need to be very clear who's doing what, because in a relationship, it's easier to butt in and nitpick because the habits you've developed in the marriage carry over into the business. We've been married twenty-six years, and certainly we've had our ups and downs, and a lot of times that's been caused by business things. But it's an ongoing trip, and we've managed to figure out how to be married and have a business together."

One business that seems to lend itself especially well to husband-and-wife involvement is running a bed and breakfast. When Richard Cox took early retirement from General Motors at age forty-eight, for instance, he and his wife, Kathy, bought a big, old farmhouse in eastern Ontario and opened a bed and breakfast.

One reason was so that Kathy, a secretary, could stay home with their daughter, Caitlin, then five.

Their business is not a moneyspinner. Kathy says without Richard's pension, they couldn't manage. And Richard, finding himself with spare time, has started another small business doing house inspections. More than anything, though, the B and B has given Kathy the chance to do the things she likes best: meeting people, baking bread three times a week, growing produce in their acre-and-a-half vegetable garden, sewing, and, of course, being with Caitlin, who is now nine. "She just enjoys hanging out with me," explains Kathy, "you know, watching me cook and work in the garden, and I enjoy having her hang out with me. She's a good little companion. And I think she's an incredibly secure little girl because her parents are always around."

For the woman working at home on her own, though, isolation can be a problem. "You need to build something into your life that gets you out," says Wendy. "You have to join the local Rotary Club or the local home business organization, and arrange a babysitter so that you can go to lunch on a certain day. That's part of the business of balancing your family life and your business life and staying sane." She mentions a group of at-home workers in one small town who meet every day for an early-morning walk — for the exercise and the social contact. Fitness and proper nutrition are real issues, she says, for the working parent at home.

Is the working mom at home that elusive creature, the woman who has it all? We know that going to a full-time job and being a mom impose a lot of emotional stress on many women. Having a business at home while you have children isn't easy, either. But there's this: it's your business, your ideas, your time to schedule, yours to make of it what you want. Running it and finding the time you want to be with your kids is still a tightrope. But it means you don't consume a big part of your day commuting, eating lunch, and attending mind-numbing meetings, and you can use that time to be there for your children. Working moms — or dads — at home may not have it all; who does? But with a little care and judgment, they may have the best bits.

14

Helping Your Kids Learn

*T*he days are gone when the word of a teacher was accepted as law and parents' influence stopped at the school door. A new generation of highly educated parents see learning as a cooperative effort involving their child, the school, and the home. They quite rightly want to have a say in their children's schooling, and school systems are responding to that feeling by being far more open than in the past about welcoming parents into the classroom.

That's one big reason why many parents who stayed home initially to be with their children when they were infants find themselves extending that time — because they realize the important impact they can have on their children's schooling by being around.

In the introduction we mentioned the warm feeling our kids got while they were growing up coming through the door and yelling, "Hi, mom," and always finding someone there. It went beyond that. Ayesha, the parent at home, saw it as her role to be involved in the school. At that point classroom parent volunteers were not part of the picture, but she was a volunteer in the school library, baked probably hundreds of cakes for school fund-raising events, and was a chaperone on a number of school trips, some of them several days in duration. This meant our kids could see their mom was part of their schooling; there was a continuum between home and school. Some of the teachers became our friends, so talking about a problem wasn't something that had to wait for meet-the-teacher night.

Something more: as a result of being at the school and at home, Ayesha got to know our kids' friends, and some of these friendships have continued to this day. Now some of those friends have moved back to the neighborhood as parents themselves and our neighbors. That's not to say it wouldn't have happened if we'd both been working, but we might not have had the same drop-in informal relationship.

Many of the parents we met in the course of our research have used being at home as an opportunity to become actively involved in their children's education. A growing minority, as we'll discuss shortly, even go the extra step and school their children at home.

Getting the Most Out of the Education System

Making your children's education part of your life as a parent begins with researching the school you want them to attend. Sandra Evans, the sequencing engineer from McMaster, says that when the older of her two daughters, Christine, was ready to start kindergarten, she visited the large local public school and sat in on classes. She soon determined that the school lacked "the personal touch." She sat in on classes at four other schools before she finally discovered a small public school still close enough for Christine to attend that had a friendly feeling and where the children really seemed to feel at home. And that's the way it's worked. Christine settled in beautifully and Sandra knows the teachers well. "I have the time to take them to activities, to make sure they're doing their homework, and," she added, "basically they feel security, knowing they can come home and find me here." Now that Sandra has returned to work, her main regret is that she feels she can't be as involved with the school.

Linda Ryan, home with her four children, finds living close

to the school helpful, too. Her children can walk to school, "and if the school calls to say one of the kids is sick I'm there in two minutes. Because I'm here, I can bring them home if they're not feeling well." She adds: "I do volunteer work at the school. I feel connected. I know their teachers well. I can talk to them, and I know what's going on at the school."

The days when a child feels unwell, a nightmare for many working parents, turn into an opportunity for the at-home parent. There's no panic over who's going to look after the sick child — he or she simply stays home. And, providing the child isn't too sick, the day can become an occasion for enjoying stories, games, and quiet intimacy. How many of us, looking back, remember those sick days at home when we were pampered and catered to as the happiest days of our childhoods!

An important part of a child's education, in fact, is that unstructured chatter that goes on between parent and child, especially the things they want to tell you as they come busting through the door after school. The working parent, arriving home an hour or two later, harried and trying to get food on the table, misses those intimacies. And by the time supper is over, the child has forgotten to tell them the important news of the schoolday. But a mother like Connie Nabtiti hears the whole story.

She and her husband Ahmad rent an apartment in Mississauga, Ontario, just a couple of blocks from the school their seven-year-old son, Sami, attends. She walks him to and from school, mainly for the talk. "Sami comes home for lunch too," she told us. "Out of twenty in his class, only three go home. I told him, it's up to you, you can come home to lunch or stay at school, but he says it's a nice break. When he comes home, I have lunch ready. It's only half an hour, but we talk nonstop. It's yip, yip, yip. We always have lunch together and we talk about what's happened in the morning and what's going to happen in the afternoon."

Being home probably allows parents to have a greater influence over their children's values, whether that includes religious beliefs or an environmentally friendly philosophy. The former leads many parents at home, especially Christians, to send their children to religion-based schools. And "counterculture" parents at home often seek out alternative schools either inside or outside the public system.

Susan Russell, the upstate New York mother who is bringing her daughters up vegetarian, sends them to a local Waldorf independent school. She is so convinced the school is giving them the right preparation for life that the divorced Russell says all her extra money goes to paying for the school.

Some families experience disruptive events that, if it weren't for the parent at home, would be potentially disastrous for the children. Deborah Fallows, author of *A Mother's Work*, told us of such an event when her husband, Jim, was transferred to Tokyo and she found herself living in a remote suburb of the city with their boys, aged five and eight, and unable to speak Japanese. The boys weren't in school, and she was on her own with them from seven in the morning until her husband got home around nine at night.

She found a book of things to do with children in Tokyo, and every single day set out with them on expeditions that took them, via subways and buses, to a playground made of rubber tires one day, an ice-cream factory the next. At shrines especially, they'd run into groups of Japanese children who were as interested in the boys as the boys were in them. It was a time, recalled Fallows, when they had few material goods, and couldn't even watch television.

She says now of her four years abroad, some of which were spent in Malaysia, "It was a tremendous gift and very lucky for us as a family. I think those years set the whole tone for our family life. I think we have really an extraordinarily close family because we were so reliant on each other. It changed us completely."

Often, too, parents spoke to us about especially sensitive children who need every bit of a parent's attention and patience in order to prepare them for school. It would be easy to dismiss these children as overprotected, except that generally there were other children in the family, so the parents had a basis for comparison.

We had no clue, for instance, that anything unusual was at work when we called on Cheryl Stewart at the bungalow she and her husband, Gary, built for themselves in rural Caledon, an hour north of Toronto. Gary operates a car rustproofing business from a workshop beside the house, and Cheryl does the books, besides being home for Ashley, aged ten, and Matthew, six. Ashley was home from school that day with a fever, and Matthew, who would be going to school later, was shooting a ball across the living room with a hockey stick. The only thing unusual perhaps was the quiet tone of voice Cheryl used when a ball whizzed past her ear. "Let's not do raisers today, okay," she said to Matthew. "Let's just do grounders." Matthew complied.

Then a simple question opened the floodgates. We asked, "What has being home meant to you?" and she burst into tears. Only as her sobs subsided was she able to explain what staying home had meant as far as her son is concerned.

"Matthew is really challenged. He's tested my parenting skills to the absolute limit," she said. "I know if I had not been here with him he would have been damaged. He's very shy, and he would cry easily. People say, 'Take him to nursery school and let him cry — he'll get over it.' But it's taken a long time to gradually bring him around. And I think a parent knows better than anyone. Ashley was less shy, and I didn't have to be as meticulous with her. But with Matthew I had to be aware of his feelings and situations."

When Matthew didn't want to go to nursery school, she and Gary talked it over, and decided to let him stay home, where he was perfectly happy. The summer before he went to kindergarten he joined the T-ball league, and because he was a good hitter he enjoyed it.

"All that summer," said Cheryl, "I prepared him with little things, buying new clothes, a backpack. I didn't know how it would go, and the first day I was shocked — he went off to school like a little trouper. The second day it was really windy, and that upset him for some reason. I could tell he was trying to muster every bit of courage he had to get on the bus, so I tried to keep things light and busy. He got on, looked out of the window, and was fine.

"It's mostly boys in his class at school. You would expect them to be wild and rambunctious the way boys are. But generally speaking they are very quiet, affectionate, not terribly physically aggressive boys, and the majority have been home-reared."

Matthew is still hesitant about going to friends' houses alone. But, said Cheryl, "the day will come, it'll come when he's good and ready. And meanwhile I'm glad I was here for him."

Home-Schooling: Organic Learning

The biggest surprise we got in our research was the number of parents who are using being home as an opportunity to teach their children themselves. And none that we met had started out with the idea they'd end up as their children's teachers.

The process starts, of course, with the decision not to put an infant in day care or with a child minder. Then the parent discovers just how much of a contribution to their child's development being home makes. They read together, play, talk endlessly — all activities that open up the world of language and images to a small child. So when it comes time for school to start, it's understandable many parents don't want the process to stop. And that's particularly true of parents who are teachers or who are in the child-development field: they ask themselves why they're devoting themselves to other people's children when they could be doing the same for their own.

Our first thought was how courageous these people were — how we'd never dream of doing such a thing as home-schooling. And then we thought back to the time when our youngest daughter, Fazia, was five, and how, in different circumstances, we might have become home-schoolers, too.

We were living in London at the time, and every day, when they weren't doing things around the house, Fazia and Ayesha would be out and about: to the park where there were other children, shopping up Putney High Street where there were lots of friendly storekeepers — and even Cockney barrowboys shouting their wares — and snooping around the furniture auction rooms that Ayesha haunted at that time. They were inseparable companions and everywhere they went there were things to see and talk about.

The school where Fazia was due to start kindergarten was a perfectly good one. But Ayesha was especially reluctant to let her go; she felt Fazia was probably learning more being at home than she would at school. Any adult who has spent a great deal of time with a small, loved child knows what marvelous chemistry is at work. Learning goes on around the clock without any need to ever say "lesson time!" New research at Hamilton's McMaster University, for instance, shows that it's quite possible to predict how well a child will read later by how much he or she learns to play with words — rhyming games, identifying objects, picking the odd-man-out in a group of words, and so on. This talent comes from an adult — the likeliest candidate is a parent — reciting nursery rhymes and poems and telling stories from the time a baby is in the cradle. Being with other children is not particularly helpful for these skills.

Well, to end the story, we finally chickened out. Keeping a child out of school was not done at that time, and, with a great deal of reluctance, we signed Fazia up for kindergarten.

Many other parents, we discovered, don't give up so easily. In fact, it is estimated there are 35,000 children in Canada and 300,000 in the United States being educated at home.

Heidi Brennan, of Mothers at Home, says she got interested in home-schooling when a neighbor introduced her to a book called *Teach Your Own* by John Holt (Dell Publishing, 1981). "I started reading that and bells and whistles went off. I was fascinated. My sister was autistic, and there was a time she couldn't go to school because her behavior was so off the wall. So my grandmother, who was living with us, started teaching her. I was in third grade and when I would come home from school I would read to her. I looked back and realized, my goodness, my sister was home-schooled. So I thought, why not put off putting our oldest in school for a couple of years? We always thought reading was one of the most important things you could do with your kids. We love books and we don't think you can start them reading too soon. I always spent hours reading with Charles, and he loved it.

"So I started out home-schooling in the most casual way. My primary goal was to help him to read because once he could read it's like you've unlocked the door to everything. Also, I'd just had a new baby, and here I was, booting Charles out the door to kindergarten and he was going to miss all these new baby experiences."

The Brennans' Washington home is a children's place, but doesn't look anything like a traditional school. The furniture has a lived-in look, there are books everywhere, a giant cut-out choo-choo, painted for Daniel's fifth birthday party, is still taped to the dining area wall, and downstairs, in the walk-out basement, are the counter-spaces and stacks of materials and the computer where four of their five children (John is only two) are home-schooled.

Heidi: "We talk to our children about everything, go places, and do things. Our pattern is to do the core subjects in the morning — you can usually do the nitty-gritty things in four mornings a week — so by lunchtime we're done. Then it's let's have fun, kids, and we have free-flowing afternoons with history, art, anything. That's the secret of good home-schooling — you create the possibilities for yourself. You don't have to be on a nine-to-three schedule. Did you know that on average children receive less than five minutes a week of individual attention from their teachers? But at home it's a tutor relationship with tutorials rather than classroom teaching.

"We had not intended our children would home-school all the way through high school. We take things one year at a time. Now I have friends who are home-schooling at the high-school stage, and we can see the possibilities. High school wasn't a bowl of cherries when I went; but now problems involving drugs and alcohol and sex and violence are worse. A lot of home-schoolers are accused of isolating their kids. Yes, we are isolating them from some things, and that's a good thing. But we talk to them about world events, drugs, everything that's in the newspaper. And we believe our kids should be exposed to jobs and careers early. Even at fourteen I believe our kids can be out in the community doing something, maybe volunteering. People say, 'Aren't you worried your children won't get to Harvard?' I say, 'We just want to raise good people.'" In any case, Harvard now admits students who were home-schooled.

Sandra Kenzie, the former nursing instructor who found a new community in the La Leche League, got interested in home-schooling after attending a workshop at a League conference. "Meredith, who is sixteen now, was in grade three, and although she was doing well, she was unhappy in school. I'd been talking about home-schooling the two younger ones and she said, 'Can I just stay home, Mom?' So I said we'd give it a try. With her it was only a matter of months she stayed home, and then she went to a private school that focuses on the arts. She had a wonderful time, but we couldn't afford for everyone to go, and Laura, the next one, really didn't want to go to school so I was quite happy to try home-schooling her and Patrick.

"People often ask me, 'How can you home-school when you're not a teacher?' A lot of people set up a classroom in their home and have school from nine to eleven. I didn't do anything like that. Until Laura got to be eight she just learned by playing store, and we did lots of baking, so she learned her fractions. I read to them a lot and we did lots of nature hikes.

"I had no idea how you teach someone to read. Megan and Patrick just learned to read, no one taught them. Laura got discouraged because she wanted to read the books I was reading to her, and they were too hard. So finally we gave up. I spent the next two years reading advanced books to her. Then one day, when she was eight, I found her on the couch with a book. I said, 'What are you doing?' She kind of looked at me: 'I guess I'm reading.' I really am becoming more and more convinced that a lot of children are labeled 'learning disabled' when it's just that they're not ready, and if you just leave them they will grow into it.

"I've seen what we do described in a magazine as 'organic home schooling.' It's based on life experiences, looking at what they're interested in and ready for. Patrick is very different from Laura. He's very academic like his dad, and basically he teaches himself. [Megan, who is taking a year off before going to university, is tutoring Patrick and a neighbor's child, Emily.] Laura didn't like to sit and read — she liked to just *do* things. At eight she could cook. People say, 'That's old-fashioned, being able to do that,' but it helps children feel they can do things and that they are an important part of family life and society. They are not being put in an artificial learning situation — they are helping out at home."

We heard a similar story from most parents: that with home-schooling, learning is not something separate that you sit down to do, but something as natural as going for a walk or baking a cake.

That's when we realized that, like most parents at home, we had been home-schoolers without knowing it. And, as grandparents, we're doing more of it than ever. We thought of mornings at the cottage when our grandchildren come into our bed at seven for a delicious long read of Roald Dahl, how talk of the mouse Gramma saw in the kitchen turns into family stories about Mice We Have Known, and by breakfast we're talking about David and Goliath, and when we get up from the table it's ten-thirty, and where did the morning go? In home-schooling, of course.

One of the breakthrough events in the modern home-schooling movement was an article in *Harper's Magazine* in November 1990, in which a Seattle-area high-school English teacher David Guterson described how, the September their oldest son was to start school, the big yellow bus pulled up in front of their home, opened its doors, waited for a few minutes, then drove away.

"Since then," wrote Guterson, "each of our three sons has missed the bus, so to speak."

A substantial proportion of home-schoolers — an estimated 60 percent in Canada — are Christians who want their children to grow up with a firm faith. But the Gutersons, like most of the home-schooling parents we met, had no firm ideological views. "I wish I could write that my wife and I had excellent reasons for deciding to home-school," wrote Guterson. "We didn't. It was in the gut." They read books about home-schooling, talked endlessly, and were full of indecision — right up until the moment the bus pulled away without their son, and they found themselves "flung headlong into a life neither of us would have predicted."

Guterson, of course, is a teacher. He's got the qualifications, you might say. Wendy Priesnitz, the expert on home businesses, was a teacher too, as are many parents who home-school. It was her teacher training, she says, that showed her how ill qualified many teachers are to teach. "Most teachers learn what they are going to teach the night before — that's why they need so much prep time," she says.

Parents say to her, "I'm only a secretary or a pipefitter — how can I educate my kids?" Her response: "I think that's one of the saddest commentaries on our society. We really discount who we are and what we know and the lives we lead. Every one of us lives a rich life if we stopped to think about it. We have so much to offer kids."

Wendy and her husband, Rolf (who is, incidentally, trained as a pipefitter) were pioneers when they began home-schooling in the 1970s (one daughter, Heidi, is now twenty-four, the other, Melanie, twenty-two). They pretty much had to figure it out for themselves. "The model we used was watching them learn how to walk and talk," she said. "You don't sit them down and tell them, if you move this muscle, it will do this. You just allow them to find out by doing it. No one doubts that their child will learn to walk, but when it comes to reading or learning the times tables, we're not as sure because we've all of a sudden separated that off as something difficult that we have to show you how to do."

Heidi and Melanie essentially grew up the way children would have grown up in the home, say, of a medieval wool merchant or saddler. Wendy and Rolf, who have lived mostly in small towns in Ontario and British Columbia, decided early on that they would start a business so that they could be home with their daughters. Heidi got a first lesson in reading when she found her bedroom, like the rest of the house, stacked with the first issue of *Natural Life*, the magazine her parents had started, each copy of which had to be sorted by postal code. Said Wendy: "Heidi remembers wanting to read and recognize the letters so that she could help, because that was the only way she could get those darned magazines off her bed and out of her room."

As the girls grew up, they found themselves at the center of the business. Wendy would be sitting at her desk, snipping out letters for headlines, while Heidi and Melanie would be on the floor, gathering up discarded letters, putting them together, learning how to read. When they were hired, employees had to understand that they would be working with two small girls probably sitting on the floor and maybe asking how to spell a word. "I guess the girls were brought up by a village," said Wendy.

Often Rolf and Wendy would take the girls into the city on

business trips, to the printer's or maybe to their accountant's, fitting in side trips to the science center or the museum. They learned firsthand what went on in factories and business offices, and also how to behave and get along with adults. Opportunities were everywhere. An unusual Native place name that Heidi noticed on a subscription order from Alberta led to weeks of research — and a visit to the museum — on Native place names. "We fed on each others' curiosity," recalled Wendy.

Through *Natural Life*, Rolf and Wendy were coming into contact with other home-schoolers, and in 1979 they started the Canadian Alliance of Home Schoolers. Wendy subsesquently wrote a book on the subject, *School Free* (Alternate Press, 1995).

How did the girls turn out? Heidi, who lives in Nova Scotia now and has her own home publishing business, says she found it confusing when she finally chose to go to high school — she didn't know you couldn't get up and walk out of a class when you felt like it. And it was difficult, having formed a mind of her own, to conform to teen music and clothing tastes. "Another big difference," she says, "was that I *wanted* to be at school, and I knew I could leave school when I no longer wanted to be there. Because of this, I excelled at school." Melanie, who never showed the least interest in learning her times tables, and so never did, now works as assistant to a stockbroker and is taking securities courses.

Some critics claim that home-schooling is "undemocratic" — that it cuts children off from their peers who are richer or poorer or of a different race or religion, amounting to the ultimate snobby private school. The home-schoolers we met say they make sure their children are involved in sports programs and other activities that bring them into contact with other kids. It's easy to understand why parents want to keep their children away from the drugs and violence endemic in many school systems. But that puts an extra responsibility on the parent at home to make sure they're not shutting their children away from the real world.

It's clear, though, that with confidence in the education system faltering, home-schooling will appear more and more attractive to parents as time goes on. David Guterson, from his own experience as a teacher, writes, "Schools *keep* children first, and any education that happens along the way is incidental and achieved against the odds."

Our own view is that you should never home-school simply to justify being home with your children. You should only do it if it's a creative learning experience that both of you enjoy. We feel concern, too, about parents who home-school simply to keep their children away from outside influences and ideas. The aim, we think, should be to open children up to the world, not close them off from it.

As for at-home parents who choose to send their children to school, many are today's unsung heroes. With school budgets being cut back ferociously in many jurisdictions, schools and community programs are more dependent than ever on volunteer help — in the classroom and to provide sport and other extracurricular activities. If it wasn't for the at-home parent, many of these activities would simply come to a standstill. As an at-home parent, you deserve a pat on the back. You're helping to hold things together.

Epilogue

When All Is Said and Done

No one ever said it would be easy. You may know that by staying home you are giving your children the greatest gifts within your power to bestow: your love and your time. But on Monday morning the driveways on your street are empty, and babies, let's admit it, are not lovable all the time.

No one is going to call you into the office, tell you you're doing a grand job, and give you a raise. More likely, you'll be wondering whether it's worth fixing the car one more time and driving across town to get that special on disposable diapers.

"Even though I'm sure I made the right choice, I still struggle with it a lot," Jennifer Rodin Lenzo, of Aiken, South Carolina, wrote to *Welcome Home*. "I miss teaching and feeling like I have tangible measurements for my success. I miss doing things on the spur of the moment and being a little irresponsible. . . . I still feel frustrated and lost quite a lot of the time. . . . I don't live near family and have moved so often that I have few friends nearby. . . . This job of raising three small, busy, wonderful preschoolers is very hard. I need patience (which I never had much of to begin with), energy, and wisdom. I love my kids so much, and I know, deep down, that I am the best person for this job. . . . I know this is right."

Sharon Nweeia, of Miami, Florida, recalled what it was like when she quit her job of ten years to stay home with her three-year-old daughter: "Never in my wildest imagination would I have suspected how lonely and frustrated I would become. I felt completely inadequate as a mother and guilty about not enjoying our time together. All my friends worked, and I felt out of my element." Then she realized: "Most of my anxiety was brought on by my friends at work who undermined the value of staying home."

Sharon joined an organization for the mothers of preschoolers and met a new circle of friends. "What you remember about working is that you received validation for what you were doing," she says. "That is not always as obvious in the home. But remember, work will always be there. The real purpose of life is to appreciate the importance of things, like relationships. It is okay to take it slow now. We've a long life to live."

As part of our research, we invited at-home parents to write to us about their experiences. Many described the frustrations of having to scrimp, and of doing a good job, yet getting no credit for it from the world at large. And then this letter arrived from Susan Steinberg, a counsellor in Don Mills, Ontario, now in her fifties:

"It was a gorgeous, sunny day in June. There I was in my suburban garden with my then four- and six-year-old boys. My days were filled. Although my husband [an obstetrician and gynecologist] was a wonderful father, he was also an absentee model much of the time. That day in June was to have far-reaching effects — well beyond what I could ever have either imagined or understood at the time.

"The words of Peggy Lee's song, 'Is That All There Is?' presented themselves to me. I only knew there had to be more than laundry, cooking, and cleaning and time spent almost totally with toddlers. Although I worked part-time in educational research, I craved more adult stimulation and had a high need to learn and grow. Little did I realize either how much of a challenge raising children in today's world could be, or how much of a far-reaching impact my decision to return to school and ultimately more fully to work would have, not only on me, but on my relationships with my children and my mate.

"I couldn't have known or understood then what a snowball effect a major change like this could have on the rest of my life. And I have never quite forgiven myself for this human error. . . . How could I have known then what I know now? I never realized the pressures I would be imposing upon myself and how hard I was making my own life. And, sadly, I never envisioned how life would change from the more evenly paced to the at-times frantic.

"How much did I miss of what was really going on with my children because I was so busy planning how I would juggle the Friday night Sabbath family dinners, the essays, and the children's school play? How many times did my actions tell my children that my class mattered more to me than simply being there to listen and to set a happy, casual tone and atmosphere within our home? I missed the fun we had together making cookies, reading books, throwing a baseball, and mostly just the casual ambience and laughter of the earlier, more relaxed years. I hadn't realized that my perfectionist, high-standard tendencies, combined with my . . . desire for accomplishment would drive my life in any but the calm way that my inner nature truly cherished.

"Money had not been the prime motive for my moving back more fully into the work force. In fact, those early years where we scrimped and did without were good ones. Now that I have known what material means can buy, I would truly say that some of those earlier, leaner years were some of the best. If I had my life to live over again, I would stay home. My work has brought great fulfillment . . . but no work reward can replace having a home environment free from tension and stress. I chose to bring my children into the world. They deserved more of the special moments we knew earlier. . . . Now, with my three sons twenty, twenty-five, and twenty-seven . . . I can clearly say I would have chosen a different option from the one I did choose."

This book, at the start, focused on the few intense months after the birth of a child when many women feel a profound conflict between returning to work and their need to be with their babies. But, as Susan Steinberg's letter makes clear, such a decision has life-long implications. When that wrinkled newborn has become a mother herself, an executive, a big wheel in the world, you'll still be looking back on that moment of choice, weighing whether or not you made the right decision.

The same holds true for the effect of the decision on your marriage. Staying home, as we've seen, can put strains on the relationship, especially if your spouse is not 100 percent behind your decision. It's extremely important to talk these things out.

Wrote Kim Pattillo, of Aurora, Ontario, "When my daughter, Lindsay, was born, I had always assumed I would want to return to my job in advertising. I enjoyed my work and had lots of friends and fun. Then an amazing thing happened — I wanted control over every aspect of her little life and I couldn't imagine anyone else doing the job. . . . I was very uptight because I thought my husband, John, wanted me to return to work, and he thought I wanted to get back to work. We finally sat down and really shared our feelings, and to my surprise, we both wanted me to be with our daughter. What a happy day it was when I decided to stay home with our daughter — and wasn't pressured either way by John.

"Life was not all a bed of roses. There were some stressful times when money was being stretched to the max, and another child, Matthew, followed two years later. As a mother at home, I have experienced absolute highs and devastating lows: the joy of watching the children grow, first steps, first teeth, first words — and the problems of self-esteem, when people who know you as a mom at home talk down to you. . . . I felt guilty that I had graduated from university and started a career only to 'give it up' for my family.

"Thirteen years later I can say this is what I was meant to do. My education has only enhanced other areas in my life and has certainly not been wasted. My husband and I are teammates when it comes to parenting and running the house. . . . We've had a few tears, been flat broke and not speaking. We are still learning, still growing, but every day our lives seem richer. I thought I might want to go back to work when the children got older, but I find at eleven and thirteen they need me more than ever. . . . This is not a job for everyone, and I have the greatest respect for friends, family, and others who have chosen a different path. Maybe that's the really neat thing — we *can* make choices, and have the freedom to follow our hearts!"

That's the large picture. But day to day, parents at home experience their greatest joy in being there for those special little moments they might otherwise have missed. Connie Nabtiti, who lunches with her little boy, Sami, every day, recounts:

"One day Sami asked me how much I made. He said, 'You work at home right? Well, how much do you get paid?' I replied that I didn't get paid. He said, 'Well, Daddy should pay you.' I told him that 'Daddy does things for me, and I don't pay him.'

"'Yeah,' he said, 'but he doesn't cook and clean. You're working here, Mom. You should get paid.' I said, well, he paid me in hugs and kisses. 'Yeah,' he said, 'but that's not the same.'"

Small moments to be treasured. But are they important enough to risk your career for? That's the fear that drives many women back to work — that if they drop out for a few years they won't be able to get back in. Facing daily work-family stresses, they worry, too, that their marriages might break up and, without a job, where would they be?

It is a hard choice to make, no doubt about it. But it's a choice that's getting easier. This really is not the 1950s: women are not as vulnerable today as their mothers were. They are better educated, better qualified, and better able to slip back into the job market when the time is ripe. The enormous expansion of home businesses and people working at home mean it's easier to achieve a balance between home and work — and to keep up your expertise to make it easier for you should you want to return later to a full-time job. In any case, as Arlene Rossen Cardozo reported in *Sequencing*, going back to the same old job wasn't an issue for many of the women she interviewed — they had moved on and wanted different jobs, even different careers.

She quotes a Manhattan literary agent who was combining her business with being home with two grade-schoolers: "Women today are being sold a romantic bill about babies . . . that somehow if you are home for a while with a baby, then it's all over. Well, it's only the beginning. Having a child to raise, to guide to maturity, to help overcome weaknesses, to encourage strengths, is a major life commitment." For more and more women, says Cardozo, the straight career line is no longer the option they choose. Interestingly, many men lately are also realizing there's more to life than a one-track career. It's just that women thought of it first.

When mothers do return to the workforce later, they may have more to offer. As a management consultant, Heidi Brennan says, "I noticed that women who had returned after their children were older had a lot more of a concept of management based on parenting. If you're a good listener with your kids, you're a good listener with employees. And I thought these women had a great sense of organization."

Is it worth putting up with the down days when you're on your own, the snide putdowns moms at home experience, the financial sacrifices? Betty Walter didn't hesitate with her answer: "I would tell young women, being a mother is potentially one of the most fulfilling and rewarding things they could ever be. Their children will be far more interesting than anyone was willing to tell them. If they are willing to devote time to their kids, they will grow so much personally, and they will never regret putting their careers on hold or cutting back on their work hours."

What's missing now is recognition. Psychologist Brenda Hunter says simply: "They need to hear a voice out there saying, 'What you are doing is wonderful!'"

Withrow Park Revisited

Summer has faded into fall and two months have passed since we spoke to the group of new mothers at Withrow Park. How have they resolved their conflicts? What decisions have they made?

Fiona McKnight has seen her hopes dashed. She had been quite sure back in the summer that she had a commitment from her superior at work allowing her to return to her job co-ordinating CD-ROM distribution on a part-time basis so that she could be with her baby, Max, then five months old, most of the time. But the deal had been turned down by higher management. "They said there's only full-time work," she reports sadly. Then her husband's firm closed down, he was laid off, and she no longer had any choice about returning full-time.

Would her husband, Bill, stay home with Max? "I just don't make enough," says Fiona. "And we have to keep his time open for interviews." Max spends two days a week with Bill's mother, and the other three days in a day-care center, which costs his parents $880 a month. "I only see him three hours a day now," she says. He's been at the day-care center for two weeks, and has picked up a bronchial condition. For now, they're surviving on Bill's severance pay, but in another couple of months that will run out. "If Bill can't work, we'll have to decide whether to pull Max out of day care," she says.

Louise Christie is much happier. "Things are going really well," she reports. The person who had replaced her in her old job working for her husband quit, and Louise has been going in half a day a week to train the new person, usually taking her baby, Hunter, with her. But she spent five and a half weeks in a rented cottage and at her in-laws' cottage the past summer, and she's still on track to eventually take a course in childbirth education.

Sarah McGarr, who probably felt the greatest conflict — torn between her long-hours job and baby Jack — is having to make her own compromises. "I'm feeling a lot better now," she says. "We found an excellent nanny we're going to share with one of the other moms in the exercise class — and I'm looking for a new job." She had searched in vain for a part-time job but there were none to be had. Now she's looking for a full-time job closer to home and with shorter hours than her old job, although she still hasn't found one. "If I don't find anything else, I will go back to my old job at the end of the month," she tells us. "I'll be telling my employer I can't stay at the office until eight-thirty, I have to leave by five. In reality that's going to be hard to manage — the work has to be done. There's a lot of pressure to stay late. I won't be able to live with that for long," she admits.

Sarah is weaning Jack in preparation for going back to work. "I would ideally like to breast-feed him at night," she says. "I could have continued while I'm working, but using a pump at work — I don't think so." Leaving Jack, she realizes, "will be very hard. I have never been apart from him except I went out one night. And that was to a baby shower. My husband says no matter what course you take it's always a huge compromise."

Lisa Howarth, so unhappy before because she was being pushed back to work after she and her husband signed for a house, is returning to work under slightly happier circumstances. She is taking a new full-time position with the Heart and Stroke Foundation that will allow her to work at home two days a week. "I put in a proposal and I was surprised how flexible they were," she says. Her baby, Ahren, will be in a day-care center three days, and at her mother-in-law's two days a week.

"I'm still at home!" Stella Margaritis announces, perhaps with a hint of pride. Through the woman whose child she used to look after, she now has the chance to look after another three-year-old on a part-time basis, which will allow her to stay home with Zoe. "She's quite a handful," she laughs. "I'm still planning on nursing her until she's about a year old."

Kareen Climenhaga, too, reports, "Everything is going along as planned. I'm still planning to stay home at least another year." She's nursing Faryn — "I think she would give me a real hard time if I stopped," she laughs.

Our interview with Sandy Lubert and Andrew Campbell, the teachers who sold their house so they could afford for Sandy to stay home, had an unforeseen result. They were intrigued to hear how other couples were managing on one income, and were particularly interested in hearing about Debbie and David Kusturin, the couple who found the kind of community they needed on their remote suburban street.

When we speak to Sandy two months later, she says they have contacted the Kusturins, and been out house-hunting in their area. Because it is not within walking distance of shopping and other facilities, and they have only one car, they decided against moving there, however. Instead, they've bought a new townhouse not far from the Kusturins'. "We'll have everything within walking distance," Sandy says happily. "We're next to a plaza with a supermarket and a library, and just down the road is a recreation center with a pool." They're also close to a new toll highway connecting directly to Andrew's school, so he can be home in half an hour.

"We've done our budget really well," says Sandy, "and we know we can do it very comfortably on one income. We were really sad about moving, but now we're excited." Her second child is expected soon, and she has started her maternity leave early. She says confidently, "I know I'm going to be happy staying home."

Appendix I
The Family Budget

*T*he first step toward managing your family finances successfully on one income is to get a handle on where all your money goes. The sample worksheet below can guide you in tracking your current spending, as well as help you find places it can be cut down.

Every family is unique, of course; you may wish to break down costs differently. To give you an idea of some average expenditures in certain categories, two "standard" budgets are included from the Social Planning Council of Metro Toronto. Both are for a family of four, but one assumes a mortgage and a car, while the other assumes a rental apartment and no car — note the large differences in housing and transportation costs!

Fixed Costs	Variable expenses	Discretionary expenses
Mortgage or rent	Food	Clothes
Property taxes	Personal care	Eating out
Heat	Alcohol and/or	Recreation, movies,
Utilities	tobacco	theater, videos,
Insurance	Household operation	papers, books, music,
(annual divided by 12)	Health care	software, gifts
Home repairs	School needs	Home furnishings
Car loan #1	Transportation	Home improvements
Car loan #2	(except car)	Charitable donations
Car insurance	Gasoline	Vacations
Other loan payments	Car repairs	*Subtotal*
Taxes	*Subtotal*	
Subtotal		

TOTAL

Total take-home pay

Surplus or *deficit*

Appendix II
The Cost of Working

Iow much is it really costing you to work? When you actually add up all the costs associated with your job, you may be surprised at how little you net. We've prepared the sample worksheet below to help you take into account all the various areas in your life where working leads to extra expenditures. Try to figure out or estimate, even roughly, monthly figures for all of the categories below that apply to you. Calculate the total and subtract it from your gross monthly pay; how much of what you earn is actually available for you and your family to use?

Child care

Transportation

  – Car expenses (Canada: 40¢/km;
    U.S.: 50¢/mi)

  – Fares, taxis, etc.

Personal upkeep

  – Clothing & shoes

  – Hairdressing, etc.

  – Drycleaning & laundry

Eating out

  – Lunches & coffee breaks

  – Family dinners out

At-work social costs

  – (Gifts, birthday lunches, etc.)

Home help

  – Cleaning services

  – Gardeners, etc.

Sloppy shopping

  – Convenience items

  – Bargains missed & coupons
    passed up

Guilt expenditures

  – Toys, games, videos, computer,
    books

  – Family meals out & outings

  – Vacations, trips

  – Clothing, jewelry

Pay deductions

  – Taxes

  – Union dues & professional fees

  – Benefit plans that duplicate
    partner's benefits

TOTAL

Gross pay — Above Total = Net Income

Standard Family Budget: Homeowners, with Car

Assumes a man working, a woman at home, a girl, 8, and a boy, 13, with gross annual income of $72,844.03 CDN.

	Monthly Amount	Percent of Total Budget
Food	644.97	10.62
Housing	1,856.82	30.59
Home furnishings & equipment	89.61	1.48
Household operation	28.65	0.47
Clothing	204.50	3.37
Health care	141.36	2.33
Personal care	73.17	1.21
Recreation, gifts, reading, etc.	327.90	5.40
Alcohol and tobacco	140.05	2.31
Transportation	361.44	5.95
Special school needs	19.09	0.31
Life insurance	29.54	0.49
Total spending	**$3,917.09**	
Income tax & social insurance	$2,153.24	35.47

Source: Social Planning Council of Metropolitan Toronto.

Standard Family Budget: Renters, No Car

Assumes a family of four, with a man working, a woman at home, a girl, 8, and a boy, 13, with gross annual income of $39,446.66 CDN.

	Monthly Amount	Percent of Total Budget
Food	644.97	19.62
Housing	717.14	21.82
Home furnishings & equipment	89.61	2.73
Household operation	28.65	0.87
Clothing	204.50	6.22
Health care	141.36	4.30
Personal care	73.17	2.23
Recreation, gifts, reading, etc.	327.90	9.97
Alcohol & tobacco	140.05	4.26
Transportation	108.54	3.30
Special school needs	19.09	0.58
Life insurance	29.38	0.89
Total spending	**$2,524.36**	
Income tax & social insurance	$762.86	23.21

Source: Social Planning Council of Metropolitan Toronto.

Note: The Social Planning budgets were last calculated in 1994. By October, 1996, the average rent for a three-bedroom apartment had risen to $986 a month.

Appendix III
Some Useful Contacts

Kids First
A Canadian organization that campaigns tirelessly for respect
and a better deal for parents at home.
P.O. Box 5256, Airdrie, AB T4B 2B3
Telephone: 403-289-1440; Fax: 403-539-0630

Mothers at Home
Founded in 1984 by three mothers at home, Linda Burton, Janet
Dittmer, and Cheri Loveles. The editors of its excellent monthly
magazine, *Welcome Home*, keep "issue" articles to a minimum and
concentrate instead on mothers describing their own experiences.
We also recommend two *Mothers At Home* publications,
"Discovering Motherhood" and "What's a Smart Woman Like
You Doing at Home?"
8310a Old Courthouse Rd., Vienna, VA 22182
Telephone: 703-827-5903; Fax: 703-790-8587

FEMALE (Formerly Employed Mothers at the Leading Edge)
One of a number of morale-boosting self-help groups for
mothers who've stepped aside from careers to be at home. Has
120 chapters throughout the U.S.
P.O. Box 31, Elmhurst, IL 60126

Mothers Are Women
An Ottawa-based group that has fought for recognition of the
importance of work done by mothers at home. It is active on
the Internet as well as producing a useful quarterly magazine,
Homebase.
P.O. Box 4104, Station E, Ottawa, ON K1S 5B1

National Moms Clubs Network
Active particularly on the West Coast.
814 Moffat Circle, Simi Valley, CA 93065
Telephone: 805-526-2725

MOPS (Mothers of Preschoolers) International
Has 1,300 moms' groups, mostly in the U.S. and Canada, but
also in nine other countries. It acts as a useful bridge by including
in its membership working mothers as well as mothers at home.
1311 S. Clarkson St., Denver, CO 80210
Telephone: 303-733-5353

La Leche League International
Breast-feeding and much more of interest to mothers at home.
P.O. Box 4079, Schaumberg, IL 601168–4079
Telephone: 847-519-7730; Fax 847-519-0035
Local branches will also be listed in your phone book.

Family Resource Coalition
For information on parent–child community organizations.
200 S. Michigan Ave., Suite 1520, Chicago, IL 60604
Telephone: 312-341-0900

Canadian Alliance of Home Schoolers
272 Highway #5, R.R.#1, St. George, ON N0E 1N0

Growing Without Schooling
2269 Massachusetts Ave., Cambridge, MA 02140
Telephone: 617-864-3100

Index